Learning with Mu

Learning with Music offers an accessible introduction to music education theory for those working in the early years. Using real case studies and rich examples, the book provides practical suggestions to develop the formative ideas of music education, such as melody, rhythm, pulse and timbre, into games and activities for every early years setting.

Chapters include a range of tried-and-tested lesson sequences and accompanying developmental benefits, allowing practitioners to confidently create tailor-made lesson plans and manage music sessions, ranging from one child through to larger groups. Each concept is grounded in child development theory, as well as music education theory, giving practitioners an insight into the research-based principles and priorities of music education for their own unique setting.

With a clear focus on the benefits of teaching music from birth to preschool, *Learning with Music* is essential reading for all early years practitioners, as well as students on Early Childhood courses.

Frances Turnbull is an Early Years Music Specialist and founder of Musicaliti, a preschool music education programme. She has presented early years music sessions in a variety of settings since 2006, after training as a secondary mathematics and science teacher. She enthusiastically follows research into the health, educational and developmental benefits of music, which she researched during her undergraduate psychology degree and Master's degree in education. Frances also teaches primary guitar and directs a local community choir, the Bolton Warblers.

Learning with Music

Games and Activities for the Early Years

Frances Turnbull

Routledge
Taylor & Francis Group

LONDON AND NEW YORK

First published 2018
by Routledge
2 Park Square, Milton Park, Abingdon, Oxon OX14 4RN

and by Routledge
711 Third Avenue, New York, NY 10017

Routledge is an imprint of the Taylor & Francis Group, an informa business

British Library Cataloguing in Publication Data
A catalogue record for this book is available from the British Library

Library of Congress Cataloging in Publication Data
Names: Turnbull, Frances S. author.
Title: Learning with music : games and activities for the early years /
    Frances Turnbull.
Description: Abingdon, Oxon ; New York, NY : Routledge, 2018. |
    Includes bibliographical references and index.
Identifiers: LCCN 2017007342| ISBN 9781138192577
    (hardback : alk. paper) | ISBN 9781138192591 (pbk. : alk. paper) |
    ISBN 9781315639871 (ebook : alk. paper)
Subjects: LCSH: Games with music—Instruction and study. |
    Education, Preschool—Activity programs. | Music—Instruction
    and study—Juvenile.
Classification: LCC MT948 .T87 2018 | DDC 372.87/044—dc23
LC record available at https://lccn.loc.gov/2017007342

ISBN: 978-1-138-19257-7 (hbk)
ISBN: 978-1-138-19259-1 (pbk)
ISBN: 978-1-315-63987-1 (ebk)

Typeset in Optima
by Swales & Willis Ltd, Exeter, Devon, UK

MIX
Paper from
responsible sources
FSC
www.fsc.org   FSC™ C013985

Printed in the United Kingdom
by Henry Ling Limited

This book is dedicated to my family: Carl, for your constant support even though you're never quite sure what I'm doing; Alex, for being as patient as a child can be while mum always has work to do; and Bob, for having all the spots!

Contents

Contents

Figures

Tables

Alphabetical list of songs

Preface

Music is minimally, if at all, addressed in early years training courses. This leaves the greater proportion of preschool and nursery workers reliant on their personal experience or informal training by older staff (more than likely also trained through personal experience). While this is a fascinating example of how word-of-mouth traditions are passed down through generations and across different geographical areas, it also suggests that there may be areas that have been overlooked. Many of the existing books geared to this market tend to struggle to balance the theory behind the practice with the actual practice, making these books either too informative or not detailed enough. Overly theoretical books are inaccessible because the language and conceptual nature of the content are difficult to apply, while practice-only books tend to minimise theoretical justification and, while easy to apply, lack on-going explanations and principles. This book aims to balance the history of music education with the theory of child development through regularly introducing songs within the theory of the book and describing the practical ways that songs have been used in real nursery or preschool settings.

Nurseries and preschools in the UK have come under intense scrutiny in the last few decades for the quality of experience they provide children before they begin formal education at primary school. Initially offering free, undirected play for children under 4 years old, childcare providers are now expected to introduce basic academic concepts to assist and support primary instruction towards the buzz word, "school readiness". Academic ability in itself is a relatively fluid concept, as towards the end of the last century it was measured using intelligence quotient (IQ) tests with the intention of finding the most suitable way to identify the abilities of the future workforce. With the rapidly changing work environment, new inventions and technologies and ever-changing information, the skills that were once valued for work have changed dramatically, as has the workforce itself. Consequently, within the last few decades executive function has been recognised as a more accurate predictor of overall success than IQ, and it includes academic, economic and personal success. Even the concept of executive function is not entirely clear, as specialists debate the more detailed aspects of it. However, there are specific skills generally agreed to make up executive function, including working (short-term) memory, co-operation, planning, problem-solving and self-control (motor).

In this educational climate of results based on a table from the Programme for International Student Assessment (PISA) (OECD, 2013), school readiness has been identified as a predictor of higher national test scores in the UK. This is significant to the UK government because countries with higher results potentially indicate countries that use the most effective teaching methodologies. Countries with better teaching methodologies are presumed to have stronger workforces, which is understood to create additional value to their national Gross Domestic Product (GDP), the value of goods and services provided by a country in a year. For this reason, school readiness has major implications for early childhood professionals in terms of inspections and expectations. Activities seen to encourage school readiness often attract government funding. These activities are identified through research, ideally practice-based research.

Various aspects of music education have been linked to executive function skills that encourage school readiness, including studies in 2014 (Lesiuk, 2014) that began to show that gross motor movement may be linked to the development of fine motor skills, and 2016 studies (Zhao and Kuhl, 2016) that link rhythm to speech development. My own research is beginning to show links between musical gross motor movement training and fine motor development, another predictor of school readiness. As a result, this book aims to provide the theoretical rationale for activities considered essential for a good musical and rhythmic grounding in an approachable and accessible way. By going beyond the science/technology/engineering/mathematics (STEM) vs science/technology/engineering/arts/mathematics (STEAM) argument, it shows that in fact the arts are essential to not only balancing the education of people but to enduring human success.

As a self-taught musician with a commitment to education, I intend this book to provide useful ideas of songs that can be easily learnt by staff and successfully taught to children. Every song may be used in every age group, providing early childhood specialists with a wide variety of material that may be used sequentially or even thematically, recognising the individual skillsets and expertise of educators. In this way, children will already be familiar with repertoire that they can sing successfully, and they will be able to play instruments along with songs, play the associated game to the song, and even move to the rhythm and pulse of the song. Material available on YouTube and SoundCloud (Musicaliti) will help both staff and children in learning the songs.

This book has been written to include past and present music education theory to help generalist early years music educators understand the need for and benefit of musical games and activities. The first chapter goes back to the beginning of music education theory and describes the most prominent approaches to music education in their purist form. While many music specialists identify with one specific specialist approach, often there is considerable overlap between approaches. The second chapter considers the impact of technology and invention on music education, considering how human understanding has changed and adapted to new information, and the influence it has had on music education. Chapter 3 proposes a way forward for music education based on international interests and educational trends. The final chapter provides more information on the resources available to the early childhood practitioner, with a considerably extended repertoire of additional songs.

In addition to the content described above, each chapter provides a sample of traditional Western children's songs that have been sung through history. Songs have been grouped into levels of complexity based on the pitches and lengths of the notes as well as the number of notes used, beginning with two notes in the *minor third*, or the traditional "nee-naw" siren sound. Despite presenting this specific selection of songs as notes and rhythms to be used in teaching musical literacy, it is helpful for children to listen to all types of music, especially music that gives enjoyment to the child. Bear in mind that vocally children have a very different physiology to adults. As their vocal folds remain undeveloped until puberty, their singing range will be significantly different to adults. Musically complex songs can only be sung accurately by children after spending a significant amount of time practising while maturing, just like young dancers, athletes or instrumentalists.

In presenting this repertoire, a simple table format has been used to guide practitioners in knowing the rhythm of the words. Rhythmic notation is included in the Appendix, and recordings are available on YouTube or SoundCloud.

Learning to read music can be done in different ways, although it is most often taught mathematically: through numbers and counting beats. While this is effective, it does not always come naturally to everybody, which is why this book presents different ways of reading the beat/rhythm. Table 0.2 presents the rhythmic notation used, the European and American musical name, the Kodály and Dalcroze movement syllables, as well as common English insect and food names. These are useful because they rely on matching

Table 0.1 Table of rhythms

Notation	Note name	Kodály	Dalcroze	Insects/Food
l	Crotchet/quarter note	Ta	Walk	Bee
∏	Quavers/eighth notes	Tate	Jogging	Spider
♪	Quaver/eighth note	Te	Jog	Spy
♫.	Dotted quaver semiquaver / dotted eighth note sixteenth note	Tim-ka	Skipping	Beetle
♫	Semiquaver quaver / sixteenth note eighth note	Tika-Te	Quickly jog	Sausages
♫	Quaver semiquaver eighth note sixteenth note	Te-Tika	Jog quickly	Hamburger
♫♫	Semiquavers / sixteenth notes	Tika-Tika	Quickly jogging	Caterpillar

Table 0.2 Applying the syllables to rhythms

⊓	⊓	⊓		
Twinkle	twinkle	little	star
tete	*tete*	*tete*	*ta*
jogging	*jogging*	*jogging*	*walk*
spider	*spider*	*spider*	*bee*

syllables to the represented beats. These are used by ignoring the lyrics of the song and saying/moving to the generic words to capture the rhythm.

It is best to try a few ways and then choose the method that feels most natural to you. Table 0.2 is an example of understanding how to relate the beat to the songs.

References

Lesiuk, T. (2014). Music perception ability of children with executive function deficits. *Psychology of Music, 43*(4). https://doi.org/10.1177/0305735614522681 (Accessed 15 August 2014).

OECD (2013). PISA 2012 Results: What makes schools successful? *Resources, Policies and Practices* (Volume IV), PISA, OECD Publishing. http://dx.doi.org/10.1787/9789264201156-en (Accessed 20 May 2016).

Zhao, T. C. and Kuhl, P. K. (2016). Musical intervention enhances infants' neural processing of temporal structure in music and speech. *Proceedings of the National Academy of Sciences, 113*(19).

Where did music education start?

Introduction

The way that we educate people has come a long way over time, and this can be seen in the vast and varied ways that people think today. The differences in ideas reflect the multiple events and developments that have occurred within society. These are usually based on ideas taken from the observation of personal experience or from developing the ideas of other people. Music education has had a similar evolution. As this book primarily addresses Western music education, the perspective and history is considered from the Western point of view (other potential views to consider include Eastern music, tribal music or world music).

Impact of psychological thinking on music education

Historically in the West, people originally believed that the body and personality could not be separated and, as spiritual beings, people or personalities were beyond explanation. This was reflected in the heavily religious influences within the arts, including within music. In the 16th century, thinkers began to suggest that the body was separate to the mind, which was considered a strange and revolutionary idea at the time. By the next century, after many fictitious, deceptive claims and old wives' tales were proven false, people began to look for evidence of proof by asking for facts that could be verified independently through the senses. When it came to education, babies, for example, seemed to be unable to demonstrate anything that was asked of them, so it was believed that babies were born knowing nothing, merely blank tablets waiting to be trained. In the 18th century, people began to think about how individual personality influenced the way people saw events, and in the 19th century they experimented on people to understand the way that the brain worked. It was around this time that people began to develop ideas concerning effective teaching, where the most popular approach to promoting successful methodologies included demonstration classes. These were held relatively publicly, sometimes at national or international conferences so that interested subject leaders could observe the effects of students learning in these new ways. From early childhood theorists (Montessori, founder of child-led educational approaches) to psychologists demonstrating mental proficiency (Binet, founder of the IQ – intelligence quotient – test), education techniques developed at the same time as individual education subjects became more specialised, including music.

Impact of the Industrial Revolution on music education

In the 20th century, as the demand for skills increased through the development of the Industrial Revolution, psychologists, educators and scientists began to consider *how* learning occurred so that children could be taught more effectively. By the late 19th century, in the Victorian era, industrial ideas were applied to education settings, including deliberately restricting life experiences to change the behaviour of both people and animals. For example, society used to limit the time children spent with their parents because it was thought that this would encourage early independence. In the early 20th century, common changes were identified in children, like the age range covering the stages of sitting, crawling, walking and talking. Specialists also considered the way that teacher and peer interaction impacted learning, from teacher-led to student-led to peer-led teaching. Some leading thinkers promoted the idea that students should be led with clear objectives, while others argued that people learnt quicker when they were free to learn according to their interest, some considered the effect of the external environment between social groupings and relationships the strongest defining characteristic, while others considered the effect of internal, individual needs as the source of explanation for all behaviour. As business became more efficient, the concept of productivity was introduced within education at the turn of the 20th century, with interest developing in testing abilities to identify which types of people were best suited to different types of work. These ideas and developments also impacted music education, where composers of the day challenged themselves to find better ways to teach music using the increased knowledge of science, the body and the mind.

Impact of social development on education

Society was changing alongside these ideas, with developments in philosophy, science and technology, and these changes were reflected in the developments of the arts. From medieval times, changes in laws began to regulate the way that people interacted culturally, and scientific knowledge began to travel around the world, where ancient Greece knowledge started to be translated and used in Latin countries. Renaissance inventions like the printing press continued to change the way and extent that knowledge was accessed, including theories and explanations for common phenomena like gravity, giving people a deeper understanding of how the natural world worked. By the early 16th century, unproven ideas like midwives' tales were challenged, with new requirements for evidence and generalisability. In the early 19th century, the first attempts were made to understand people through psychology: from the way that they thought, to repairing bodily injuries. At the same time, different ways of passing on knowledge were explored through experiments on both people and animals, with philosophical ideas developing based on personal experiences. Some of these philosophies were used to guide judgements made by governments and law makers, seen clearly in the way the law has changed to accommodate human-centred thinking and racial and gender equality.

Impact of social development on music education

Table 1.1 shows that music as a discipline has developed substantially from the beginning of recorded history where it began as vocal training for part of society, developing into a religious activity during the gradual decline of the Roman Empire. Music education reflected these changes – the heavy religious emphasis gradually developed into human-centred and emotive music. Through developments in the Industrial Revolution, new instruments were invented and perfected, providing the same musical accuracy as the human voice, and standardised musical notation was introduced which allowed musical influences to travel over distance and time. Orchestras of varied instrumentalists developed, along with operas that combined instruments and voice, with the purpose of moving the audience to experience the emotion of the composer. The audience changed too, from having music composed only for the aristocracy to it being written to appeal to a wider audience, it gradually became more accessible to the public. The increased access to music led to an increased interest in learning to perform music. Consequently, different ways to teach music were developed, the main foci of which were movement, vocal development and instrumental rhythms. Musical philosophers developed ways of understanding and appreciating differences in historical music compared to modern music, while composers explored new ways to express the social and political changes of the time. Table 1.1 compares the time lines of a selection of scientific discoveries with musical periods and education or music education events.

Music education today

While music education has gradually become more accessible to everyone, music education has received increased public interest in recent years for specific reasons, having been in and out of the news in different ways. New evidence of additional benefits of musical education have been suggested through various studies, along with impressive claims from supporters, only to be challenged in small ways and found to

Table 1.1 Table comparing scientific inventions, musical composer periods and music education developments

Philosophy/Science/Psychology developments	Musical periods	Music/Education
476–1000 Greek and Arabic universities develop scientific studies **742–814** Charlemagne introduces cultural and educational reform **1000–1300** High Middle Ages European scholars decipher Greek and Arabic texts **1200** Latin translations of Greek intellectual writings **1175–1253** Robert Grosseteste devises scientific process of observe, law, example **1219–1292** Roger Bacon develops scientific process to observe, hypothesis, experiment, independent verification	*Medieval/Early music* **991–1033** Guido d'Arezzo **1098–1179** Hildegard von Bingen **1150–1201** Léonin **1160–1230** Pérotin **1300–1377** Gaillaume de Machaut	• Education mainly available in monastery and cathedral schools • Medieval universities in Italy, France, England, Spain • Vocal music based on religion • Recorder, trumpet, bagpipe, shawn (oboe), harpsichord
1398–1468 Gutenberg invents printing press **1473–1543** Copernicus identifies the sun as centre of universe **1493–1541** Paracelsus founded toxicology **1561–1626** Francis Bacon introduces empiricism to science **1596–1650** René Descartes introduces mind vs matter (rationalism) **1564–1642** Galileo described gravity	*Renaissance* **1440–1521** Josquin des Prez **1510–1585** Thomas Tallis **1525–1594** Giovanni Pierluigi da Palestrina **1543–1623** William Byrd **1567–1643** Claudio Monteverdi	• Music based on modes • Composers begin to reflect art, mythology and astronomy (da Vinci, Boticelli, Michelangelo) • Music dominated by church • Chanting and instrumental music
1629–1700 Agnostino Scilla pioneered fossil study **1632–1704** John Locke describes the Tabula Rasa, introduces empiricism **1643–1727** Isaac Newton discovers calculus	*Baroque* **1653–1706** Johann Pachelbel **1678–1741** Antonio Vivaldi **1685–1750** Johann Sebastian Bach **1685–1759** George Frideric Handel	• Increase in non-religious and instrumental music • First orchestra • Opera used to impact audience mood
1711–1776 David Hume proposes the mind is based on empirical senses **1712–1778** J. J. Rousseau proposes people live and learn in freedom	*Classical/Enlightenment* **1712–1778** Jean-Jacques Rousseau **1732–1809** Joseph Haydn	• Increased value in human rights • Freedom of religion

Philosophy / Psychology / Science	Composers	Developments
1724–1804 Immanuel Kant introduces idealism through independent thought	1756–1791 Wolfgang Amadeus Mozart 1770–1827 Ludvig van Beethoven 1782–1840 Niccolò Paganini 1792–1868 Gioachino Antonio Rossini	• Increase in musical instruments including piano
Early Romantic 1770–1831 Georg Wilhelm Friedrich Hegel introduces phenomenology of spirit 1809–1882 Charles Darwin proposes evolution 1813–1855 Soren Kierkegaard explores anxiety and existentialism 1848 Phineas Gage accident shows brain can function after damage	*Early Romantic* 1809–1847 Felix Mendelssohn 1810–1849 Frédéric François Chopin 1811–1886 Franz Liszt 1813–1883 Wilhelm Richard Wagner	• Music describes nature, painting, poetry • Virtuosos composed music to show brilliance • Opera developed into long stories
1832–1920 Wilhelm Wundt develops experimental psychology 1841–1877 Douglas Spalding identifies psychological imprinting through structuralism 1824–1880 Pierre Broca identifies speech production area	*Middle Romantic* 1825–1899 Johann Strauss II 1833–1897 Johannes Brahms 1838–1920 Georges Bizet 1879–1958 Rudolf van Laban dance (Impressionist)	• Instruments could be played better and more easily thanks to the Industrial Revolution
1842–1910 William James writes *Principles of Psychology* 1849–1936 Ivan Pavlov demonstrates conditioning 1850–1909 Hermann Ebbinghaus carries out significant work on memory 1856–1939 Sigmund Freud founds psychoanalysis 1859–1952 John Dewey introduces educational democracy 1870–1952 Maria Montessori demonstrates benefits of early years education 1875–1961 Carl Jung founds analytical psychology 1878–1958 John Watson experiments with behaviourism 1879–1955 Albert Einstein developed theory of relativity	*Late Romantic* 1840–1893 Tchaikovsky 1841–1904 Antonín Dvořák 1844–1900 Friedrich Wilhelm Nietzsche 1845–1924 Gabriel Urbain Fauré 1858–1924 Giacomo Antonio Puccini	• Music is written for the public, not only aristocracy • 1865–1950 Dalcroze devises movement-based music education

(continued)

Table 1.1 (continued)

Philosophy/Science/Psychology developments	Musical periods	Music/Education
1882–1960 Melanie Klein develops methods for child analysis	*Romantic*	• 1882–1967 Kodály devises singing-based music education
1886–1969 Bartlett's theory on memory	1862–1918 Achille-Claude Debussy	• 1895–1982 Orff devises rhythm-based music education
1884 Pavlov's dogs	1864–1949 Richard Georg Strauss	• 1898–1998 Suzuki devises group music to teach beauty
1889–1951 Ludwig Wittgenstein developed philosophy of language	1865–1957 Jean Sibelius	
1889–1976 Martin Heidegger developed phenomenology	1872–1958 Vaughan Williams	
	1875–1937 Joseph Maurice Ravel	
	1881–1945 Béla Bartók	
1890–1947 Kurt Lewin theorises organisational psychology	*20th century*	• 1927–2015 E.E. Gordon develops music teaching methodology
1896–1934 Lev Vygotsky develops social learning	1882–1971 Igor Fyodorovich Stravinsky	• 1932–2013 Bennett Reimer promotes equal musical opportunity
1896–1980 Jean Piaget theorises on stage development	1898–1937 George Jacob Gershwin	• 1937–now Keith Swanwick promotes the musical process: perform, listen, create
1896–1981 David Weschler develops intelligence scale	1906–1975 Dmitri Dmitriyevich Shostakovich	• Elliott promotes paraxial music
1902–1994 Karl Popper developed arguments on falsification	1912–1992 John Milton Cage	• Welch promotes all musical development
1903–1989 Konrad Lorenz shows effects of imprinting	1913–1976 Edward Benjamin Britten	• 1957– now Lucy Green promotes informal learning
1904–1990 Burrhus Skinner develops behaviourism	1918–1990 Leonard Bernstein	• 1970–2000 Postmodernism and deconstructivism pushes the traditional limitations in music, combining styles and focussing on specific techniques
1905–1980 J. P. Sartre develops humanism		
1905–1982 Ayn Rand develops individualism		
1907–1990 John Bowlby theorises on importance of attachment		
1907–1967 Kenneth Spence develops discrimination learning		
1908–1970 Abraham Maslow identifies hierarchy of human needs		
1908–1961 Maurice Merleau-Ponty develops phenomenology		
1908–1986 Simone de Beauvoir develops feminism		
1912–1954 Alan Turing develops functionalism		
1913–1999 Benjamin Bloom creates taxonomy of learning based on objectives		

1915–2016 Jerome Bruner develops cognitive learning theory including scaffolding

1917–2005 Urie Bronfenbrenner develops the ecology of learning

1921–1996 Paolo Freire argues for critical pedagogy

1926–1993 Donald Broadbent identifies selective attention

1926–1984 Michel Foucault develops post-structuralism, post-modernism, queer theory

1928–2016 Alvin Toffler promoted customised education

1928–now Noam Chomsky develops the cognitive study of language and mind

1930–2002 Pierre Bourdieu theorises on social values

1939–now David Kolb develops experiential learning for business

1943–now Howard Gardner develops theory of multiple intelligence

1944–now Roger Scruton develops validity of aesthetics

1940–now Saul Kripke develops philosophy of language

1956–now Judith Butler develops gender, feminist and queer theory

2001 Human Genome published

2010 First synthetic genome created

2012 Higgs boson discovered at CERN

21st century

1928–2016 Einojuhani Rautavaara

1943–now Brian Ferneyhough

1944–now Michael Nyman

1944–now John Tavener

1947–now John Adams

1954–now Judith Weir

1967–now Julian Anderson

1973–now Tansy Davies

- Post-modernism, polystylism and eclecticism remain
- Multimedia and technology combined with music is increasing
- More female composers are recognised

be only valid for a small group of the population. An example of this is the Mozart effect (McKelvie and Low, 2002). After the initial results were published showing that students who listened to classical music before tests achieved higher academic scores, the governor of Georgia, USA, proposed that every new born child received a CD of classical music to improve the learning potential of those children. Within a few years, other researchers found different results when they tried to replicate the study. Further detail indicated that the effect was only seen in a group of American college students (significantly older than babies or primary children) and indicated that they were able to recall significantly more facts in a test straight after listening to classical music while revising. However, within weeks, a retest indicated that the increased knowledge gain had not been permanent as their results now matched their peers. In fact, it was later shown that the same results were achieved by students who revised while listening to a story being read, or while chewing gum. Although the promotional angle was that music enhanced learning, this study showed that people learn more effectively when more areas of the brain are being used at the same time, supporting the idea of multi-dimensional learning.

Musical education in research

Music is not the only educational area to experience disparate claims – consider the on-going debate of the benefits of phonics, and the introduction of "new" maths, and "discovery learning". However, instead of listing all the contentious educational issues, what may be more useful is to identify common themes and areas of clear success, and to evaluate critically the contribution these ideas have made to our understanding of the learning process, and how these may be effectively applied. With influences from areas including biology, neurology, physiology, philosophy, pedagogy, politics, economy, sociology and mathematics, it may be valuable, then, to understand the prominent music education theories in order to appreciate where music education may be headed. For example, musical instruments discovered from stone-age times show that the ability to make music has been honed by people since humanity first invented a way to record events. This demonstrates that there has been a human need for music since the beginning of time.

Music education in history

From the first written accounts of education, musical training in ancient and biblical times originally only involved vocal and aural teaching – musical people chanted and sang without accompaniment. Primitive wind instruments made from bird bones have been discovered, dating from 40–70,000 years ago, using breath in a different way. With technological advances, alternative instruments developed, for example, the harp (seen in ancient Egyptian paintings in 3000 BC) developed into the harpsichord, which required a different type of physical effort – pushing keys that struck the strings of an instrument – eventually led to the development of the piano (1709). The beat and the notes, rhythm and melody, were the most important features that determined the quality of the music. Over time, more nuances were introduced where music could be graded into how loudly or quietly, quickly or slowly it was played, and even whether it reflected activity or emotion. This led to the first operas being written (1597), with the specific intention of evoking emotion in the audience. In ancient times, different note combinations described scales and harmonies where qualities like meaning, importance, good and evil were attributed to them. In medieval times, notes played together were considered pleasing or displeasing, however, many of these judgements were based on the personal views of an aristocracy that could afford to financially support the composers of the style of music they favoured. Musicians out of favour had to rely on income as music teachers, and with the aristocracy only able to provide limited support, an increasing number of music teachers looked elsewhere for students. New students came from varied backgrounds and so music teachers needed to find different and creative ways to teach people with very different skills from very different backgrounds.

Specific interest in music education seems to have developed at the same time as the growth of international interest in the mind and, subsequently, learning progressed. Along with the theories that were developing through psychology, a few composers began to experiment with the most effective ways to teach by applying new ideas to their classrooms. Initially, adult students received these experimental methods, all performing more accurately almost immediately, which led to these composers becoming involved in teaching school children and adapting their techniques accordingly. Most of the leading music education ideas are referred to as "approaches" rather than methods. The argument is that a "method" suggests a step-by-step routine that covers all eventualities, while the original teachers of the "approaches" realised that progression of knowledge was not necessarily sequential. In addition, although the content of the sessions was based on the same principles, the delivery of the session and interpretation of the principles were based on the personality, skills and specialisms of the individual teacher.

Song Level One: Cobbler cobbler

Level One songs start with two notes, the ambulance ni-naw sound, *so-mi.*

> *Cobbler, cobbler, mend my shoe*
> *Get it done by half past two*
> *Half past two is much too late*
> *Get it done by half past eight*

Figure 1.1 Song using so-mi notes

Table 1.2 Cobbler cobbler rhythm table

⊓	⊓	⊓	I
Cobbler,	cobbler,	mend my	shoe
⊓	⊓	⊓	I
Get it	done by	half past	two
⊓	⊓	⊓	I
Half past	two is	much too	late
⊓	⊓	⊓	I
Get it	done by	half past	eight

We played this with younger children by "hammering" shoes or tapping shoes on the floor to the beat and pretending to fix them. This helped to prepare them for playing the older version. The important part of this song was distinguishing between two beats and one beat. Older children played this game in a circle or in pairs. In a circle, each child tapped the shoe (or knee) of the friend on their right on the beat. In this way, they felt the beat of the friend on the left, as well as giving the beat to the friend on the right. This game was even played in pairs by tapping the right shoe/knee of the friend sitting opposite. We made this game a little more challenging by then changing direction. It was great for developing teamwork and co-operative play as it helped to develop the ability to slow down or play faster – working together at keeping the beat. It was also good for literacy development as it introduced the idea of syllables/breaking down sounds to make words.

The Dalcroze music education

This approach was named after **Émile Jacques-Dalcroze (1865–1950)**, a Genevan composer and music teacher who wanted to improve the performance of his adult music students. Influenced by the scientific advancements of the day, he developed exercises to associate musical rhythm ideas with physical experiences, which he named "eurhythmics". He recognised the relationship between space, time and energy, related to the physics equation for speed, distance and time, and used this in his exercises. For example, in order to travel a greater distance (or play a longer note) it would either take a longer time or need more energy.

Jacques-Dalcroze used the idea of physical movement with his highly proficient adult music students, finding that their musical performance improved remarkably once they could express musical ideas through the body. He appears to have adopted this idea from his experience of Middle Eastern and African cultures during his travels. Ahead of his time in some respects, the relationship between experience and application has been explained in the 21st century through non-invasive brain scans like MRIs and PETs. Studies have found that brain cells, or neurons, light up when thinking about something that has been experienced before, which can create the sensation of experiencing it again. Because it is literally the memory or idea of doing something that has activated these cells, the cells have been called "mirror neurons".

By devising exercises that made music theory a lot clearer and more accessible, Jacques-Dalcroze used a 20th-century concept of "experiential learning", a process that Kolb (1983) observed in adult education and business management. By taking part in an activity, thinking about principles that apply, relating them to a bigger picture and then applying them to new situations, people have been found to use skills acquired this way as part of their "toolkit" or repertoire in making future decisions about unknown situations. In the Dalcroze approach, students move according to the rhythm, learn how to write down the beats by remembering the movements they made, move again in the same context with greater understanding, and then finally use those movements in a newly invented (improvised) context.

The modern Dalcroze approach is a tri-part system that includes training in eurhythmics, Kodály's sol-fa (found in the next section) and improvisation (spontaneously invented performance). Despite improvisation being included as a separate specialism in the Dalcroze approach, in Kolb's theory, improvisation is the culmination of learning as it involves experimentation of skills in new ways. In addition to rhythm, the Dalcroze approach considers disciplines of music as harmony, composition, pedagogy, plastique animée, movement technique and expression. The Dalcroze subjects consider the nuances of music, such as beat, metre, dynamics, articulation, accents, shape of the measure, binary and ternary beats, polyrhythms, tempo, duration, augmentation, diminution, excitation–inhibition, complementary rhythm, phrase, rests, syncopation, metric transformation, unequal beats, as well as the relationship between time, space and energy. Exercises often involve quick reaction (stop–start), follows or imitation (memorisation) and canon (repeating the same pattern one or two beats later).

Dalcroze in research literature

Writings about the Dalcroze approach are mainly authored by practitioner teachers, although there are a few academics that have focussed on clarifying the techniques. These include Juntunen (2004; Juntunen and Hyvonen, 2004; Juntunen and Westerlund, 2001, 2011), Caldwell (1993, 1994) and Pope (2005, 2010), and because of the focus on the body, generally they use a phenomenological framework to investigate the experience of practising Dalcroze.

Dalcroze has been interrogated through multicultural and multi-age lenses, and despite the origins in adult music education, has found most application in the preschool and primary areas of education. As a result, Dalcroze is mostly associated with children's music education, however, modern Dalcroze groups are making a significant effort to bring Dalcroze training into mainstream adult professional music and dance courses.

Criticisms of the Dalcroze approach

Among its detractors, the Dalcroze approach has been criticised for its seemingly limited application in special education situations, although the experiential strength of the approach has been found to increase accessibility to music in both children and adults with limited ability. Another criticism is that because of the focus on gross motor movement, it is a predominantly child-focussed method of music education and is often considered inappropriate for adults in spite of the potential extended applications. Word-of-mouth feedback often reveals that the movement experience is more enlightening for adults with theoretical music training. The final major criticism is the exclusive commitment to the approach that is expected and, up to now, this purism has been the only way to develop further within the field.

The Dalcroze approach originated in Geneva, Switzerland, where further training is available at the **Institut Jacques-Dalcroze** (www.dalcroze.ch). However, Dalcroze societies can be found in many countries where research still continues, and work is actively being done to incorporate this way of learning in music courses in universities and conservatoires. Regular training sessions are held which are open to the public, where licence qualifications may be earned (subject to sufficient music theory training) in both written and practical work, with the highest level being the Diplome, roughly equivalent to the work required for a PhD. In the UK, in addition to regular publications, residential week-long summer schools are held each year during the July/August (northern hemisphere) summer holidays, with academic conferences held biannually. More information on courses, events and international links can be found at **Dalcroze UK** (www.dalcroze.org.uk), where specialist Dalcroze books and DVDs can also be found.

Dalcroze for babies (0–18 months)

This section addresses Dalcroze for non-walking babies. While most babies begin walking at around 12 months, normal development ranges from early walkers of 6–9 months through to later starters of 18–24 months. Babies' spontaneous responses to situations are mainly introverted, often only identifiable through small gestures like eye movement and head turning. It is thought that babies feel a continuous connection to the mother or primary caregiver which develops through experiencing independence, and that they adapt to their environment based on where they appear to fit. They can show signs of recognition, enjoyment, dislike and fear for not only people but objects and situations, indicating that unlike the original blank tablet theory, babies are born complete and competent yet inexperienced individuals, challenging how we address and care for them.

Dalcroze warm-ups involve physical movement, and in pre-walkers this is achieved through baby massage techniques and gross motor limb movement. Suitable songs may be chosen to reinforce the relational aspect of learning, and adult body language, eye contact, and confidence play a big part in the child responding co-operatively.

Baby massage can be as simple or as complex as interest or training allows. From gentle heart-shaped movements on children's chests or backs to stroking or "milking" arms and then legs, to full body strokes, circular shapes on palms of hands and soles of feet, and gentle head massage. These actions help to develop proprioception, the child's ability to determine where their body ends and their carer's body begins. This skill is essential in developing an internal body map of their skills, towards being able to anticipate what they will be able to reach or the amount of effort they will have to put into stretching, reaching and grasping to hold on. Some classes encourage explicit adult awareness of child consent as well as child autonomy by redressing the power balance through vocalising the question, "can I massage you?" to the child, maintaining eye contact, and determining the response by the accompanying behaviour. At this age, studies appear to show that babies still feel physically connected to those nearest to them. As they develop the concept of being separate, figuring out where their fingers end and yours start, they begin to learn about appropriate and inappropriate touch. As a care provider, this activity also acts as an opportunity to identify potential child protection concerns, with the proviso that children are reassured by safety and care. Most often, the most successful adult behaviour is a calm, caring attitude, being alert to detail like gesture and eye movement and what it may imply, while being completely in the moment with the child, modelling enjoyment, confidence and happiness while singing.

The next skill from a Dalcroze perspective is limb manipulation. Simple repetitive motion appears to be the most successful way to warm up limbs prior to further activity (from crawling and walking, to simple lap bounces, swinging and swaying in arms). Choosing a suitable song while maintaining eye contact, indicates enjoyment and exclusive focus on the child. Psychologically, babies have advanced skills in reading body language, being acutely aware of changed focus or lack of interest. Interaction like continuous eye contact conveys their importance as individuals, the value you place in their company, and this ultimately works towards their self-image, self-confidence and expectation of how people will respond to them.

Typical activities include lifting arms up and down either simultaneously or alternating up and down arms, and the same with legs, up and down. In addition, crossing the midpoint of the body develops proprioception (bodily awareness in space) by encouraging interaction between neural pathways. Previously it was thought that this encouraged the left "cognitive" side of the brain to interact with the right "creative" side of the brain. We now understand that by touching the left hand/elbow to right foot/knee and vice versa, and even crawling using right hand/left foot, left hand/right foot combinations, the left part of the brain learns about different ways to control the right part of the body and vice versa. Varied movement is important developmentally because the more new experiences the brain is exposed to, the easier it is for the brain to recover in situations of injury or illness later in life. Studies have shown that although neural messages may usually follow one route, other areas of the brain are able to compensate for any changes by rerouting messages, and this is made easier through multiple early experiences. Consequently, despite the pride that some parents take in their children appearing to "skip" developmental skills such as going from sitting to walking without crawling, the awareness that develops from lifting and balancing on all fours, and crossing the midpoint through alternating legs and hands through crawling, is more essential than we may have realised.

Dalcroze for toddlers (18 months–3 years)

For this purpose, toddlers are considered to be new walkers up to approximately 3 years old. While toddlers generally appear to have short attention spans, it has been found that self-chosen activities or those in which they show an interest can keep them focussed for hours at a time. A lot of toddler time is taken up with exploration and repetition, leading to many practitioners recognising the remarkably advanced, scientific way that toddlers investigate natural phenomena. By trying different ways to get the same result, toddlers' actions are not actually as haphazard or meaningless as they appear; the on-going repetition develops both their understanding of the detail of how things work and an understanding of how their own body works. They begin to respond in a more extroverted way, and often have a good sense of humour. From language to facial expressions to movement, toddlers are developing an understanding of where they fit in the world. They make decisions about themselves and the people surrounding them based on appearances, reactions and behaviours. In new walkers up to 3 years old, imitation is non-judgemental, while physical development is fearless because of their insatiable curiosity. As body language is the most fluent language that toddlers use, they imitate everything involved in being an adult, including emotions like confidence and embarrassment.

Dalcroze for toddlers is an exercise in imitation and physical development. Movement is an essential part of day-to-day learning, and games involving opposites can be used to great effect, developing concentration as well as physical confidence.

Popular imitation games usually include making and naming sounds for animals, vehicles for transportation, weather, and popular characters like superheroes. In order to develop the neural association of length to slow and continuous, these can initially be extended into movements. For example, the extended "mooooo" of a cow; the short, sharp quack of a duck; the swaying of a windy day; short sounds of plip-plopping rain; long sounds of flying superheroes; or short sounds of running superheroes. These can be further extended by comparing them to instrument sounds – short, sharp moves can be compared with wooden instruments (e.g. drums, guiros), while flowing moves like flying or swimming can be compared with long, metal sounds (e.g. triangles, bells). A musical story could even be developed where instruments are played in sequence, symbolising characters or events, and represented pictorially as a reminder of what happens next. This development from concept to movement to sound not only creates a pattern for encoding toddlers' own creations, but also acts as a decoding pattern for understanding others' creations, where existing pieces of music may be used and understood for their relationships to movements, events and characters.

Physical development is spontaneous and joyful so, as a result, effective games involve playful ideas like humour, suspense, gentle surprise and quick reward. When playing music (recorded or live, like a tambourine or drum tap), toddlers tend to copy adults, so it is essential to be prepared to demonstrate the movements that you want to develop. Contrary to previous ideas, toddlers are conceptual thinkers – they respond to stories and continuity of associated ideas. Songs and games involving ridiculous movements, slowing down while building tension and then suddenly changing to a quicker beat, and games involving simple sequences like walking under a number of arches in a circle, help children to begin to associate movements with sounds. This makes it easier to later associate sounds with pictures, words and even music notation. At this stage, all types of spectrums are extreme – it is fast or slow; it is quiet or loud; it is up or down; it is high or low; it is big or small – which are also useful language development opportunities. Because of the experimental nature of toddlers, safe props can also be used to develop preposition words like "on", "in", "under", and "around".

Dalcroze for preschoolers (3–5 years)

Preschoolers are considerably more sophisticated than toddlers in both their thinking and movement. They are still hugely reliant on body language for meaning, and a lack of talking between themselves does not stop them from communicating through eyes, touch and gesture. Their increased confidence in their growing independent ability makes preschoolers more likely to fiddle and fidget if their attention is not completely engaged. The imagination of the preschooler is exceptionally vivid; while it can sometimes seem that they cannot distinguish between reality and fantasy, research shows that it is their limited communication ability that leads adults to think that way. Preschoolers are aware that they can do a lot more than they could a year or even a few months ago. From going to the toilet, asking for food and fetching toys, they value their independence and recognise unfair changes in the balance of power. In situations where they are trusted, they tend to respond responsibly, but in situations where they are disempowered, whether because of a lack of time or misunderstanding, they are liable to seem irrationally upset and frustrated. It is at this stage that they learn to manipulate people that they feel are not authentic.

Dalcroze for preschoolers involves imagination and independence. Creating opportunities for either can be time-consuming in preparing areas or using props that are safe (unable to harm selves or others), authentic (really work) and proportionate (right size).

Many preschool games involve imagination (which is based on reality). Children will play-act as the important people in their lives, doing the important jobs they see in their lives, and unselfconsciously acting in unexpected ways. This behaviour can indicate where they place their priorities and what they have observed as the behaviour that they are expected to use as adults. As these are unselfconscious games, it is useful to create safe spaces for them to "practise" being grown-up, with self-regulating limitations (safe toys, not too high, dangerous or precarious, etc.). It is also useful to have generic items that can act as anything, like pieces of plain fabric that could be wings, clothes, walls, beds, etc. Pretending to be different people allows children to practise expressing behaviours and emotions, helping children to develop the way in which they will ultimately view themselves.

Preschool children thrive on responsibility and independence, yet few settings use these skills. Along with the relational benefit of learning to care for siblings and friends, children have sufficient interest and energy to not only learn about caring for others but also to learn about caring for things, creating a pleasant working environment, packing away and cleaning up. Games and activities where children work together can be particularly powerful as they learn to work with different personalities, and as an educator, being aware of groupings that support and encourage each other can benefit the group tremendously. Allowing children to not only take responsibility but be accountable for their actions is a "gift" that children respond to and take pleasure from achieving.

Song Level Two: **Pease porridge**

Level Two songs use simple rhythms and three notes that are far enough apart to hear the difference clearly, *so-mi-do*.

Figure 1.2 Song using so-mi-do notes

Table 1.3 Pease porridge rhythm table

	⊓		-
Pease	porridge	hot	
	⊓		-
Pease	porridge	cold	
	⊓	⊓	
Pease	porridge	in the	pot
			-
Nine	days	old	
	⊓		-
Some	like it	hot	
	⊓		-
Some	like it	cold	
	⊓	⊓	
Some	like it	in the	pot
			-
Nine	days	old	

Pease porridge hot, pease porridge cold
Pease porridge in the pot, nine days old
Some like it hot, some like it cold
Some like it in the pot, nine days old

Sitting in a circle, we used this game to reinforce the steady beat by giving children a rhythm stick to pass. Younger children held the stick for each line of the song until the rest, after which they passed it to the friend on their left. Older children tapped the stick on the floor until the rest and then passed it to their left. This game developed teamwork well when it began slowly enough for all children to recognise which friend they needed to pass the stick to, and how long they needed to wait, or what they needed to sing next. When there was little to no hesitation in the song as children sang and passed, it indicated that we were singing at the correct speed for that group.

The Kodály music education

This approach was named after **Zoltán Kodály (1882–1967)**, and was recognised in 2016 on the UNESCO Intangible Heritage list (UNESCO, 2016). Despite it being referred to as an approach, there is more sequential methodology than can be found in other approaches.

As a Hungarian student, Kodály collected samples of national folk songs as a way of understanding how music remained in public consciousness, and used the themes he identified as principles in his music education technique. While in England, he came across the work of John Curwin, an English minister who had devised hand signals to teach his choir and congregation new songs before the printing press had been invented. Taking these ideas back to Hungary, Kodály created a sequence of learning music called solfége or sol-fa, taken from the syllables used: do, re, mi, fa, so, la, ti, do. This not only aided in teaching musical accuracy but also helped singers as well as musicians gain a better grasp of musical notation. Once devised for the adult students in his conservatoire, Kodály worked on an approach for children, limiting songs by the number of notes that were used in order to maintain musical accuracy, and only gradually increasing the scale, pitches and rhythms once the previous songs were correctly produced. His approach is known for the concept of PPP: Prepare, Practise and Present, where concepts were subtly taught through practical experiences such as chants and games and, once these were secure, the concepts were identified and practised again, and finally explicitly presented to the group, building confidence skills. Kodály's methodology became known by his presentations at musical and educational conferences, where his pitch and rhythm-accurate students would perform to the amazement of educators who still used traditional rote learning. His influence spread widely until at one point almost half of all primary schools in Hungary were primarily music education schools. Used more widely in America, this approach is gaining interest in both Europe and the Far East.

By teaching concepts through physical involvement, Kodály also falls into Kolb's version of experiential learning. Students experience the concept by playing the game, get formally introduced to the concept by name and description, learn how to apply it more generally, and then use it in new work, ensuring that concepts are securely known.

Kodály's approach is based on being able to sing before putting the music onto an instrument. Using a steady beat, simple metres introduce students to the variety of music they may encounter. Deliberate focus and mention is made of the form of the music or how repeated parts may be and whether they are long or short, high or low, quick or slow, and loud or quiet. Finally, simple notation is introduced based on speech syllables, including the associated rests. The intermediate level covers the major trichord and pentatonic scales, introducing major pentachords and hexachords. Pitches are matched with absolute letter names at this stage, with more advanced notation/rhythms being presented. The advanced level of the Kodály approach introduces syncopation and compound metres, as well as minor scales and modes, adding to the aural repertoire. Dotted rhythms are introduced at this stage with quavers and semiquavers, along with the minor hexachord and pentachord scales.

Games use a variety of techniques including dances in parallel lines and circles, body percussion at different levels, props like tennis balls thrown up for high notes or bounced for low notes, conducting for keeping clear beat divisions and, most importantly, the introduction of inner hearing in order to experience multiple pitches and rhythms simultaneously.

Kodály in research literature

While Kodály mostly wrote music books, different people helped him to develop his approach, with writings by Lois Choksy (1999) and others (Barton and Hartwig, 2012; Benedict, 2009; Bugos, 2011; Coppola, 2009; Earl, 1987; Spurgeon, 2004). In research literature, the Kodály approach is often combined with the Orff approach (see the next section), as Orff specifically introduces tuned and untuned percussive instruments, along with a focus on body percussion. Although Kodály intended his method for adults, children's music education was an afterthought, as the prolific spread of his approach in America has ironically limited the use of his approach to mainly children's education or specialist music teachers.

Criticisms of the Kodály approach

The focus on the introduction of limited notes and scales is the most common criticism of the Kodály approach, with pieces of research using current playground songs and chart hits to show that children are capable of far more complex pitches and rhythms. This argument, however, could be seen as misunderstanding the reason behind simplifying the pitches and rhythms, specifically in the ability to identify and internally hear/imagine the melody. Another criticism is the limitation to folk song and classical music as "good" music, with little regard to contemporary music. As children will come across different genres, it is suggested that it may be useful to expand the concept of good repertoire. Finally, the words used for rhythms are contended by classical and folk musicians as they suggest that the words make it more difficult for children to eventually learn commonly used notation. These are what make this theory an approach and, as such, they can all be managed effectively by a self-aware teacher.

The Kodály approach originated in Kecskemét, Hungary, where the **Kodály Institute of the Liszt Ferenc Academy of Music** provides further specialist music training as well as visitor weeks and weekends (www.kodaly.hu). Kodály societies can also be found in many countries, having become particularly well known in America, and these international societies support local educators in their music training. In the UK, in addition to regular publications, residential week-long summer schools are held a few times each year during the northern hemisphere summer holidays, where experts from the Institute often attend. More information on courses, events and international links can be found at the **British Kodály Academy** (www.britishkodalyacademy.org), where specialist Kodály books and DVDs can be bought.

Kodály for babies (0–18 months)

This section addresses Kodály for non-walking babies. While most babies begin walking at around 12 months, normal development ranges from early walkers of 6–9 months through to later starters of 18–24 months. Babies' spontaneous responses to situations are mainly introverted, often only identifiable through small gestures like eye movement and head turning. It is thought that babies feel a continuous connection to the mother or primary caregiver which develops through experiencing independence, and that they adapt to their environment based on where they appear to fit. They can show signs of recognition, enjoyment, dislike and fear for not only people but objects and situations, indicating that unlike the original blank tablet theory, babies are born complete and competent yet inexperienced individuals, challenging how we address and care for them.

Kodály warm-ups are all singing and chanting practice, and as babies will be in the care of one or more adults, it is these adults that will be vocally warming up. This provides not only a familiar routine for the babies but also a fantastic example of preparation before performing or singing. As relationship is such a major part of this age group, singing directly to little ones using focussed eye contact and body language builds and strengthens this relationship, especially uninhibited, animated singing. Although research shows that babies can recognise pitch and rhythm inaccuracies, relationship and attention are far more important to them as they attempt to imitate the way songs are sung and actions are performed.

Singing a variety of songs from different genres is a fantastic way to introduce music to babies, whether rap (a form of chant!), chart-topping hits (that they will probably hear more frequently at home or in the car) or traditional nursery rhymes with child-friendly themes. At this stage, before they start to mimic, they are building their mental repertoire of songs to be accessed once they are able to be more vocal. Developing babies' inner hearing is easily done at this age by singing the beginning of a familiar song and leaving out the last word or last phrase and watching them for a response, whether vocal, eye contact or physical, and then "together" completing the song.

Kodály for toddlers (18 months–3 years)

For this purpose, toddlers are considered to be new walkers up to approximately 3 years old. While toddlers generally appear to have short attention spans, it has been found that self-chosen activities or those in which they show an interest can keep them focussed for hours at a time. A lot of toddler time is taken up with exploration and repetition, leading to many practitioners recognising the remarkably advanced, scientific way that toddlers investigate natural phenomena. By trying different ways to get the same result, toddlers' actions are not as haphazard or meaningless as they appear; the on-going repetition develops both their understanding of how things work as well as an understanding of how their own body works. They begin to respond in a more extroverted way, and often have a good sense of humour. From language to facial expressions to movement, toddlers are developing an understanding of where they fit in the world. They make decisions about themselves and the people surrounding them based on appearances, reactions and behaviours. In new walkers up to 3 years old, imitation is non-judgemental, while physical development is fearless because of their insatiable curiosity. As body language is the most fluent language that toddlers use, they imitate everything involved in being an adult, including emotions like confidence and embarrassment.

Modelling is the most important concept at this level because the feedback occurs so much later. From asking respectfully to waiting politely, providing examples of behaviour is essential to later displays of behaviour. Musically, we sing a lot of two and three note songs with actions and regular rhythms so that children learn to identify accurately the notes they hear and are able to sing them back successfully when they are ready. Children are more likely to sing the ends of the songs first, then the ends of the lines; for example, in Twinkle, twinkle, stopping after "Twinkle, twinkle little star". As children become more confident in holding instruments, we tap to the beat using different instruments. With songs they know well, we can tap the words instead of singing them, developing the ability to play together.

Movement songs can involve walking and stopping, jogging and walking, jumping and stopping, and alternating between fast and slow. This can be done with the teacher tapping simple instruments like a triangle, drum or tambourine the beat is easier to distinguish on these instruments than maracas or egg shakers), while the children walk slowly, quickly or stop. These can easily become a storyline to a theme or take on the characters of a favourite or popular television or film character. At this age, children communicate a great amount through body language, learn through imitation, and are easily distracted by what they see; expect to lead by example rather than instruction, building up to children responding to audio signals.

Movement songs can also involve introducing the experience of simple shapes that children can create in a group. Songs that involve standing in circles prepare children for experiencing the visual and physical space necessary to achieve that form. Walking in a circle prepares their fine motor response through gross motor experience. Opportunities to practise these can be created by drawing a circle on the floor (chalk/tape) and every so often walking thoughtfully and deliberately along the line. Using songs that create bridges and walking under can also be done at this age. By having half of the children in multiple pairs creating bridges around a room, the long line of remaining children can walk from bridge to bridge, similar to creating a "dot-to-dot" experience, rather than all the children wandering haphazardly under any bridge.

Finally, songs that involve rehearsing life events and emotions are invaluable. Simple props like scarves can become clothes or mops, swords or wings, as children develop skills like empathy by acting out old and young, happy and sad, cross and surprised, sick and better etc.

Kodály for preschoolers (3–5 years)

Preschoolers are considerably more sophisticated than toddlers in both their thinking and movement. They are still hugely reliant on body language for meaning, and a lack of talking does not stop them from communicating through eyes, touch and gesture. Their increased confidence in their growing independent ability makes preschoolers more likely to fiddle and fidget if their attention is not completely engaged. The imagination of the preschooler is exceptionally vivid; while it can sometimes seem that they cannot distinguish between reality and fantasy, research shows that it is their limited communication ability that leads adults to think that way. Preschoolers are aware that they can do a lot more than they could a year or even a few months ago. From going to the toilet, asking for food and fetching toys, they value their independence and recognise unfair changes in the balance of power. In situations where they are trusted, they tend to respond responsibly, but in situations where they are disempowered, whether because of a lack of time or misunderstanding, they are liable to seem irrationally upset and frustrated. It is at this stage that they learn to manipulate people that they feel are not authentic.

Taking advantage of their independence, preschoolers enjoy jokes and silliness, like songs that play on words. Get them to act out the jokes within the context of songs, so that it is clear how long they have to develop their character before the next part of the song is sung. Songs involving the minor third and major sixth can be used to work towards songs where children may sing successfully. Be aware that because of their vocal development, preschoolers' vocal folds are immature for many years and, as a result, their singing voice is much higher than many adults, much like their speaking voice. For them to sing successfully, it is useful to model the same pitch to them, so an adult singing at a pitch that is comfortable for them. The best way to encourage pitch matching is by singing the falling minor third, like the ambulance siren, "hello, everyone", and having the children imitate the sound. If one-to-one, keep singing the same pitch as the child, whether higher or lower, until the child is unable to sing any higher or lower, and they can then experience what it feels like to sing the same sound. This will ensure early success at singing.

Children are also able to start recognising substitutions of words to represent ideas and pictures to represent a beat. Tapping or clapping to a beat can be tricky at this age if the children have not had a lot of musical experience at home, but walking to a beat is more natural (even so, on average only half the children will manage this accurately). At this stage, there is more success in differentiating between fast and slow than in matching the beat as the children learn to gain greater control over their bodies, specifically their limbs.

Children are now also ready to be introduced to a greater variety of shapes, including spirals (walking in a straight line and being led into smaller circles), concentric circles, parallel lines where the head couple walks or dances down the centre, and parallel lines where each side crosses over. As with all ages, repetition is key, so allow repetition as often as possible. Be aware that children are still reading body language more accurately at this age than they ever will again, and that they will at once be aware of boredom, embarrassment or frustration in the same way that they can also read patience, acceptance and encouragement in all of their key worker's activities.

Song Level Three: **Let us chase the squirrel**

Level Three songs use simple rhythms and four notes that are closer together than the Level One and Two songs, *do-mi-re-do*.

> *Let us chase the squirrel*
> *Up the hickory, down the hickory*
> *Let us chase the squirrel*
> *Up the hickory tree*

We used this song with younger children to introduce them to the idea of keeping a beat by tapping instruments in time or tapping on body parts in time. New walkers began to walk to the beat. Older children walked in a circle (holding hands or not, depending on group ability) and began to play the game. The game involved one "squirrel" that stood

Figure 1.3 Song using so-mi-re-do notes

Table 1.4 *Let us chase the squirrel* rhythm table

⊓	⊓	I	I
Let us	chase the	squir-	rel
⊓	⊓	⊓	⊓
Up the	hickory,	down the	hickory
⊓	⊓	I	I
Let us	chase the	squir-	rel
⊓	⊓	I	-
Up the	hickory	tree	

outside the circle and waited for the last line of the song to catch one of the "hickory nuts" walking in the circle. As the children were encouraged to walk to the beat, only one child was caught, and they held hands, making a bridge across to the inside of the circle. The "hickory nuts" continued to walk under the bridge, and each one that was caught was added to the bridge until all the children joined in.

The Orff music education

This approach was named after **Carl Orff (1895–1982)**, a German composer and educator who focussed on rhythmic playing as a group. A World War I veteran, Orff began teaching music in a school set up to focus on the arts (dance, art and music), and he was engaged to teach the musical component. His musical recordings led to him being invited to write musical lessons for the radio, which were played on Bavarian Radio. Working with various graduates of the school, musical textbooks were devised to accompany these lessons until World War II began, during which time the arts school was destroyed. The publication of Orff's ideas of interacting music with dance were seen as a reaction to the devastation of war and led to a new form of musical tuition for children that spread internationally.

Orff's approach to teaching was that students learn by doing and have technical explanations later. As there is no systematic programme or sequence of skills to be taught, it is considered an approach rather than a method, and is based on modelling intuition and in-the-moment creativity. Common themes within the Orff approach include singing, playing and dancing, with percussive instruments that can be tapped or scraped, both tuned, such as xylophones (wooden), glockenspiels (metallic) and marimba (larger xylophones), and untuned, such as drums, tambourines, wood blocks, maracas and guiros.

Often the music uses a simple background drone (repeated rhythm or beat) that continues through the song, while other instruments repeat ostinati (short rhythmic patterns) that are played in turn or built up, creating a complex sound. Tuned percussion is introduced with limited notes, ensuring that a pleasant sound is created or modelled early on, preparing children for more complex songs later. Songs are often improvised, or made up on the spot, following a pre-planned formula of pattern 1 or A, or the chorus, to pattern 2 or B, or the verse, back to pattern A, the chorus, also termed ABA. With more independent, confident groups, the pattern can change to ABACADA, where B and C and D are entirely different, but return to the original A pattern.

Modes play a big part in Orff music, as they do in Dalcroze and Kodály, because of the interesting and unexpected sound contrasts. Modes are scales that originated in the Middle Ages and today can be played using only the white keys of the piano, giving each scale a particularly emotional feeling (happy, sad, holy, etc.) through the different tonal patterns. The Ionian mode can be played from C–C; the Dorian mode can be played from D–D; the Phrygian mode can be played from E–E; the Lydian mode can be played from F–F; the Mixolydian mode can be played from G–G; the Aeolian mode can be played from A–A; and the Locrian mode can be played from B–B. Within Orff training, using modes helps to ensure that songs are always in the right key, with some educators removing keys from glockenspiels or xylophones to ensure that any chosen notes harmonise successfully by creating a pleasant sound. When children are confident in singing new songs, they are considered ready to formally learn how the music was made. Instrumental playing begins with body percussion in the Orff approach, with clapping, chanting, singing, stamping and patting, sometimes called "patsch" (knee tap). Despite being designed to teach children generally, it has achieved significant success with children who have special needs, building physical confidence, co-ordination and developing concentration and self-control. The flexibility of the instruments allows for incidental inaccuracy while still sounding pleasant, making it ideal as a therapy for injury and illness as well as for the elderly.

Orff in research literature

The Orff approach features quite widely in research, where various techniques have been used to measure at what age children can match rhythms accurately, through to how it can be used as a therapy for autistic children. It is often used alongside the Kodály approach, has been compared to African music education and even used for school readiness, such as language development. With works also written specifically for child education (Keetman, 1954), books and papers appear to use this approach in order to compare its efficacy with other methods (Benedict, 2009; Bugos, 2011; Casarow, 2012; Coppola, 2009; Gault, 2005; Pollatou et al., 2005; Thresher, 1964).

Criticisms of the Orff approach

The main criticism of the Orff approach is that it presumes children will only want to play or will only be capable of playing repeated motifs or rhythms. As with the Kodály approach, the Orff argument is that simplifying skills makes them easier to identify in more complex pieces. The approach is also criticised because it removes the potential for failure by physically removing notes that may clash, leading to a false experience of success. The Orff argument is that early success leads to on-going persistence, whereas early failure destroys self-belief. Finally, the Orff approach is criticised for its focus on nationalistic or folk song to the exclusion of current music, similar to all the approaches discussed so far. The Orff argument is that this is a starting point to learning music. When viewed as an approach to initial interest and success, or as part of an on-going programme of musical development, these can be viewed as initial scaffolding blocks to be used for a time, much like tracing letters or the building blocks of the number line.

The Orff approach, also called Orff Schulwerk (schoolwork), was developed in Munich and then Salzburg, Germany, where the current **Seminar and Information Centre of Orff-Schulwerk (IOFS)** provides further specialist music training (www. orff-schulwerk-forum-salzburg.org/english). Orff societies can also be found in many countries supporting local educators in their music training and has developed a particularly strong following in Australia. In the UK, as well as producing regular publications, residential week-long summer schools are held every two years during the northern hemisphere summer holidays, where experts from other countries often attend. More information on courses, events and international links can be found at **Orff UK** (www. orff.org.uk), where specialist songs and games can be accessed.

Orff for babies (0–18 months)

This section addresses Orff for non-walking babies. While most babies begin walking at around 12 months, normal development ranges from early walkers of 6–9 months through to later starters of 18–24 months. Babies' spontaneous responses to situations are mainly introverted, often only identifiable through small gestures like eye movement and head turning. It is thought that babies feel a continuous connection to the mother or primary caregiver which develops through experiencing independence, and that they adapt to their environment based on where they appear to fit. They are able to show signs of recognition, enjoyment, dislike and fear for not only people but objects and situations, indicating that unlike the original blank tablet theory, babies are born complete and competent yet inexperienced individuals, challenging how we address and care for them.

Orff for babies involves the exploration of body sounds and percussion instrument sounds and actions. Babies naturally respond to sound in different ways, but most often manage the beating action of a stick on a drum, as well as shaking instruments. While their home experience of music determines their ability to match and maintain a steady beat, the focus is on introducing different sounds when they are ready or show an interest, developing their ability through natural interests.

Singing without music helps to focus acutely on the rhythmic quality of language, as do chants. This is particularly interesting with the current research interests in using music in speech development and the potential links of rhythm to dyslexia (Corriveau and Goswami, 2009; Goswami, 2011; Goswami et al., 2011, 2013; Huss et al., 2011; Goswami, 2011). Chanting can also be used to develop speech and language through naming body parts to a particular rhythm. Moreover, this can be utilised to name items around the home or nursery, different family members and other objects in which the child is naturally interested; for example, dinosaurs, princesses, teddies or sports.

Orff instruments can be used with adult assistance to help to identify instrument sounds and how they may work together, for example, using a single drum or wood block (short sound) with half of the children, and a metal instrument, like a triangle or chime bar (long sound) with the other half of the group. These can be played as the whole group sings along, with the short sound instrument being tapped more frequently than the long sounding instrument, creating a variety in tone and rhythm.

Orff for toddlers (18 months–3 years)

For this purpose, toddlers are considered to be new walkers up to approximately 3 years old. While toddlers generally appear to have short attention spans, it has been found that self-chosen activities or those in which they show an interest can keep them focussed for hours at a time. A lot of toddler time is taken up with exploration and repetition, leading to many practitioners recognising the remarkably advanced, scientific way that toddlers investigate natural phenomena. By trying different ways to get the same result, toddlers' actions are not as haphazard or meaningless as they appear; the on-going repetition develops both their understanding of how things work as well as an understanding of how their own body works. They begin to respond in a more extroverted way, and often have a good sense of humour. From language to facial expressions to movement, toddlers are developing an understanding of where they fit in the world. They make decisions about themselves and the people surrounding them based on appearances, reactions and behaviours. In new walkers up to 3 years old, imitation is non-judgemental, while physical development is fearless because of their insatiable curiosity. As body language is the most fluent language that toddlers use, they imitate everything involved in being an adult, including emotions like confidence and embarrassment.

Children this age are more independent and so more able to take turns passing around instruments. This gives them opportunities to hear the instruments they are playing as well as being the audience and hearing the instruments being played. Listening to songs where they identify the sound of a hidden instrument is useful, and even recording their voices can be fun where they try to identify their own and their friends' voices. Timbre (pronounced "timber" or "tamber") considers the "voice" of the instrument; for example, the sound of the drum compared to a triangle, compared to a ukulele, compared to a recorder. This distinction helps children to identify instruments by their characteristics, and different songs or parts of songs can involve playing the different instrument types.

Choosing songs that name characteristics, qualities or emotions helps to build children's musical associations as well as their vocabulary. Another technique is to assign personalities from well-known book stories, television or film characters to the instrument players. For instance, playing an instrument "like a fairy" would involve high and quick notes, whereas playing "like a troll" would be slow and low. Opposites are a good way to begin to understand the distinctions or dynamics in music, where we look at high/low, fast/slow, quiet/loud. More advanced musical concepts would be happy/sad, heavy/light, and these opposites in songs help to develop singing accuracy through singing high and low notes alternately.

Introducing routine actions helps to establish the concept of the on-going beat as children begin subconsciously to associate actions with specific words, then tapping with specific words. An example of this in *Twinkle, twinkle* is the star actions on "twinkle", and pointing action for "up". The extension to this is walking or clapping to the beat – clapping on the "twin" part of "twin-kle", or tapping knees. This skill is then transferred to tapping, rubbing, shaking or strumming the instruments.

Orff for preschoolers (3–5 years)

Preschoolers are considerably more sophisticated than toddlers in both their thinking and movement. They are still hugely reliant on body language for meaning, and a lack of talking does not stop them from communicating through eyes, touch and gesture.

Their increased confidence in their growing independent ability makes preschoolers more likely to fiddle and fidget if their attention is not completely engaged. The imagination of the preschooler is exceptionally vivid; while it can sometimes seem that they cannot distinguish between reality and fantasy, research shows that it is their limited communication ability that leads adults to think that way. Preschoolers are aware that they can do a lot more than they could a year or even a few months ago. From going to the toilet, asking for food and fetching toys, they value their independence and recognise unfair changes in the balance of power. In situations where they are trusted, they tend to respond responsibly, but in situations where they are disempowered, whether because of a lack of time or misunderstanding, they are liable to seem irrationally upset and frustrated. It is at this stage that they learn to manipulate people that they feel are not authentic.

Body percussion can be a lot of fun at this age, as well as helpful in learning body parts. Tapping in four beats, usually each line of a song, and then changing body parts for each line helps to introduce children subconsciously to the concept of form and structure, similar to sentence construction – one thought per line. It also helps to explain the later concept of music that is written in 4/4 timing (4 crotchet /quarter note beats per bar). It is helpful to be clear about the difference between *pulse* (the on-going beat, like your heart beat) and *rhythm* (the beat of the word syllables), and focus on one or the other.

Keeping an accurate beat at this age and stage is dependent on many factors, not least of which is experience or how much musical activity children have done at home and how much natural interest children have. While the common view is that people are born with it or not, research shows that all babies are born with the ability to recognise whether music is in time or not (they naturally have perfect rhythm), and that from days old babies can recognise whether the key of music they hear changes, showing that they have perfect pitch and know when music is out of tune.

This is important for music education because it shows that the brain is already prepared to sing and play in tune but, like all other skills, it needs to be developed to be maintained. As a result, only half of a preschool group will be able to walk accurately to a beat – partly because of their home experience and partly because of their understanding of what is being asked of them. It is useful to develop this skill, though, as it is easier in the long term to match walking and jogging to the beat than clapping and tapping, mainly because of the size and weight of the limbs involved (legs are bigger and slower than arms and hands).

Song Level Four: Frosty weather

Level Four songs use simple rhythms and the whole anhemitonic pentatonic scale, *la-so-mi-re-do*. This means that all the notes are at least a tone away from each other, so they are easier to sing and repeat successfully.

Figure 1.4 Song using la-so-mi-re-do notes

Table 1.5 Frosty weather rhythm table

Fros-	ty	wea-	ther
Snow-	y	wea-	ther
⊓			
When the	wind	blows	we
	⊓		
All	stick to-	ge-	ther

> *Frosty weather*
> *Snowy weather*
> *When the wind blows*
> *We all stick together*

When we sang this song, children walked in a circle holding hands while singing the first two lines of the song. In the third line, they let go hands and turned around on the spot. On the last line, children all walked towards the middle and took four steps back before singing again. This song developed timing through co-ordination, planning and anticipation as well as concentration skills as children had to co-ordinate the words and movement sequences to allow the game /dance to continue successfully.

The Suzuki music education

Shinichi Suzuki (1898–1998) based his music education on the way that language is learnt after moving to Germany to further his violin study, and personally struggling to learn German as a Japanese citizen. His motivation for developing his music method was that by teaching music he hoped to return the beauty of life after having experienced the horrors of war. As Suzuki was originally a violinist (self-taught), his method was first written for violin students and this has been developed over time to include most concert instruments, including harp, guitar and organ. His ideas are known as a method because there is a clear sequence of songs and skills that are learnt over time, and it is most famous for welcoming children from the moment they can show an interest and hold a smaller version of an instrument, even from as young as two years old. Despite the high standards of music that young children could achieve, Suzuki's motivation was for children to develop "noble hearts" or good characters, not to become musical prodigies.

Suzuki sessions include a lot of parental involvement, especially in early childhood, with a commitment to attend lessons, listen to recordings and practise every day. Learning begins, like language, by doing before reading, without an audition process, as Suzuki believed that "everybody was capable of producing beautiful music". The focus on memorisation does not include an introduction to music theory, which is left to the teacher, as is playing in groups and regular performances. Each teacher follows the same progression of songs, where competition is discouraged in favour of supportive camaraderie.

Many of the teachers trained in the Suzuki method also attend Dalcroze and Kodály training for the application to movement and singing. Sessions for the youngest children develop ways in which children learn to perform together (in unison) by beginning with movement and singing, to become familiar with the piece they are learning.

Suzuki in research literature

The Suzuki method is not well represented in research, suggesting that there is not a lot of academic interest in it. This is despite the extensive influence of Suzuki's methods in most developed countries. Authors that have written about this method include Suzuki (Suzuki et al., 1973) as well as others (Barton and Hartwig, 2012; Coppola, 2009; Custodero, 2005; Liperote, 2006).

Criticisms of the Suzuki approach

As well as the considerable benefits, there have been a few criticisms of Suzuki's approach to music education. Teachers have criticised the slower process of development of musical skill, and this has been attributed to the slower process that needs to be taken with younger children. Criticisms have also been voiced about children needing to use more effort than they would had they been bigger. This has been partially addressed through ensuring smaller instrument versions were available, and where this is not possible (e.g. the double bass), physical growth is essential. Finally, musicians and music teachers have criticised the note and rhythmic perfection as having little personality because of a lack of dynamics when using the group teaching method. The Suzuki argument would look to the purpose of music as being to unite rather than being expressive.

The Suzuki method was developed in Matsumoto, Japan, where the current **Talent Education Research Institute** provides further specialist music training (www. suzukimethod.or.jp). Suzuki institutes can also be found in many countries, supporting local educators in their music training, and has developed a particularly strong following in America. Regular training opportunities exist all over the UK in the various instrumental options, including early years teacher training. Also in the UK, residential week-long summer schools are held during the northern hemisphere summer holidays, which also feature leading experts from other countries. More information on courses, events and international links can be found at the **British Suzuki Institute** (www.british suzuki.org.uk), for parents, children and teachers interested in this approach.

Suzuki for babies (0–18 months)

This section addresses Suzuki for non-walking babies. While most babies begin walking at around 12 months, normal development ranges from early walkers of 6–9 months through to later starters of 18–24 months. Babies' spontaneous responses to situations are mainly introverted, often only identifiable through small gestures like eye movement and head turning. It is thought that babies feel a continuous connection to the mother or primary caregiver which develops through experiencing independence, and that they adapt to their environment based on where they appear to fit. They can show signs of recognition, enjoyment, dislike and fear for not only people but objects and situations, indicating that unlike the original blank tablet theory, babies are born complete and competent yet inexperienced individuals, challenging how we address and care for them.

As with all ages, the approach of *doing first* is most effective. Playing music and singing songs together naturally attracts the interest of little ones. Hearing the regular beat and changing notes of the melody often inspires movement, and this can be encouraged by moving together and even by taking turns in making movements. The Suzuki approach is that all music that is heard is of the highest quality, so early exposure to high quality or live music is greatly encouraged. Musical experience should associate beauty with life, working towards developing a character that values all that is good. Interactive play should be enjoyable for both the adult and child.

Suzuki for toddlers (18 months–3 years)

For this purpose, toddlers are considered to be new walkers up to approximately 3 years old. While toddlers generally appear to have short attention spans, it has been found that self-chosen activities or those in which they show an interest can keep them focussed for hours at a time. A lot of toddler time is taken up with exploration and repetition, leading to many practitioners recognising the remarkably advanced, scientific way that toddlers investigate natural phenomena. By trying different ways to get the same result, toddlers' actions are not as haphazard or meaningless as they appear; the on-going repetition develops both their understanding of how things work as well as an understanding of how their own body works. They begin to respond in a more extroverted way, and often have a good sense of humour. From language to facial expressions to movement, toddlers are developing an understanding of where they fit in the world. They make decisions about themselves and the people surrounding them based on appearances, reactions and behaviours. In new walkers up to 3 years old, imitation is non-judgemental, while physical development is fearless because of their insatiable curiosity. As body language is the most fluent language that toddlers use, they imitate everything involved in being an adult, including emotions like confidence and embarrassment.

As children begin to interact more, the Suzuki approach would be to encourage a common repertoire of songs that are used regularly. Using ways that interest and engage children, music should be a daily, shared activity between adult and child where repetition is encouraged towards mastery, whether in the tune, in the lyrics or on an instrument. Techniques like letting children complete the last line are also encouraged, and turn-taking in instrument play can be used to work towards activities that involve completing the last line. Furthermore, opportunities for parents to interact are valuable so that experiences can be shared and continued regularly in a loving environment.

Suzuki for preschoolers (3–5 years)

Preschoolers are considerably more sophisticated than toddlers in both their thinking and movement. They are still hugely reliant on body language for meaning, and a lack of talking does not stop them from communicating through eyes, touch and gesture. Their increased confidence in their growing independent ability makes preschoolers more likely to fiddle and fidget if their attention is not completely engaged. The imagination of the preschooler is exceptionally vivid; while it can sometimes seem that they cannot distinguish between reality and fantasy, research shows that it is their limited communication ability that leads adults to think that way. Preschoolers are aware that they can do a lot more than they could a year or even a few months ago. From going to the toilet, asking for food and fetching toys, they value their independence and recognise unfair changes in the balance of power. In situations where they are trusted, they tend to respond responsibly, but in situations where they are disempowered, whether because of a lack of time or misunderstanding, they are liable to seem irrationally upset and frustrated. It is at this stage that they learn to manipulate people that they feel are not authentic.

Teaching preschool music provides opportunities to engage and shine in ways that are not only limited to academic or extrovert behaviour. The Suzuki method subtly engages all the senses of the child, developing an internal knowledge and confidence in their own abilities and a curiosity to develop skills through repetition in different ways according to their interests. One challenging task is co-ordinating the group to work towards a single common goal, such as playing together. One approach is to use group games, which have a clear focus and are usually engaging enough to hold the children's attention. Developing the playing or performance into the concept of a game, listening to when different parts should be played, can improve the group's sense of accuracy in timing. One of the most useful concepts at this age is to use gross motor movements to define fine motor activity.

Song Level Five: **Love somebody**

Level Five songs include simple time, and introduce the 6/8 timing, like rocking songs, with the notes limited to *so-fa-mi-re-do*.

> *Love somebody, yes I do,*
> *Love somebody, yes I do,*
> *Love somebody, yes I do,*
> *Love somebody, but I won't say who*

Figure 1.5 Song using so-fa-mi-re-do notes

Table 1.6 Love somebody rhythm table

♫	♫	♫	♩
Love some-	body,	yes I	do
♫	♫	♫	♩
Love some-	body,	yes I	do
♫	♫	♫	♩
Love some-	body,	yes I	do
♫	♬♬	♫	♩
Love some-	body, but I	won't say	who
♫	♫	♫	♩
Love some-	body,	yes I	do
♫	♫	♫	♩
Love some-	body,	yes I	do
♫	♫	♫	♩
Love some-	body,	yes I	do
♫	♬♬	♫	♩
Love some-	body, and it's	you, you	you!

Love somebody, yes I do,
Love somebody, yes I do,
Love somebody, yes I do,
Love somebody, and it's you, you, you!

We used this song with younger children as a scarf/hiding song, where they played/ danced with the scarf for the first three lines, and then hid on the fourth line, then danced with their heads covered for the next three lines, and took the scarf off for the last line. Older children used this as a guessing game, with one person in the middle with their eyes closed or blind-folded, and the rest of the group in a circle around them. The teacher chose one child to sing the last line on their own by giving them something to hold. All the children sang the first three lines and the chosen person sang the fourth line. The teacher took the object away and the child in the middle took off the blindfold or opened their eyes, and walked around the group to listen to the voices as they all sang the next three lines. Finally, in the last line, the middle person chose the person they thought sang the solo, and sang the last line to that person. (Cheaters skipped their turn!)

The Gordon approach to music education

The Gordon approach to music education is an applied process of musical instruction developed by the American professor, **Edwin Gordon (1927–2015)**. His focus on musical development for preschool children resulted in identifying musical aptitude tests and stages of musical development, coining the term "audiation" to describe the ability to imagine music without physically hearing it, and developing music learning theory. Using his scientific background training, Gordon identified processes of musical development that he considered common to all, which were ultimately applied to various instrumental training programmes, most notably, piano, wind and string instruments.

Gordon identified types and stages of audiation that considered the process of learning music all the way through to the original composition and analysis of music. Music education, he considered, began with listening to, then reading, then writing music, both familiar and unfamiliar, after which music could then be recalled and performed from memory. The next progressive skill involved creating and improvising original music, first through performance, then through reading, and finally through writing. Gordon's stages of audiation began with momentary retention, then imitation of patterns, through to establishing tonality and metre. This developed to retaining tonal and rhythmic patterns, then recalling tonal and rhythmic patterns, and finally to anticipating tonal and rhythmic patterns.

Taking this research into audiation further, Gordon identified two types of learning: discrimination learning and inference learning. Discrimination learning involved the ability to repeat tones and rhythms, creating a verbal association, partially synthesising these, creating a symbolic association through notation, and then finally analysing the tones and rhythms ("composite synthesis"). Inference learning involved the process of creating new music through unfamiliar patterns by a separate process of using all the discrete skills of discrimination learning, devising original improvisations in response to existing music and, finally, demonstrating theoretical understanding of the introduced patterns, for example, intervals, time and key signatures and other aspects of music theory.

Gordon's aptitude tests were designed to help teachers identify the most appropriate ways to teach children, including identifying which children were most likely to benefit from private teaching.

Gordon in research literature

Most of the references to the Gordon music education approach in literature were written by E. E. Gordon (Gordon, 1980a, 1980b, 1986, 1989, 1999), and are either included as books or articles (Gordon, n.d.a and n.d.b, 2003, 2010, 2013). In addition, many of the publications are only available from GIA Publications, also known for their publications of sacred music. Additional authors include Liperote (2006), Apfelstadt (1984) and others (Coppola, 2009; Cox, 1998; Earl, 1987; Rauscher et al., 1997; Spurgeon, 2004; Welch et al., 2004).

Criticisms of the Gordon approach

The Gordon, or "Music Learning Theory", approach has been most criticised for being too prescriptive. As an independent theory, it is seen to limit potential access to the wide diversity of musical styles and practices that exist. While critics have acknowledged the detail of the pedagogical process of music education, exclusive focus on the method is warned to lead to strict conformity to musical ideas. Despite this constant view, Gordon has consistently encouraged the use of his ideas alongside others, with a view to enhancing other concepts through his deeper understanding of the musical processes being taught.

The Gordon approach was developed in America, where the current **Gordon Institute for Music Learning (GIML)** provides further specialist music training, (www.giml.org). Gordon's music approach is in comparatively fewer countries than the other approaches discussed in this chapter, but as publishers as well as educators, there are many resources available from GIML to support national and international educators in their music training. In the UK no clear representation is apparent, although various methods pioneered by Gordon are used in academia; for example, musicianship testing.

Gordon for babies (0–18 months)

This section addresses Gordon for non-walking babies. While most babies begin walking at around 12 months, normal development ranges from early walkers of 6–9 months through to later starters of 18–24 months. Their spontaneous responses to situations are mainly introverted, often only identifiable through small gestures like eye movement and head turning. It is thought that babies feel a continuous connection to the mother or primary caregiver which develops through experiencing independence, and that they adapt to their environment based on where they appear to fit. They can show signs of recognition, enjoyment, dislike and fear for not only people but objects and situations, indicating that unlike the original blank tablet theory, babies are born complete and competent yet inexperienced individuals, challenging how we address and care for them.

In the Gordon approach, music is first introduced through listening and then by inviting the children to imitate what they have heard. Singing, moving and chanting are all involved as babies will naturally wiggle and move to music, more so when adults dance with them, allowing them to feel their bodies being moved in synchronisation with the beat, or being bounced to the beat on the adult's knee. Providing opportunities for babies to respond is an often overlooked aspect of music sessions at this age. Opportunities are possible in movement, instrument play and vocalisation by identifying moments when babies are ready and willing to respond, and then providing an expectant pause for babies to move, tap or vocalise.

While Gordon's approach lists "creating and improvising unfamiliar music" as the highest musical achievement, it should be noted that from the youngest ages children are considerably more imaginative than adults in making up songs, for both song content as well as the variety of tones and rhythms. Because the content has few restrictions, some adults do not consider children's songs as "real music", particularly those unable to identify the different timings and key changes. As children become more "institutionalised", creativity tends to diminish significantly unless original contributions are recognised and encouraged.

Gordon for toddlers (18 months–3 years)

For this purpose, toddlers are considered to be new walkers up to approximately 3 years old. While toddlers generally appear to have short attention spans, it has been found that self-chosen activities or those in which they show an interest can keep them focussed for hours at a time. A lot of toddler time is taken up with exploration and repetition, leading to many practitioners recognising the remarkably advanced, scientific way that toddlers investigate natural phenomena. By trying different ways to get the same result, toddlers' actions are not as haphazard or meaningless as they appear; the on-going repetition develops both their understanding of how things work as well as an understanding of how their own body works. They begin to respond in a more extroverted way, and often have a good sense of humour. From language to facial expressions to movement, toddlers are developing an understanding of where they fit in the world. They make decisions about themselves and the people surrounding them based on appearances, reactions and behaviours. In new walkers up to 3 years old, imitation is non-judgemental, while physical development is fearless because of their insatiable curiosity. As body language is the most fluent language that toddlers use, they imitate everything involved in being an adult, including emotions like confidence and embarrassment.

As babies develop their language skills, vocalisations begin to resemble words more closely, and toddlers become more able to fill in the "gaps", indicating their successful recall and retention of the music with which they are familiar. Songs with words are still more meaningful at this age than syllables, and tapping to the beat can be introduced, gradually acquainting children with matching pictures to words, and words to beats. In this way, toddlers can begin to recognise the rhythmic structure of music, typically in four beats per line.

Toddlers are also adept at creating original music, usually with more recognisable vocabulary, and are even able to retain and recall the original compositions that they have made up. Finding ways to keep these original pieces of music helps to recognise the significance of their original contribution; recording devices are useful for this process.

Gordon for preschoolers (3–5 years)

Preschoolers are considerably more sophisticated than toddlers in both their thinking and movement. They are still hugely reliant on body language for meaning, and a lack of talking does not stop them from communicating through eyes, touch and gesture. Their increased confidence in their growing independent ability makes preschoolers more likely to fiddle and fidget if their attention is not completely engaged. The imagination of the preschooler is exceptionally vivid; while it can sometimes seem that they cannot distinguish between reality and fantasy, research shows that it is their limited communication ability that leads adults to think that way. Preschoolers are aware that they can do a lot more than they could a year or even a few months ago. From going to the toilet, asking for food and fetching toys, they value their independence and recognise unfair changes in the balance of power. In situations where they are trusted, they tend to respond responsibly, but in situations where they are disempowered, whether because of a lack of time or misunderstanding, they are liable to seem irrationally upset and frustrated. It is at this stage that they learn to manipulate people that they feel are not authentic.

Gordon for preschoolers combines movement with tone and rhythm, and children this age will be more able to recognise neutral syllables to identify tones or rhythms. As many of these approaches borrow from one another, examples of neutral tone names used by Gordon come from Kodály: do-re-mi-fa-so-la-ti-do, while examples of rhythms include ta (crotchet/quarter note), te-te (quaver/eighth note) and tika-tika (semiquaver/sixteenth note). Children will be more confident at recalling and retaining what they have heard as they practise the length of a crotchet beat (or quarter note) compared to a minim (half note), and they will also be able to start "writing" what they have heard using teacher-made notation cards. Movement and notation cards are useful as initial gross motor introductions of more complex skills, including handwriting and mathematical processes, like addition, especially when used in music that the children have made up themselves.

Preschoolers, depending on their experience and familiarity with music, will be able to improvise competently or make up their own songs. The more graphic songs are usually attempts to impress peers, but their own spontaneous songs are insights into the views, opinions and experiences of the little artist that is developing. Songs with clearer lyrics will be more common, with fewer key and timing changes, so they may even be easy enough for the adult, teacher or group to learn, respecting and validating the child's original contribution.

Song Level Six: Polly put the kettle on

Level Six songs use more combined rhythms than before, extending the notes to *la-so-fa-mi-re-do*.

Figure 1.6 Song using la-so-fa-mi-re-do notes

Table 1.7 Polly put the kettle on rhythm table

⊓	⊓	⊓	l
Polly	put the	kettle	on
⊓	⊓	⊓	l
Polly	put the	kettle	on
⊓	⊓	⊓	⊓
Polly	put the	kettle	on, we'll
l	l	l	-
All	have	tea	

Polly put the kettle on
Polly put the kettle on
Polly put the kettle on
We'll all have tea
Suki take it off again
Suki take it off again
Suki take it off again
They've all gone away

Younger children enjoyed using this song as an instrumental experience, while older children enjoyed acting out the "story". Using appropriate props, such as scarves and blocks, for example, children pretended to be Polly putting a kettle on a stove and drinking tea. This game was extended by helping children to recognise the syllables /rhythms/ beats in the musical phrases, and either jogging or walking to the beats.

Summary

By considering social development, it is easier to understand how these approaches to learning music came about. Scientists and teachers wanted to create systems that could be applied to a bigger group of people and, after finding a little success with one method, they worked hard to develop it into a more detailed and far-reaching concept. Looking at these approaches individually, it is clear that some elements cross over, and it is more than likely that, given the dates of their lives, these different music educators were aware of each other and their ideas. While rhythmic movement was emphasised by Jacques-Dalcroze, the other approaches also used games and movement to emphasise rhythm. Kodály used singing to develop internal hearing, and Gordon called his internal experience of music "audiation". Jacques-Dalcroze adopted Kodály's solfége system in his training, and even Suzuki and Orff's training used unaccompanied singing. Percussive instruments feature prominently in the Orff approach, but again were used with the other approaches to develop various musical concepts, from rhythm through interval awareness to improvisation techniques. Interestingly, these ideas all originated from the scientific perspective involving experimentation through observation, intervention and result. This also describes the action research model that many teachers use in order to implement group learning interventions – finding out how children can best learn difficult concepts. The next chapter considers advances that affect child development and how these specifically apply to music education.

Song Level Seven: Stop on a spot

Level Seven songs use more combined rhythms than the Levels One–Six songs and the full range of notes, ti-la-so-fa-mi-re-do.

> *I'm gonna walk, walk, walk, walk*
> *Walk, walk, walk*
> *I'm gonna walk, walk, walk and*
> *Stop on a spot!*

In this song, children walked to the beat while the teacher tapped an instrument. When the teacher stopped, the children found a spot to stop on. The teacher varied this beat: playing twice as quickly, so that children were jogging; twice as slowly, so that children were walking slowly; tapping lightly so that children tiptoed; tapped

Figure 1.7 Song using ti-la-so-fa-mi-re-do notes

Table 1.8 Stop on a spot rhythm table

♫ ‖	‖	‖	‖
(I'm gonna) walk,	walk,	walk,	walk
‖	‖	‖	♫
Walk,	walk,	walk	I'm gonna
‖	‖	‖	‖
Walk,	walk,	walk	and
♪	‖	‖	-
Stop on	a	spot!	

loudly so that children stomped, etc. This game developed children's self-control, balance, listening skills and spatial awareness. Younger children jingled bells or tapped drums and stopped on the teacher's cue, building suspense and anticipation through self-control.

References

Apfelstadt, H. (1984). Effects of melodic perception instruction on pitch discrimination and vocal accuracy of kindergarten children. *Journal of Research in Music Education, 32*(1), 15–24. https://doi.org/10.2307/3345277 (Accessed 9 July 2014).

Barton, G. and Hartwig, K. (2012). Where is music?: A philosophical approach inspired by Steve Dillon. *Australian Journal of Music Education*, 2, 3–9.

Benedict, C. (2009). Processes of alienation: Marx, Orff and Kodály. *British Journal of Music Education*, 26(2), 213–224. https://doi.org/10.1017/S0265051709008444 (Accessed 14 April 2014).

Bugos, K. M. (2011). *New York State Early-Career Teachers' Selection and Use of Pedagogical Approaches in Elementary General Music*. Ann Arbor, MI: ProQuest LLC.

Caldwell, J. T. (1993). A Dalcroze perspective on skills for learning. *Music Educators Journal, 79*(7).

Caldwell, J. T. (1994). *Expressive Singing: Dalcroze Eurhythmics for Voice* (1st edition). Englewood Cliffs, NJ: Pearson.

Casarow, P. (2012). *Uniting Orff and Kodály: Best of Both Worlds*. Clearwater, FL: Clearwater Christian College.

Choksy, L. (1999). *The Kodály Method I: Comprehensive Music Education*. Upper Saddle River, NJ: Prentice Hall.

Coppola, C. (2009). Two perspectives on method in undergraduate music education. *Teaching Music, 17*(1), 60.

Corriveau, K. H. and Goswami, U. (2009). Rhythmic motor entrainment in children with speech and language impairments: Tapping to the beat. *Cortex, 45*(1), 119–130. https://doi.org/10.1016/j.cortex.2007.09.008 (Accessed 6 April 2017).

Cox, G. (1998). Musical education of the under-twelves (MEUT) 1949–1983: Some aspects of the history of post-war primary music education. *British Journal of Music Education, 15*(3), 239–253. https://doi.org/10.1017/S0265051700003922 (Accessed 14 April 2014).

Custodero, L. A. (2005). Observable indicators of flow experience: a developmental perspective on musical engagement in young children from infancy to school age. *Music Education Research, 7*(2), 185–209.

Earl, G. S. (1987). *With Music in Mind: Kodály Principles of Music Education Applied to Beginners at the Piano*. London: British Kodály Society.

Gault, B. (2005). Music learning through all the channels: Combining aural, visual, and kinesthetic strategies to develop musical understanding. *General Music Today, 19*(1), 7–9.

Gordon, E. E. (1980a). Developmental music aptitudes among inner-city primary children. *Bulletin of the Council for Research in Music Education, 63*, 25–30.

Gordon, E. E. (1980b). The assessment of music aptitudes of very young children. *Gifted Child Quarterly, 24*(3), 107–111.

Gordon, E. E. (1986). A factor analysis of the musical aptitude profile, the primary measures of music audiation, and the intermediate measures of music audiation. *Bulletin of the Council for Research in Music Education, 87*, 17–25.

Gordon, E. E. (1989). Audiation, music learning theory, music aptitude, and creativity. In *Suncoast Music Education Forum on Creativity* (Vol. 75, p. 81). ERIC. http://eric.ed.gov/?id=ED380341 (Accessed 12 April 2017).

Gordon, E. E. (1999). All about audiation and music aptitudes: Edwin E. Gordon discusses using audiation and music aptitudes as teaching tools to allow students to reach their full music potential. *Music Educators Journal, 86*(2), 41–44.

Gordon, E. E. (2003). *A Music Learning Theory for Newborn and Young Children: 2013 Edition*. Chicago, IL: GIA Publications. Retrieved from www.giamusic.com/search_details.cfm?title_id=3153 (Accessed 12 April 2017).

Gordon, E. E. (2010). *Essential Preparation for Beginning Instrumental Music Instruction*. Chicago, IL: GIA Publications. www.giamusic.com/search_details.cfm?title_id=11105 (Accessed 12 April 2017).

Gordon, E. E. (2013). *Basics of Vocal and Instrumental Harmonic Improvisation*. Chicago, IL: GIA Publications. www.giamusic.com/search_details.cfm?title_id=22052 (Accessed 12 April 2017).

Gordon, E. E. (n.d.a). *AMMA and ITPT*. Chicago, IL: GIA Publications. www.giamusic.com/search_details.cfm?title_id=3311 (Accessed 12 April 2017).

Gordon, E. E. (n.d.b). *Guiding Your Child's Musical Development – Edwin E. Gordon*. Chicago, IL: GIA Publications. www.giamusic.com/products/P-3603.cfm (Accessed 12 April 2017).

Gordon, R. L., Shivers, C. M., Wieland, E. A., Kotz, S. A., Yoder, P. J. and Devin McAuley, J. (2014). Musical rhythm discrimination explains individual differences in grammar skills in children. *Developmental Science, 17*(6), 809–1049.

Goswami, U. (2011). A temporal sampling framework for developmental dyslexia. *Trends in Cognitive Sciences, 15*(1), 3–10. https://doi.org/10.1016/j.tics.2010.10.001 (Accessed 6 April 2017).

Goswami, U., Huss, M., Mead, N. and Verney, J. P. (2013). Perception of patterns of musical beat distribution in phonological developmental dyslexia: Significant longitudinal relations with word reading and reading comprehension. *Cortex, 49*(5), 1363–1376.

Goswami, U., Wang, H. L. S., Cruz, A., Fosker, T., Mead, N. and Huss, M. (2011). Language-universal sensory deficits in developmental dyslexia: English, Spanish, and Chinese. *Journal of Cognitive Neuroscience, 23*(2), 325–337.

Huss, M., Verney, J. P., Fosker, T., Mead, N. and Goswami, U. (2011). Music, rhythm, rise time perception and developmental dyslexia: Perception of musical meter predicts reading and phonology. *Cortex, 47*(6), 674–689. https://doi.org/10.1016/j.cortex.2010.07.010 (Accessed 6 April 2017).

Juntunen, M.-L. (2004). *Embodiment in Dalcroze Eurhythmics*. Oulu, Finland: University of Oulu.

Juntunen, M.-L., and Hyvonen, L. (2004). Embodiment in musical knowing: How body movement facilitates learning within Dalcroze Eurhythmics. *British Journal of Music Education, 21*(2), 199–214.

Juntunen, M.-L., and Westerlund, H. (2001). Digging Dalcroze, or, dissolving the mind–body dualism: Philosophical and practical remarks on the musical body in action. *Music Education Research, 3*(2), 203–214.

Juntunen, M.-L., and Westerlund, H. (2011). The legacy of music education methods in teacher education: The metanarrative of Dalcroze Eurhythmics as a case. *Research Studies in Music Education, 33*(1), 47–58. https://doi.org/10.1177/1321103X11404653 (Accessed 29 December 2013).

Keetman, O. (1954). *Orff-Schulwerk Music for Children*. Mainz: Schott & Co.

Kolb, D. A. (1983). *Experiential Learning: Experience as the Source of Learning and Development* (1st edition). Upper Saddle River, NJ: Financial Times/Prentice Hall.

Liperote, K. A. (2006). Audiation for beginning instrumentalists: Listen, speak, read, write. *Music Educators Journal, 93*(1), 46–52.

McKelvie, P., and Low, J. (2002). Listening to Mozart does not improve children's spatial ability: Final curtains for the Mozart effect. *British Journal of Developmental Psychology, 20*(2), 241–258. https://doi.org/10.1348/026151002166433 (Accessed 2 January 2014).

Pollatou, E., Karadimou, K. and Gerodimos, V. (2005). Gender differences in musical aptitude, rhythmic ability and motor performance in preschool children. *Early Child Development and Care, 175*(4), 361–369.

Pope, J. (2005). A Dalcroze approach to musical analysis. In D. Forrest (Ed.), *Celebration of Voices: XV National Conference Proceedings, A* (p. 305). Parkville, Vic.: Australian Society for Music Education. http://search.informit.com.au/documentSummary;dn=813775793478131;res=IELHSS (Accessed 16 August 2014).

Pope, J. (2010). Dalcroze Eurhythmics: Interaction in Australia in the 1920s. *Australian Journal of Music Education, 2*, 135–147.

Rauscher, F. H., Shaw, G. L., Levine, L. J., Wright, E. L., Dennis, W. R., Newcomb, R. L. (1997). Music training causes long-term enhancement of preschool children's spatial-temporal reasoning. *Neurological Research, 19*(1), 2–8.

Spurgeon, A. (2004). Proposed changes for the undergraduate elementary music education curriculum. *General Music Today, 17*(3), 28–32.

Suzuki, S., Mills, E. and Murphy, T. C. (1973). *The Suzuki Concept: An Introduction to a Successful Method for Early Music Education*. Berkeley, CA: Diablo Press, Incorporated.

Thresher, J. M. (1964). The contributions of Carl Orff to elementary music education. *Music Educators Journal, 50*(3), 43–48. https://doi.org/10.2307/3390084 (Accessed 18 April 2014).

UNESCO. (2016). *Safeguarding of the Folk Music Heritage by the Kodály Concept – Intangible Heritage*. www.unesco.org/culture/ich/en/BSP/safeguarding-of-the-folk-music-heritage-by-the-kodaly-concept-01177 (Accessed 1 April 2017).

Welch, G., Hallam, S., Lamont, A., Swanwick, K., Green, L., Hennessy, S., Cox, G., O'Neill, S. and Farrell, G. (2004). Mapping music education research in the UK. *Psychology of Music, 32*(3), 239–290. https://doi.org/10.1177/0305735604043257 (Accessed 9 July 2014).

2 | How has technology impacted music education?

Introduction

The idea of music education goes back to the beginning of time. The first written record of music being taught is in ancient historical writings from the days of the Hebrews in Egypt. Historical evidence of instruments and pictures of musical performances show that people have used music for different reasons, including marking significant life events, entertaining, soothing and even medical procedures.

The social value of music

Music has been accepted as a language that can be recognised by all, and access to music and the opportunity to make music are generally considered to be the right of every person. Music has always been included in the history of public education to some degree, but it is also one of the first subjects to be challenged for its relevance and value during times of austerity. The most common reason given is that the value of music is not easy to quantify in terms of social welfare, economic necessity or life expectancy. Ultimately, as much as music pervades society, from high-level entertainment to bedtime lullabies, it has been difficult to measure or identify an objective value for the part that music plays in everyday life; neither is it particularly obvious how or whether musical skills could or should be considered essential to human survival. This view of the social value of music is gradually changing. The financial value of music-based tourism is now being used and recognised to calculate the national economic value that music holds. Music has also been recognised for the significant health benefits that it holds for groups with memory or movement disorders, like dementia and Parkinson's, and other high-stress, at-risk patient groups such as neonatal, oncology and intensive care, although this is not in the mainstream yet.

The skill value of music

Music once held great value in education for its own sake. Historically, in the first schools in ancient historical writings, music education meant *training in singing*. Over time, and with the development of the printing press, music education evolved from musical ability into musical literacy, or training in reading music, so that music could continue to be played after composers' deaths. People unable to read notation or perform on instruments often identify musical skill as something they would have liked the opportunity to learn or develop. However, within the group of society that can play or perform, a distinction has been made between those that can read music and those that cannot. This has led to the split view that those that can read musical notation are "qualified" musicians because they can (in theory) play any style of music, including music from centuries ago – although, those who only read notation are restricted to playing music that already exists. In contrast, those that cannot read music yet learn to play instruments or sing proficiently are considered less qualified because they cannot play music that they have not heard before – yet, not only can they play almost any music they hear (also known as "playing by ear"), they are often able to create new music, too. Most musicians fall somewhere within this spectrum, with a small minority able to both read and play by ear proficiently. This divide is unfortunate as it unnecessarily enhances a split in an already small community.

The educational value of music

In ancient times (roughly 500–1000AD), music education was considered essential training for a well-rounded education. This was necessary to learn about valuing "the good things in life", specifically the arts. This view was within a culture that had no requirement for educational training for anyone except those interested in professions that depended on accessing information through books. As a result, the concept of public or group education was initially only available to people at college or university level. It is only as people recognised that a wide range of learning experience at a younger age acted as preparation for learning effectively later in life that schools developed from the 6th century. They began as interested parents and educators with financial means privately employing specialists to prepare their children for further study. Gradually, the national benefits of public education became clear, leading to the modern concept of "schooling" for older children, with the first known state-run school set up as the Beverley Grammar School (Northumbria, 700AD), while earlier education experiences were left to the ability (and financial means) of the child and/or parents. Research demonstrated that earlier educational training produced a more skilled workforce, and with more calls to reduce child labour, state provision for primary education became mandatory, with only the "able" or affluent continuing to secondary and then, if required, university.

It was during this transitory process that academic interest in music diminished. In developing the national budget, various skills were deemed more essential than others for the future workforce, once known as "reading,'riting and 'rithmetic", the "three Rs". By reducing the teaching focus in this way, fewer resources were available to train teachers in music, leading to music being considered irrelevant for all but the truly gifted and talented. Historically, the greatest argument to include music came from the religious sector, but as religious influence in education reduced over time, so did the argument and support for music.

The economic value of music

The developments achieved during the Industrial Revolution clearly demonstrated the benefits of only using essential resources to make a greater profit. As this model was so successful in business, it was applied to education too, with the implication that it was not thought essential that all people would benefit from a broad education. Therefore, "essential knowledge" was divided into subjects that could be chosen (or avoided), depending on student interest or ability. Music was compartmentalised into a specialism, requiring highly skilled teachers with more specialist training than most general teachers received. One of the results of compartmentalisation was that as technological advances and information sharing expanded during the 1980s, for example, the educational "necessities" focussed on science, technology, engineering and mathematics (STEM) subjects, with financial assistance made available to schools supporting this focus. This has resulted in music tuition again being restricted to those who had higher abilities or the financial means. However, small countries like Finland are committed to making education relevant for now and the future. It is now (at the time of writing in 2016) reorganising its curriculum by removing compartmentalised subjects and instead focussing on phenomena: teaching the skills needed to understand/improve problems/events of the world suited to the interests of each child. Not only will students be more properly prepared for careers that follow their interests, they will not be learning skills more or less irrelevant to their careers. This has the potential to limit student opportunities if they change their interests, so it is essential that broad opportunities are still available. This view also requires a high level of general teacher training (i.e. Finland requires all teachers to have master's degrees), but also comes with unexpectedly high student engagement and negligible behaviour management. Larger countries are looking at these smaller countries with great interest, aware that their more diverse population and economic spread would benefit from a better system, but one that is manageable on a bigger scale. Musically, this would allow interested children the opportunity to develop their proficiency regardless of their financial background, alongside other interests.

The creative value of music

Employers have often chased a form of scientific formula to try to gain the commercial edge on competitors and hire the best employees, with leading employers even using psychometric tests (e.g. IQ tests) to identify the most successful way to find and employ the most appropriate staff. Today, as the focus on STEM skills is increasing, employers are beginning to identify those with creative skills in addition to STEM training as preferred candidates because of the breadth of implicit skill they bring to business, such as problem-solving, experimentation and flexibility. Recent research (Sala and Gobet, 2016) has challenged the current value and validity of music education research because studies are too specific or too small to reproduce, so results cannot be repeated. This means that many of the results published cannot be proven and cannot be generalised to any other population groups. Consequently, we are unable to categorically state that creative subjects, like art, dance, drama and music, improve business or academic achievement. However, there is a growing body of larger studies and repeatable research that suggests that long-term music training improves essential aspects of health, social interaction and emotional management.

Historical value of music

History has shown that music education has experienced a transformation. From being considered essential, music education now needs to meet specific criteria before being made available, leading music education specialists along a road of having to quantify its value. This is partly due to the evolution of society, technology and, subsequently, education. For example, after society spent centuries entertaining unexplained ritual and tradition, science began to question the relevance and validity of generally accepted truths, from the "world being flat" to gravity itself, leading to incredible inventions and advances. These advances led to a questioning of the claims of true medical benefits for behaviours and supplements, saving future generations from poisonous and even deadly fashion trends and remedies. While some of this knowledge was available to a minority of the population quite quickly, advances in social and educational circles led to specialists identifying the most appropriate ways to share knowledge more effectively. The next part of the chapter identifies individuals that contributed to the development of educational understanding, and it is interesting to see that several themes are repeated. Sometimes this is because students were intrigued enough to pursue their teacher's interests, but in other cases these themes arose as an important issue, important enough to be identified separately in different countries or even at different periods in history. The next section addresses the history of early childhood education and its influence on music education through a number of these themes, which help to show the progress of thinking on education.

Song Level One: **Rain rain**

Level One songs start with two notes, the ambulance ni-naw sound, *so-mi*.

> *Rain, rain, go away*
> *Come again another day*
> *Rain, rain, go away*
> *All the children want to play*

We found these notes easy to learn and repeat, which is why this song is so useful: one note is high: the other is low; some notes are one beat: some are two. This straightforward introduction to music gave new learners the confidence to sing in tune. When we played

Figure 2.1 Song using so-mi notes

Table 2.1 *Rain rain* rhythm table

l	l	Π	l
Rain,	rain	go a-	way
Π	Π	Π	l
Come a-	gain a-	nother	day
l	l	Π	l
Rain,	rain,	go a-	way
Π	Π	Π	l
All the	children	want to	play

this game with young children, we tapped body parts, heads and knees for high and low notes. When we played this game with older children, we used paper plates with pictures, one with a cloud, and one with a raindrop. The cloud plate was the "high" note while the raindrop plate was the "low" note. Children had to jump to the right plate depending on the note we sang. The extension to this introduced numeracy skills by asking children to jump on the plate once for one beat and twice for two beats.

Music education implications from child development

Understanding child development and how ideas have developed over time is essential in all teaching. This is because the ideas that we believe to be true are subconsciously expressed in our behaviour towards and expectations of our students. Music is a multifaceted activity and experience, and magnetic resonance imaging (MRI) scans have shown that while playing music or even just imagining playing an instrument, every area in the brain indicates increased blood flow. This demonstrates that the areas of the brain associated with movement, speech, problem-solving, spatial awareness and social interaction, in fact every area, experience a change while playing music. This clearly has implications for the *developing* brain, and now that we know that the brain *can* adapt to new information at any stage in life, it also has implications for changes to the brain while physically playing music. To date, these implications are not clear because most music education causal studies are either difficult to replicate or only have slightly higher results than the null hypothesis (in a quantitative study, the null hypothesis states that no effect occurred). We could, however, assume that multiple areas of development appear to be affected by music education, and one way to begin to understand this is to consider how child development theory has advanced.

The way we now think about child development has changed significantly. Ideas that we now accept automatically were often thought to be extreme and overzealous at the time that theorists presented them. For example, from thinking that babies were empty vessels incapable of any ability without input, we now recognise that babies are born with advanced abilities in order to learn. Over time, various philosophers have added to our thinking in different ways, slowly building up a model of understanding how children learn. These ideas have led to the varied approaches to education undertaken in different countries, from viewing children as mini-adults to be trained to work as soon as possible, to following children's interests with no constraint – and all the possibilities in between. Indeed, many of our own ideas about education and childcare can be found in these ideas. To use information successfully, it is essential to examine all ideas and arguments carefully, as faulty thinking can have undesirable or even dangerous consequences. A clear example is the idea of "tabula rasa" (blank tablet), which has been

51

used to argue that children must be directed and controlled from birth as they have no free will and are incapable of original ideas. This led to early and pressurised education systems in different countries that resulted in a combination of high achievement with a high level of social breakdown and personal crises.

By looking at relevant thinkers over time, this section identifies overarching themes in education and how they may be applied to music education. All of the ideas presented below generally identify a purpose to education and a method of achieving the purpose. The educators' and thinkers' ideas have been divided into themes to show how they proposed to achieve their aims. These are: the effects of relationship; external motivation; internal motivation; sequential development; child-centred pragmatism; physical learning; independence development; universal education and citizenship; and play.

Song Level One: See saw up and down

Level One songs start with two notes, the ambulance ni-naw sound, *so-mi*.

Figure 2.2 Song using so-mi notes

Table 2.2 See saw rhythm table

I	I	⊓	I
See	saw,	up and	down
⊓	⊓	⊓	I
In the	sky and	on the	ground

See saw, up and down
In the sky and on the ground

Pretending to be on a see saw, younger children stood up tall for the higher notes and crouched low down for the lower notes. This was developed with children tapping their shoulders for higher notes and then tapping their knees for lower notes. As children became more confident with this, we tapped the number of beats in each bar/word.

The importance of relationship in education

Research shows that relationship was recognised most as integral to successful learning. When children experience a relationship with their teacher, learning content often feels easier to understand and remember. This experience has been explained as a result of there being fewer barriers put in place to accepting new information, and can be seen clearly when following the progression of learning in early childhood. Thus, models of learning and growth acknowledge increasing degrees of influence from the central character to the furthest influences based on the increasing relationships being built and the strength, or level of influence, that they hold. While external influences were being explored by scientists, philosophers and psychologists also recognised internal influences unrelated to external ones. They developed ways to explore, as scientifically as possible, the internal ideas described to them by patients, which became the discipline of psychoanalysis. Psychoanalysis became popular at the turn of the 20th century as it was one of the first comparatively scientific applications recognising the effect of internal motivational forces on behaviour and development. Consequently, it was used in many different ways to discover and uncover unexplained situations, behaviours and "truths" behind situations where rational reasons were unclear. One major area of interest involved research into the effects of maternal deprivation on infants as the result of circumstance.

René Spitz on relationship

René Spitz (1887–1974), an Austrian infant psychologist, identified principles to be used in infant psychoanalysis (Spitz, 1946a, 1946b, 1950; Spitz and Wolf, 1946). Using observation through creating film, he found disturbing behaviours in infants as a result of maternal deprivation in foundling homes (homes for abandoned children). This resulted in Spitz identifying three main infant reflexes, including smiling, stranger anxiety and syllabic or semantic communication, as well as providing advice for infant care in foundling homes. This also provided sufficient evidence to show that children could thrive developmentally, despite not having natural parents. Educationally, this was a huge step forward, indicating the significant level of dependence that human infants experience at birth, common developmental behaviours observable, and the important fact that a substitute carer could successfully raise a child. Within music education, parents often provide their children with a substitute because they are unable to teach their children themselves, for different reasons, and Spitz's work demonstrates that children can learn from others successfully.

Harry Harlow on relationship

Harry Harlow's (1905–81) controversial research with rhesus monkeys conclusively demonstrated the extreme effects of isolation from infancy (Harlow, 1958; Harlow et al., 1950). The intention was to discover rehabilitative approaches that could be used with human primates. This impacted the local culture of the day, where physical affection was associated with spoiling children, and nurseries finally recognised the value in encouraging physical affection in infants. More recent research has identified that the stress hormone, cortisol, is reduced in response to physical touch, while immunity increases in response to touch. Educationally, this area has been difficult to navigate because of the ethical problems of what constitutes appropriate behaviour, whether affection is unwanted or welcomed and, subsequently, whether caregivers will be accused of abuse. These same issues arise in music education, particularly when children are learning to hold instruments or manipulate their fingers, where much of the blanket advice is to avoid contact. To find a balance, current advice is that in any situation, the student is asked for permission with a full description of how the teacher intends to move the child's body/ fingers/instrument and, if in any doubt (e.g. if the child is too young to understand), insist on parents attending the session to either watch the teacher interacting or to help the child themselves to avoid misunderstanding while supporting learning.

John Bowlby on relationship

Psychoanalysis also helped to identify the integral relationship between parents/carers and children in post-war England with work by **John Bowlby (1907–90)**. He identified the response that individuals experience when threatened, naming it the attachment behavioural system (Ainsworth and Bowlby, 1991; Bowlby, 1977, 1958). Through researching evacuee children post-World War II, Bowlby demonstrated that infants used caregivers as a base for exploration and a haven for safety and protection, which led to further research in attachment. Within education, this concept changed the whole Westernised social view of raising children to be independent by creating parental distance early on. Identifying generational effects, Bowlby provided completely humane evidence on the importance of care in the young, compared to Harlow's non-human primate experimentation, challenging the need for animal models in educational research. Within music education, the music specialist can be viewed as the caregiver, showing the importance of the child development qualities of music teachers for beginners.

Mary Ainsworth on relationship

Attachment theory is a concept that recognises the instinctive need for infants to bond with one main carer. It was developed by **Mary Ainsworth (1913–99)** into a social experiment called the Strange Situation (Ainsworth, 1967, 1979; Ainsworth and Bell, 1970; Bell and Ainsworth, 1972) that classified the type of attachment that existed between parent (carer) and infant. Importantly, relationship classification was shown to have the capacity to determine the potential health of a child's future relationships. Depending on the infant's response to a parent breifly leaving the child in a room with a stranger, Ainsworth was able to determine the behaviour of a parent towards the child, helping to identify supportive bonds (60–70% of Western population), as well as cases of mental health and even abusive relationships between parent/carer and child. This provided the therapist with avenues of therapy to support the development of the child and the health of the parent/carer. Educationally, this concept is used to recognise that the parent is the first and foremost educator, along with the importance of assigning key individuals to take responsibility for each child within group care situations. Within music education, this recognition of individuality is met well because of the nature of the private teaching methodology: demonstrate-imitate-explain-perfect-improvise/teach. This process automatically identifies the music teacher as the specialist responsible for guiding the student.

Jerome Kagan on relationship

In the wake of the World War II, psychologists were tasked with identifying ways to predict personality development because of the inexplicable events that had occurred during the Nazi regime. **Jerome Kagan (born 1929)** identified few personality correlations from childhood to adulthood, but identified *biology* and *environment* (Kagan, 1966; Kagan et al., 1964, 1987, 1988) as the major forces affecting personal development. He identified brain state, bodily movement, bodily feeling, facial expression and muscle tension as key identifiers of states of emotion impacting personality development. He further suggested that inhibited infants were more likely to be inhibited adults, but that this may change depending on genetic and environmental influences. Educationally, this united the nature–nurture debate (whether biology had a stronger influence over development than environmental), showing the relevance and importance of both. Within music education, biology has often been used as a reason for musical inability, however, this theory suggests that the environment (whether physical or emotional) can be used to support ability. This has led to many interventions and inventions that have created access for people who would not normally be able to use instruments, including support structures to hold instruments and even new instruments in order for people with disabilities to access music education successfully.

Berger and Cooper on relationship

Research has shown that the parental role in early childhood music education has a significant impact on development. Developing a theory that describes three levels of musical play as *unfinished play*, *extinguishing play* and *enhancing play*, **Berger and Cooper** (2003) identified ways in which adults extend or interrupt musical play. Through verbal requests and body language, children requested and benefited from uninterrupted musical play when the appropriate materials were available. Berger and Cooper showed that children's focus and concentration was extended purely by adults valuing the vocal feedback and willingness to remain flexible in timing, even during structured music sessions. **Cooper and Cardany's** (2011) later research showed that the increased rate of learning in early childhood suggested that this was a critical period for learning music. As a result, they concluded that opportunities should be made to focus on music at these early stages. Finally, **Barrett** (2011) shows that the relational interactions between parents and young children help to develop the children's identities, especially in the development of musical identities. Together, this research indicates that later musical identities are formed well before the first instrumental lessons, based on early relationships.

Research in general education has shown the significant effect that parenting has on child development, along with providing a broad range of opportunities for children to experience new situations. Implications for general as well as musical early childhood education is that the physical affection provided to infants by familiar caregivers provides the support that children need to develop the social, physical, academic, creative and emotional skills necessary to learn successfully.

Song Level Two: **Andy Pandy**

Level Two songs use simple rhythms and three notes that are far enough apart to hear the difference clearly, *so-mi-do*. This develops to include the fourth note, *la-so-mi-do*.

> *Andy Pandy, sugar and candy, all jump up*
> *Andy Pandy, sugar and candy, all jump down*
> *Andy Pandy, sugar and candy, all jump in*
> *Andy Pandy, sugar and candy, all jump out*

For younger children, we played instruments as we sang the words so that they could learn the tune. For older children, this game involved standing in a circle and children following the actions: jumping up, down, into the circle and out of the circle. As a change, we introduced the parachute, experiencing mixed success.

Figure 2.3 Song using so-mi-do notes

Table 2.3 Andy Pandy rhythm table

⏐♪	⏐♪	⊓♪	⏐♪
Andy	Pandy	sugar and	candy
⏐	⏐	⏐	-
All	jump	up	
⏐♪	⏐♪	⊓♪	⏐♪
Andy	Pandy	sugar and	candy
⏐	⏐	⏐	-
All	jump	down	
⏐♪	⏐♪	⊓♪	⏐♪
Andy	Pandy	sugar and	candy
⏐	⏐	⏐	-
All	jump	in	
⏐♪	⏐♪	⊓♪	⏐♪
Andy	Pandy	sugar and	candy
⏐	⏐	⏐	-
All	jump	out!	

How external motivation impacts education

Since the beginning of time, people have been fascinated by the ability of others to learn, gaining information and skills from another. Falling within the psychological area named "theory of mind", which is the ability to be aware of another's state of mind, this theory can be observed in early childhood. As scientific investigation proved to be successful and well received, professions interested in human development, such as psychology, psychiatry and psychometrics, began to adopt the principles of hypothesis, experiment, observation and conclusion. However, with no direct access to internal brain processes, those interested in development began to experiment with the effect that external influences had on individuals. In the same way that laws of gravity and inertia had been discovered, the intention was potentially to identify "laws" or guiding principles that could be applied to people, and this approach experienced varying degrees of success.

John Locke on external motivation

The father of the concept of "tabula rasa", or blank tablet, **John Locke (1632–1704)** based his civil rights philosophies on his progressive religious beliefs (Petryszak, 1981). His views on education conflicted with the traditional views of his day, which were that children were born evil and had to be trained to be good. He proposed that although people were born with empty minds, they were greatly influenced by their first impressions, environment and experiences. Educationally, this view recognises the long-term effects of decisions and activities undertaken in the first few years of childhood. Within music education, this view indicates that the first impressions that an infant or young child has of a music teacher have the potential to impact their musical development for life, a view also held by Kodály, who stated that the state of a town's musical interest and ability was directly affected by the enthusiasm and inclusivity of the town's music teacher.

Johann Heinrich Pestalozzi on external motivation

Using the scientific principles of observation, **Johann Heinrich Pestalozzi's (1746–1827)** approach to education used physical activity and practical object lessons as a basis for developing internal ideas (Bowers and Gehring, 2004; Niland, 2009; Sengupta, 2003). His process of action-experimentation-reflection became a recognised process in children's learning. Implications for education are that children move from practical experience to theoretical understanding. In music education this is observable as children often begin to play through memorising as opposed to reading/calculating notation. As this skill progresses, they lose the need to rely on an earlier practical demonstration, a concept that can be applied throughout education.

Kurt Lewin on external motivation

Taking a mathematical and physics approach to education, **Kurt Lewin (1890–1947)** identified behaviour as a result of forces acting on an individual to achieve goals, much like the scientific principles of movement being dependent on force and mass (Adelman, 1993; Lewin, 1946, 1947; Lewinet al., 1939). In itself, this implied that if internal and external forces could impact a person's success, then one could be affected by both nature (internal) *and* nurture (external). He further applied this theory to group dynamics, using his training in Gestalt theory which viewed events as complete in themselves with separate identities and qualities to their additive parts. He then identified group members as being dependent on each other for the group to exist, especially if the group was formed to complete a task. Observing that belief systems could change within discussion groups, he introduced terms including *feedback,* taken from electrical engineering; *unfreezing,* the process of changing beliefs or ideas; *participant observation,* through concrete and personal experience; and *cognitive aids,* which could be models or examples to help group thinking. Finally, Lewin is credited as the author of *action research,* describing steps as: identifying an idea; research; plan; implementing first step; evaluate; amend; implement next step. Lewin viewed collaboration with participants as essential, whereas today this view is not considered as important. Implications for education is the recognition that group and individual behaviour will vary considerably based on the perceived forces acting on the group, and that group adhesion is determined by purpose, and so goals should be clearly understood by all. Implications for music education are that different dynamics exist within solo rehearsal compared to group rehearsal, and that, particularly within group performances, a unified purpose, usually conducting, is essential for cohesion.

Lev Vygotsky on external motivation

The process of observation was also used by **Lev Vygotsky (1896–1934)**, a Soviet psychologist who identified social interaction as a major influencing force on development (Vygotsky, 1967, 1978, 1979). He emphasised the importance of making meaning and the subsequent role that community played. Contrary to Piaget's view of development before education, Vygotsky argued that learning was a human function that occurs regardless of development. Educationally, his view is comparable to Csikzsentmihalyi's concept of flow being a perfect balance of skill and opportunity (see p. 94); Vygotsky defined his zone of proximal development as a perfect balance of student interest and opportunity created by a more experienced peer or teacher. The implications for both education and music education are identical. This theory elevates the importance of a child's environment and so it is essential to be acutely aware of the social environment to which children are exposed because of the power of peer influence. As such, it is necessary to create a suitable environment to foster the on-going learning that Vygotsky identified, and to pay close attention to the child in order to identify when to step in and help, what level to teach, and when to step back. This approach is ideally suited to individually planned project work, fitting the child-led interest paradigm perfectly. In teacher-led situations, the teacher will need to set the standard of instruction at a single level, with the implication that it will simultaneously be set too high *and* too low for most of the students.

Erik Erikson on external motivation

Up to the 19th century, all observational research had been objectively external, but as the new century began, with the psychoanalytical influence of internal motivation, **Erik Erikson (1902–94)** used his psychoanalytical training to focus on the impact of society on individual personality development (Erikson, 1956, 1959). As education is (arguably) an external process applied to individuals to elicit change, the impact of social behaviour on personality and subsequent individual behaviour is a more natural, potentially unavoidable, development. Erikson saw development as strictly sequential, dependent on conflict resolution, as did Sigmund Freud. However, Erikson also identified conflict within relationships, showing a need to develop trust, identity and to help the next generation. He considered development and growth as on-going processes, where adolescence was key to identity development. His stage theory addressed all ages beginning with children developing trust/mistrust from 0–1½ years, with the implication that parental attachment should be protected at this stage, and the political implication for establishing and protecting maternity leave. Early childhood (1½–3 years) should be focussed on developing will by extending autonomy as much as possible, as opposed to the idea of preparation for formal education. Preschoolers (3–5 years) develop purpose through play, where initiative and enthusiasm could be directed and encouraged to prevent feelings of guilt. School ages 5–12 years fall in line with Pestalozzi's thinking of children contributing to their education by earning sufficient money to pay for their schooling themselves, developing their sense of industry and usefulness. Adolescence (12–18 years), Erikson's most emphasised period, should allow for freedom in developing interests, opportunities to freely discuss and collaborate and discover strengths and identity to prevent role confusion. Young adulthood (18–40 years) should develop opportunities for intimacy, both romantically and within friendships and families, avoiding isolation. Adulthood (40–65 years) should create situations in which to generate oneself through care, preventing stagnation. Finally, maturity (65+ years) could lead to ego integrity or despair in developing wisdom to pass on to the next generations. While this theory is more descriptive than testable, it provides useful ideas on environmental principles that may support society at specific age levels, through both education and through music education.

Burrhus Skinner on external motivation

Returning to the scientific application of observation, **Burrhus Skinner's (1904–90)** theory considered the causes of behaviour from primarily external sources, acknowledging that we have a mind but stating that without suitable tools it was difficult objectively to identify internal causes (Ferster and Skinner, 1957; Skinner, 1938). As a result, he did a lot of animal experimentation to identify the results of repeated actions, which he named positive and negative reinforcement. The familiarity of these terms is testament to the ease with which his ideas can be and have been indiscriminately used in education, despite punishment being shown to weaken behaviour. Skinner's principles have been widely used to modify behaviour in both individuals and large groups, and criticism of this approach includes trying to apply animal findings to human participants, the institutional approach taken with children, and the comparatively short-term changes. In both education and music education, an example of reinforcement behaviour includes sweets and/or stickers to help motivation. However, by ignoring the impact of the mind, learning becomes a process that is driven by external results, removing the opportunity to learn for learning sake, thus limiting the potential for on-going change.

Abraham Maslow on external motivation

Various psychologists identified that the environment can impact development, but **Abraham Maslow (1908–70)** was the first to identify specific areas within the environment (Maslow, 1943, 1959). Developing ideas on human fulfilment, Maslow took a humanistic approach to human potential, theorising that people's basic needs must be met while they are developing more advanced needs. While his progression is sometimes portrayed so that higher levels cannot be reached before reaching lower levels, his original approach stated that if higher levels were not being achieved, the reason *may* be that lower level needs had not been met, recognising that individuals may be at different stages on multiple levels simultaneously. This concept has been useful in education, instigating the start of free school meals in many countries, as well as child safeguarding and enhanced programmes of before and after-school care and holiday clubs in order to ensure that children are physically, socially and emotionally ready for academic learning. In terms of music education, Maslow's hierarchy of needs provides a useful checklist to determine why children may not be succeeding, and to assess whether there are additional measures that can be put in place by parents or government agencies to support their development.

Urie Bronfenbrenner on external motivation

The environmental perspective became significantly more detailed with **Urie Bronfenbrenner's (1917–2005)** ecological systems theory (Bronfenbrenner, 1977, 1986;

Bronfenbrenner and Condry Jr, 1970; Bronfenbrenner and Morris, 1998). Looking at the child's perspective, Bronfenbrenner detailed the child's immediate influences, from family to social, cultural, institutional and even the national forces that act on them. Applying this theory within education led to the HeadStart American programme and SureStart English programme, where the intention was that children could be assisted directly to attain their expected development and thereby reach their potential. In practice, the system has still battled to access those hardest to reach, indicating that while this system is comprehensive, and is certainly helpful in getting more government departments communicating with each other, there are still some areas in which details may be misunderstood or overlooked. From an educational and music education point of view, this system identifies a potential syllabus of interests that could be used by educators to identify suitable interests within development.

Albert Bandura on external motivation

With an understanding of Skinner's behaviourism, **Albert Bandura (born 1925)** identified the effects of social behaviour on individuals, devising a shockingly-effective experiment known as the "Bobo Doll". A child would watch a televised show of an adult interacting with an inflatable, weighted doll. The interaction would involve one of four behaviours: the adult would treat the doll gently and be praised; treat the doll gently and be punished; treat the doll aggressively and be praised; or treat the doll aggressively and be punished. The child would then be left in a room with the doll, and each time every child was found to replicate the behaviour of the adult, more so when praised, less so when punished, but they would repeat the gentle or aggressive behaviour that they had observed. Thus, Bandura theorised that people can both affect their environment and be affected by their environment, known as "reciprocal determinism". He devised the Social Learning Theory based on the behaviour that adults modelled to children. He found that self-efficacy (self-belief) made a huge difference in the goals that people set, and that self-regulation developed through observation or modelling. His interests in moral agency led to his theory that people could suspend their moral or humane beliefs if actions were sufficiently justified and they were distanced from personal responsibility. The implications for education as well as society are that behaviours originate from modelling, whether at home or socially, and that environments can affect the development of individuals in as much as individuals can affect their environments. This effectively disqualifies popularly held beliefs that smaller children are unable to understand complex adult interactions, and that children will achieve their potential regardless of their environment. Within music education, music was originally taught by demonstration, using imitation through modelling. Descriptions and explanations of behaviour developed as music became more formalised, so that there are now two extremes on the scale of practical music education: only teaching through music; or only teaching through language – the second of which has been the route of many school music lessons. In terms of environment, philosophical theorists are considering the environment as a third teacher or silent teacher because of the effect it has on development, suggesting that while environment is not the only factor influencing behaviour, it plays a significant role within the process of development with long-lasting consequences.

Creating suitable external environments were found to be particularly beneficial in music education. These ranged from establishing a sense of routine (Addessi, 2009) to creating musical play situations such as musical stories and being introduced to a wide variety of songs (Barrett, 1997, 2006, 2011, 2012). While these situations were not guaranteed to produce musicians, which could only be confirmed through longitudinal study, there was enough of a correlation for music education researchers to identify a relationship between developing musical skills through external influencers and young children.

Using scientific principles in research studies is beneficial because, in theory, anyone suitably trained would be capable of replicating the situation and, therefore, replicating the results which would corroborate the original idea. Mainly using observation, theories involved what we now call action research, because changes or interventions would often be put in place followed by more observation of the results. With varying theories on the importance of the environment, it is clear that the environment is considered a major factor by some of the greatest thought leaders in human development, with significant implications for the development of society. However, contrary to studies in the natural world, the anomalies experienced with humans could not be sufficiently explained by laws in the same way as biology, physics, chemistry and mathematics, leading to additional routes of enquiry.

Song Level Three: All around the buttercup

Level Three songs use simple rhythms and four notes that are closer together than the Level One and Two songs, *so-mi-re-do*.

All around the buttercup
One, two, three
If you want an awesome friend
Just choose me

With younger children, we played this game by holding hands in a circle. One child walked around the circle until the last line, then stopped, swapping places with the nearest child, who walked around the circle. With older children, we stood in a circle holding raised hands as one child wove in and out between each child, and then chose a new person on the last line. Once children were confident with this, we developed the game so that each new person chosen formed a chain behind the one who started

Figure 2.4 Song using so-mi-re-do notes

Table 2.4 *All around the buttercup* rhythm table

⊓	⊓	⊓	‖
All a-	round the	butter-	cup
‖	‖	‖	-
One,	two,	three	
⊓	⊓	⊓	-
If you	want an	awesome	friend
‖	‖	‖	-
Just	choose	me	

weaving in and out, until there were fewer and fewer children in the circle, but one long, weaving line. Through this, children learnt about bridges, sewing and shapes, as well as learning the co-operative skills of playing games, anticipation and self-control from turn-taking.

How to develop internal motivation through education

Without prior experience, understanding or explanation, it can be difficult to understand many phenomena that occur naturally, from gravity to human behaviour, to life and death. Over time, the scientific methodology to test natural phenomena (hypothesis, experiment, observation and conclusion) was shown to be easy to reproduce, and led to many discoveries which either proved commonly held theories and beliefs to be right or wrong. After scientists of human nature tried to use this formula on human development and understanding, the extensive anomalies showed that people were much more complex than natural elements and minerals. Looking back to the origins of psychology and philosophy, it can be seen how the significance of individuality and the effects of internal motivation may be responsible for the scientific anomalies.

Jean-Jacques Rousseau on internal motivation

In order to understand and explain natural events, religious ideas began to dominate the world in medieval times. Religious leaders interpreted meanings of sacred scriptures, sometimes exploiting them for their own political or economic benefit. In the West, one prevalent interpretation of Christianity led to the concept of "original sin", where human character left to its own devices was deemed to be evil. This led to teachings that at birth people were evil and had to have their instinctively evil traits trained out of them as early as possible. Bucking this trend, one of the earliest philosophers, **Jean-Jacques Rousseau (1712–78)**, went against the grain and instead promoted the idea of inherent goodness of character. He suggested that by giving children freedom to explore a neutral environment they would learn successfully and become good citizens (Bertram, 2010; Niland, 2009). His ideas were based on philosophies and beliefs, written in an imaginary story, which unfortunately provided no objective evidence to prove this thinking. However, his intention was to create a society of responsible citizens that would work towards the greater good. Within education, this type of thinking gives children the benefit of support, and is altogether more respectful of the child as an individual, recognising that individual fulfilment holds greater social potential than coercive group thinking. Within music education, this theory can be translated into presuming that all children are musical and that it is their environment that encourages or discourages individual development. Indeed, in the era of non-invasive interventions, this has been found to be the case.

Johann Heinrich Pestalozzi on internal motivation

Despite the limited political view of many nations, freedom for children to explore their individual interests has been a theme for centuries. Basing his ideas on Rousseau's commitment to freedom in childhood, Pestalozzi used physical activity and object lessons in his methodology, limiting the focus on language and creating freedom for children to pursue their interests. His "psychological method of instruction" aimed to identify "laws of human nature", where he encouraged children to create their own judgements and reasoning to work towards what we now call a holistic education based on "hands, heart and head". Pestalozzi's principles of learning included: respect for personality; protected development potential; demonstrated love without chastisement; a focus on practice before explanation, reinforced by explanation once learnt, and then reinforced further by repetition with understanding. His commitment to improving social conditions, using a balanced education and teaching through a process of "action–experimentation–reflection", led to almost eradicating national illiteracy in Switzerland. Interestingly, he intended schools to involve self-sustaining production, allowing children to finance their own learning, and he completely disapproved of rote learning (memorisation based on repetition). The implications for education are multiple, from viewing teaching from a position of respect, not discipline; using observation and reflection to guide teaching approaches and interests; and the most challenging, empowering children to be self-sustaining early on. The implications for music education are clearly in using respect, observation and reflection in teaching, and challengingly, in finding ways to provide music education for all.

Sigmund Freud on internal motivation

As psychologists recognised the impact that individuality had on behaviour, one area within psychology developed into a theory of internal motivation called psychoanalysis. This was a set of beliefs created by **Sigmund Freud (1856–1939)** and developed by others, mainly in Europe, to identify explanations for behaviour, particularly unexplained behaviour (Britzman, 2015; Freud, 1905; Sawyer, 1997; Winner, 1982). Freud identified three different ways in which people see themselves: as the id (instinctive behaviour); superego (moral conscience); and ego (mediator between instinct and conscience), recognising that even forgotten experiences from the past may impact future behaviour. Psychoanalysis argues that irrational behaviour originates in the unconscious; the conscious needs to be tricked into revealing the unconscious; disturbances develop when the conscious and unconscious experience conflict; and intervention is necessary to reconcile the two. One educationally significant aspect of psychoanalysis associates events in early childhood as well as biology as causes for irrational behaviour and, as a result, many ideas on child development rehabilitation are based in psychotherapy. Educational implications are difficult, especially in one-to-many group situations, but by bearing in mind the key points it is easier to devise principles for teaching. Educationally, if irrational behaviour originates in the subconscious, then children displaying this type of behaviour will be unable to explain the reason for it, so explanations will need to be accessed indirectly, for example, through fantasy like role play, small world toys, drawings and storytelling. Often a spontaneous event or situation will have occurred to set off the behaviour, bringing the conscious and subconscious into conflict, and without intervention, similar situations will result in similar behaviours. While intervention for adults often involves talking therapy, for children unable to make full use of language, alternative therapies have been devised, including play, drama, art and music therapy, where therapists are trained to identify the meanings of behaviours and suggest ways in which the conscious can learn to accept the conflict of the unconscious. Within music education, often the provision of technical skill with sufficient opportunity is enough for a student to access a healthy outlet for emotional expression, leading to additional benefits including performance confidence (through repeated rehearsal), physical and emotional self-control, and persistent self-motivation.

Alfred Binet and Henry Goddard on internal motivation

As society developed with the changes of the Industrial Revolution, the needs of the growing population were considered, including educational needs. **Alfred Binet (1857–1911)**, with his multifaceted psychological interests, undertook the task to create a test to differentiate teaching for children with lower abilities from that for children with average abilities (Bilhartz et al., 1999; Kaviani et al., 2014; Peterson, 1924). Using a system of questions relying on the individual's ability to consider variable solutions to problems, he used testing to investigate or access internal processes. Recognising that the scores provided from his 30-question test would only provide limited information, he cautioned that: qualitative or background information was essential in making decisions; comparative population groups had to be similar; developmental timings differed greatly between children; and environmental factors had such a deep impact on the scores that scores could not be regarded as permanently fixed. However, when American psychologist **Henry Goddard (1866–1957)**, keen on maintaining social meritocracy, came across the test in his studies, he adapted the test so that the scoring was accepted as an indication of social class, changing the purpose of the test from widening access to education for all to limiting the actual level of teaching quality within social classes. The effects of this social exclusion can be felt even today, with societies for those with high scores on intelligence quotient (IQ) tests, despite the lack of evidence of improved career options, financial achievement or social impact. Sadly, this approach was also applied to musical aptitude, with many musical groups and institutions insisting on a minimum of academic musical proficiency, often through the grading system. This limiting tactic effectively eliminated multiple generations from recognising their inherent musicality, relegating them to the realms of the audience, while the chosen few received the tuition and training required to perform. Had Binet's original test intentions been honoured, teachers would be better prepared to extend the opportunities of those with different backgrounds in order to catch up with others of more affluent backgrounds.

John Dewey on internal motivation

Around the same period, towards the end of the 19th century, in America the concept of rote education, the well-accepted and traditional method of public education, was criticised by more educational thinkers for the lack of recognition of individuality and enforced conformity. **John Dewey (1859–1952)** advocated that individual thinking should be used to create change, not just to explain or represent existing situations, and that education should be equal for all and based on practical usefulness (Campbell, 1991; Dewey, 1997, 2013; Miettinen, 2000). He argued that curriculum content should be balanced with child-led interest so that children would gain useful skills to serve the greater good, incorporating pragmatism with progressive education. This, he argued, would equip individuals with the skills needed to make informed decisions, solve increasingly complex problems, and thus recognise the benefit of education. His qualitative teaching requirements included a love for students, a love for subject enquiry and teaching methods, and a love for sharing information, concepts which now attempt to be represented by quantitative measurements including breadth of subject knowledge and student achievement. Educationally, this resulted in the child-led movement where, despite Dewey's warnings of being over-permissive, the American system in particular appeared to reduce the authority of the teacher by restricting interference and guidance. This significantly reduced the amount of content being taught, demonstrating how difficult it is to balance curriculum guidance with individual freedom. Within music education, there has always been a tendency for the teacher to be the authoritative instructor although there is more individual choice within private lessons. Most teachers now present some instruction before students are able to make informed choices.

Jean Piaget on internal motivation

While individuality was being promoted in America with varying levels of child-centred learning taking place, in Europe, **Jean Piaget (1896–1980)** was developing a genetic theory on how children think (Piaget, 1951, 1976; Piaget and Cook, 1952; Piaget et al., 1969). His ideas on children's cognitive development were based on scientific principles of experimentation, but he only used his own children for the majority of his studies. Statistics have since shown that small representations lead to skewed conclusions, so they cannot be generalised to larger groups because there are so many differences, for example, differences between how biology and environment can influence development. Using his experiments, Piaget suggested that children automatically developed their motor skills through sensory exploration from birth to 2 years old, used symbolic play and manipulated objects from 2 to 7 years, developed logical thought from 7 to 11 years, and finally began thinking in an abstract way from 11 to 16 years. Research has since shown that sequential development depends on a child's environment, and that Piaget significantly underestimated children's abilities. However, his recognition of the internal differences between child and adult thinking made educators aware of the ways that differences needed to be addressed. Educationally, this created a general awareness of standardised growth progression that has been useful in identifying situations where interventions may be introduced in delayed development as well as in premature birth. Within music education, this progression helps educators to understand the child's need to move and explore rather than sit at different ages.

Carl Rogers on internal motivation

Despite the European approach to identifying a sequence of development, Americans progressed their ideas on individualised development through **Carl Rogers (1902–87)**, another psychotherapist (A. Rogers, 2014; Rogers and Dymond, 1954; Rogers and Koch, 1959). Developing ideas on "the true self" from working with troubled children, Rogers applied his theory of personality development to a number of fields, including education. He argued that traditional educational approaches were ineffective because people naturally resisted new ideas. Thus, teachers should act as mediators, only presenting information if relevant to students, as teaching should be learner-centred. Although this ensured that information was relevant, this perspective also held the potential to limit additional interests. Educationally, this view is used actively in the home-schooling sector. Within traditional school settings, schools tend to teach all subjects throughout primary school and allow children to specialise according to their interests as they progress through secondary or high school. Within music education, all musical foundations are taught initially, with more exam bodies creating opportunities for students to specialise in their chosen genre the higher they proceed through the grading system.

John Bowlby on internal motivation

Around the same time, in the early 20th century, British psychologists came to the fore. Popular ideas within European society still idealised limited contact between parents and children to prevent children growing up "spoilt". After qualifying in both medicine and psychoanalysis, **John Bowlby (1907–90)** began working with children evacuated from London during World War II, identifying links between prolonged parental separation and crime. He suggested that the bond between a carer and infant, which he called the attachment behavioural system, was an evolutionary development that was essential to the successful development of adult relationships. This finding has helped to promote safeguarding, learning and development by being used in the development of assigning "key people" in early childhood education, specifically, and more generally by providing evidence that affection in childhood by parents and responsible carers resulted in more secure, competent and successful adults. Within music education, this is often the norm because within schools there is rarely more than one music teacher, and private teaching is based on the premise of the same individual teacher developing the child's skills within a trusted relationship.

69

Jerome Bruner on internal motivation

American contributions on child development began to move away from philosophical theory when **Jerome Bruner (1915–2016)** used scientific experiments to demonstrate the internal motivation involved in decision-making (Bruner, 1957, 1991; Bruner et al., 1949; Wood et al., 1976). His contribution to educational pedagogy has been considerable, as his approaches have been referred to and adopted in many national educational systems. Bruner supported a child-centred approach, using real-world problems to aid engagement and progression to further stages. His concept of the spiral curriculum is frequently used in early education to remind and reinforce essential or challenging learning skills. His scaffolding concept, where more experienced peers aid younger or less experienced students, has been well publicised and this approach is most recommended in many private or small-group lesson situations because it is found to be so effective, both in mainstream and music education.

Paolo Friere on internal motivation

While Bruner's theory considered the internal motivation of children in response to decision-making, **Paolo Friere (1921–97)** considered internal motivation from experience (Freire, 1996). His humble beginnings and subsequent extensive educational experience and contribution provided him with substantial insight into the necessary skills to overcome external disadvantage. From his experience, Friere argued that equal education could change external circumstances purely through the internal motivation of knowledge. By identifying the political and cultural agendas prevalent within education systems, he argued that awareness and openness of agendas was necessary to prevent multiple standards within education. This is an extremely important insight in settings with diverse populations that include deprivation, both within mainstream and music education.

Lawrence Kohlberg on internal motivation

Around the same time, in the 1950s–1960s, **Lawrence Kohlberg (1927–87)** explored the impact of "moral development", building on Piaget's concept of children's moral development (Kohlberg, 1963, 1964; Kohlberg et al., 1983; Piaget, 1997). Due to specific life experience, like Freire, Kohlberg claimed that people inherently emulate role models, including the moral example that they set. His ideas were based on several unsubstantiated assumptions, presuming that all people wanted to live in fair societies, and that all people wanted to explore their environments, which were assumptions that were never tested. Subsequent research has shown that role models do in fact elevate moral thinking but this cannot show changes in moral reasoning. Educationally, moral discussion has been shown to impact moral reasoning, and this has been used to address sensitive and national issues including sex education and, most recently, Prevent, a British values awareness programme created to safeguard communities against terrorist radicalisation. Within music education, songs and works can open discussions on viewpoints and values. This leads to musical philosophical questions such as whether songs are defined by lyrics or by their music, and whether lyrics could or should be altered to reflect changes in society, or whether they should simply be discarded.

Mihalyi Csikszentmihalyi on internal motivation

As the 20th century progressed, society and government began to highlight the concept and usefulness of education, and tension between business skills and educational principles became apparent. As a result, government stepped in to support finding a balance. The challenge of providing businesses with a suitably qualified workforce had to balance with an education system designed using responsible research that would help to develop successful communities. Psychologists began to look at additional areas that may affect education in order to understand deeper issues. Hungarian psychologist **Mihalyi Csikszentmihalyi (born 1934)** researched the relationship between happiness and creativity and found that the combination of having the right level of opportunity and skill made work seem effortless (Csikszentmihalyi, 2008), hence his concept of flow (see p. 94). Educationally, this fits with the concept of the educator as a support or scaffold, ensuring that sufficient skills are in place for the next challenge. Csikszentmihalyi's most recent work (Csikszentmihalyi et al., 2017) argues that academic success can be best predicted by what he terms "work orientation", where he lists a number of areas that are part of this term. To date, governments have been looking at interventions based on home and social influence, however, according to Csikszentmihalyi, the internal motivations of achievement, endurance, cognitive structure, order, play and low impulsivity are better predictors of fulfilling long-term educational goals. Within music education, the concept of flow describes the ultimate creative ambition, and it is at the point of matched skill and challenge that music students begin to take personal responsibility for their musical development.

Howard Gardner on internal motivation

With the frustratingly agenda-heavy IQ testing and lack of substantive educational benefit, American **Howard Gardner (born 1943)** considered education with a view to recognising and enhancing individuality (Gardner, 1983, 2003; Gardner and Hatch, 1989). He identified what he called "multiple intelligences", which were eight different ways that people process information. Instead of being used as a pedagogical concept of finding multiple ways to present learning content, however, it ended up being applied quantitatively to test individuals in order to identify their specific ways of learning. This may have been more effective had the human brain been more like a computer as previously thought, with specialist "compartments" or areas dedicated to singular processes. In fact, the development of scans like functional magnetic resonance imaging (fMRI) and positron emission tomography (PET) has shown that processes follow pathways within the brain which may actually divert in cases of accident or illness. This explains why some skills remain or can be relearnt, despite damage to the brain. Consequently, the idea of limited learning opportunities actually ended up limiting learning as an experience instead of the specialised learning that was anticipated, which would have been the case with computer-like brains. This is quite a criticism, yet the greatest criticism of this theory is the lack of empirical evidence to support the different learning styles identified, which ironically may have brought these results to the fore earlier. This theory influenced both mainstream and music education by resulting in a generation of teachers working to identify and group children according to their preferred learning styles, which reduced the children's developmental opportunities and experiences with other styles.

Angela Duckworth on internal motivation

With vocational success identified as the ambition of education by both business and government, American psychologist **Angela Duckworth (born 1970)** identified specific qualities of high achievers after analysing both business and teaching practice (Duckworth et al., 2007; Von Culin et al., 2014). She called the group of skills "grit", a term that described the persistent focus displayed by successful learners despite their environmental circumstances or perceived biological ability. The implications for education suggest that nations with high ambitions for learners should develop the skills associated with grit, regardless of background or environment. Nonetheless, current criticisms claim over-exaggeration of results, only a modest correlation between grit and success, and most potentially damaging, "grit" as the renamed personality trait of conscientiousness, which has been generally accepted in psychological circles as a quality that cannot be taught. Results remain to be seen through new research publication. Educationally, this theory opens up opportunity beyond the nature (born with it) or nurture (affected by environment) debate by allowing for individual choice, which may explain why children from similar backgrounds or even the same families can be so different. Within music education, many success stories have resulted from personal interest, persistence, detailed repetition and other skills associated with conscientiousness.

Lauren Sosniak on internal motivation

Parental involvement was balanced with teacher relationship in **Lauren Sosniak's (1952–2006)** study on talent development (Sosniak and Gabelko, 2008). She discovered that people who became most successful in their fields were given unremarkable opportunities without an over-emphasis on parental involvement. One of her studies involved interviewing the development of concert pianists, and she found that their development occurred in three distinct stages: their initial teachers related very well to them as children and made lessons enjoyable; they moved on to more advanced teachers once they began to love to play their instrument to improve themselves; finally, they were able to take extensive criticism from demanding master teachers once they had developed the necessary techniques. Interestingly, there were no child prodigies in the interviewee cohort and, on average, it took 17 years of development from the very first lesson to becoming extremely accomplished and rising to challenges beyond their grasp. This long-term view of knowledge development, encouragement for small achievements, and interdependency of personal contact with others who believed in the student suggested that "unusually successful learning may be within the reach of a large proportion of our population", showing the importance of relational learning (Sosniak and Gabelko, 2008) (see p. 289).

Spanning nearly 300 years, educational research appears to have been continuously emphasising the benefits of recognising individuality in learners, and challenging the benefits of rote learning in more and more detail. This should lead us to question why it is used now – and why it was ever used in the first place – to determine whether it should continue to be used. Rote learning appears to be used in instances where curriculum developers (educators or government) see little benefit in teaching the principles of facts that are considered essential, for example, times tables and parts of speech. Not so long ago, education's primary focus was "mental arithmetic" or quick problem-solving. In other words, rote learning is used when the process appears to be secondary to producing correct results quickly, like a machine. This type of thinking answers the second part of the question posed: why was rote learning ever used? In an age of industrialisation, where the machine was considered advanced because it saved time, money and effort, human thinking was compared to machine and computer programming (as recently as the 1980s). However, we have progressed from the wonder of repetitive machinery to the power of information transfer, with essential information stored in transient locations and accessible on demand. We currently understand the brain to be a powerhouse of information that is capable of using multiple pathways to transmit the same information should the usual pathway be unavailable and, because of this if for no other reason, it is worth rethinking the approach we use in education. It is not so much about *what* is stored, but knowing how to *access* and *use* it is essential, demanding individual creativity and thinking. The implication for educational development is that competitive tests and examinations, single moments of individual performance, are out-dated, irrelevant and should ideally be replaced by process-driven and collaboratively unifying project work. The major problems of the world, from health to famine to crime, are all complex situations that would be resolved more quickly and more expediently through process and collaboration, resulting in greater universal benefit. The implications for music education are that the traditional practice of only "playing by the dots" in individual or private teaching settings is also outmoded and restrictive, more explanatory teaching methods should be identified or devised, and learning should involve more group collaborative learning, leading to more unique musical composition.

Song Level Three: Johnny works

Level Three songs use simple rhythms and four notes that are closer together than the Level One and Two songs, *so-mi-re-do.*

Figure 2.5 Song using so-mi-re-do notes

Table 2.5 Johnny works rhythm table

Π	Π	Π	I
Johnny	works with	one ham-	mer,
Π	I	Π	I
One ham-	mer,	one ham-	mer
Π	Π	Π	I
Johnny	works with	one ham-	mer,

Π	Π	I	-
Now he	works with	two	
Π	Π	Π	I
Johnny	works with	five ham-	mers,
Π	I	Π	I
Five ham-	mers,	five ham-	mers
Π	Π	Π	I
Johnny	works with	five ham-	mers
Π	Π	I	-
Now his	work is	done!	

Johnny works with one hammer, one hammer, one hammer
Johnny works with one hammer, now he works with two

Johnny works with two hammers, two hammers, two hammers
Johnny works with two hammers, now he works with three

Johnny works with three hammers, three hammers, three hammers
Johnny works with three hammers, now he works with four

Johnny works with four hammers, four hammers, four hammers
Johnny works with four hammers, now he works with five

Johnny works with five hammers, five hammers, five hammers
Johnny works with five hammers, now his work is done

We sang this action song with both younger and older children. We began singing and banging one fist on the floor ("one hammer"), then both fists ("two hammers"), both fists and one foot ("three hammers"), both fists and both feet ("four hammers"), both fists, both feet and nodding head ("five hammers"). This developed the children's rhythmic skills, gross motor co-ordination of left and right hands and feet, as well as giving practical experience of numeracy skills like sequential counting.

Educational theories on sequential development

One aspect of the theory of development that is important to educational study is *how the theory is applied*. Science shows that people all develop differently, from walking and talking to later developments, for example, the onset of puberty and the menopause. Yet, if we use time (i.e. age) as a standard measurement, it is easier to identify and compare individual behaviour or development with most of the population, despite it being inequitable or unfair. Most theories that generalise population behaviour claim to be useful for individuals by using the theory of the bell curve, where most people fall into a central majority range, and people with lower or higher results fall into the minority ranges on each side. With the developments in scientific methodology and the focus on being able to generalise information, many early theories on child development were sequential. Theorists identified what they considered to be uniquely different stages that appeared common to all, and these theories are referred to as stage development theories, where an individual's behaviour is compared to the expected sequence of behaviour.

Jean-Jacques Rousseau on sequential development

One of the earliest observations of sequential development was suggested by Rousseau. His concept of freedom in development came from his belief in three developmental stages, loosely what we would call childhood, adolescence and adulthood (Bertram, 2010). Rousseau considered childhood to span from birth to 12, during which time children were guided by internal senses like emotion and instinct. From 12 to 16, Rousseau described adolescence as the beginning of reason, where children are able to receive instruction, after which they attain adulthood. Many of these principles are still used today, from the age span of primary and secondary schools, to the legal age of consent. Within music education, these developmental stages appear to be adhered to in public primary education, and music is taught more formally or traditionally after the age of 12 years.

Rudolf Steiner on sequential development

Historically, the next concept of sequential development was termed by **Rudolf Steiner (1061–1925)** as "phases of development" (Steiner, 2013). Steiner's holistic approach to education linked 7-year cycles to astrology, and explained age-specific behaviours through astrological qualities assigned to the planets, beginning with the "Moon phase" involving psychic forces from ages 0–7 years. His educational expectation of children was based on freedom of choice, where formal education was restricted until children indicated an interest or readiness to develop additional skills. One example of this is the gradual introduction to reading only beginning at 7 years of age, a controversial concept in the UK where education begins at the age of 4. Government education systems and teachers seem to battle between group teaching for expedience and teaching the right content at the right time. The compromise is usually finding ways to prepare children for the content that is considered most appropriate, relevant or beneficial.

This same compromise exists in music education, where games and physical activity are often found to be effective preparation to introduce new musical concepts.

Maria Montessori on sequential development

Again, the scientific approach of observation (Montessori, 1912, 1914) was used by the first Italian female doctor, **Maria Montessori (1870–1952)**. She saw the benefit of peer teaching and observed that development appeared to follow 3-year cycles. Consequently, she divided children into four mixed-age groupings or planes of development. By allowing children to choose their own activities for their own length of time, this approach introduced equity to all children regardless of background and heritage. By encouraging older children to demonstrate new skills to younger children, this approach valued the unique contribution of each individual, developing ideas like individual and group responsibility. Educationally, many of Montessori's ideas were tested scientifically, as she was a qualified doctor, however the educational community of the day only saw value in the result, not the process, so she destroyed her original research notes. However, these ideas are being demonstrated by others, such as the efficacy of peer teaching, and creative entrepreneurial skills from following individual interests. Within music education, private lessons encourage students to develop their own interests, while group lessons have been developed by studies from Lucy Green, a music education researcher, who showed that the use of peer teaching specifically during adolescence appeared to increase interest in music education for longer (Green, 2002, 2008, 2010).

Jean Piaget on sequential development

Following on from Montessori's hope for humanity resting in children, Piaget developed a theory of knowledge, or epistemology, with the same hopes (Piaget, 1976). Using observation-based conclusions, Piaget created situations to experiment on the way that children thought. He became interested in child development while working in intelligence testing, and discovered that children seemed to get the same questions wrong at similar ages, indicating that they thought differently to adults. Combining his training and interests in sociology, biology and psychology, he devised four developmental stages to describe the physical and psychological changes observed in childhood, which were further subdivided into more specific processes: the sensorimotor stage from birth to 2 years; the pre-operational stage from 2 to 7 years; the concrete operational stage from 7 to 11 years; and the formal operational stage from 11 to 16 years. He was one of the first to research children through naturalistic observation (i.e. not in a laboratory), and using psychometrics (intelligence tests) and psychiatric methods (psychoanalysis). Criticisms against his work include: experimentation was limited to his own three children; his strict stage progression; and his omission in recognising that background, culture and environment affect development. Educationally, Piaget's ideas and principles made European and American education more child-centred, interactive and constructed (building new knowledge based on previous knowledge). Within music education, the recognition of different ways of thinking allows for more appropriate approaches to be used.

Erik Erikson on sequential development

Identity development was a feature of Erikson's stage development theory, possibly as a result of his multiple heritage (Erikson, 1956, 1959). He developed an eight-stage level theory on psychosocial development from birth to death. Despite being presented sequentially, Erikson explained that his identified conflict was merely an indication of the most obvious conflict at the ages stated, that all conflicts were experienced in every lifetime, and that conflicts could be resolved at any point, not only during the stated ages. Subsequent research has provided some evidence that those that resolve adolescent conflicts are best equipped to resolve the conflicts of early adulthood, and are most successful in intimate attachments during early adulthood. Educationally, this theory provides *principles* in which children may be given opportunities to resolve crises healthily. In the early years, for example, from 0–2 years, children who are able to implicitly trust their carers should develop hope; from 2–4 years, children who are encouraged to act autonomously and not shamed into "good behaviour" should develop will; from 4–5 years, children who are given opportunities to use their initiative and not respond out of guilt should develop purpose; from 5–12 years, children who are recognised for their achievements in the work that they produce and not their failures should develop competence. Within music education, similar principles may be applied, supporting Sosniak's assertion that early music teachers would promote love for the subject.

Jerome Bruner on sequential development

Returning the focus of research to the process of how knowledge is acquired, Bruner devised three stages of cognitive representation (Bruner, 1966). Organising lessons through discovery from the child's view, he identified the first stage of knowledge representation as "enactive", based on experience and physical manipulation of objects observable in children under a year. The second stage involving a visual summary of images was called "iconic", with reality represented by a picture that was observable in children aged 1–6 years. The final "symbolic" stage described the storage of information in codified form, such as language, observable in children over 7 years old. He supported learning that introduced simple skills which could be built on later using more complex skills, and promoted the concept of information sharing by more experienced learners, now termed "scaffolding". These principles are easily seen in both general and music education, with children creating physical experiences, developing this into pictures in books, and finally developing it into descriptive speech or writing. Within music, children play the games, play the music, and then learn the concept, which is expressed in a new way.

Lawrence Kohlberg on sequential development

The efficacy of scaffolding can easily be seen through the studies of Kohlberg. While some of the approaches above have attempted to explain knowledge acquisition by developing an overarching explanation for learning within a lifetime, others, like Kohlberg, focussed on a smaller area of learning in greater depth (Kohlberg, 1963, 1964; Kohlberg et al., 1983). Kohlberg was interested in Piaget's theory on moral development due to his life experience of smuggling Jewish people into Palestine, his incarceration and subsequent escape. His theory of the development of moral reasoning led to his concept of ethical behaviour consisting of six constructive stages founded on the assumption that all people wish to live in a co-operative society based on justness and fairness. He examined the words and deeds of people that he considered public role models, believing their words and actions influenced their followers, yet he never tested this. Modern research has shown that this observation creates moral elevation but cannot show whether moral reasoning had been impacted. Using discussions with school children, Kohlberg was able to show that moral discussion successfully impacted moral reasoning. Educationally, this shows the power of collaborative discussion in learning, and the process of learning, from situations being right or wrong, through to giving the right answers to look good, to developing principles to live by. Within music education, this process is useful to know in understanding the level of thinking of students from the answers that they provide.

Observationally, there appears to be a lot of potential in accepting the concept of developmental skill progression within education as well as in medicine. Clearly the benefits are that the concept helps the professional in determining whether the child falls into the average, below-average or above-average grouping, and therefore how much help may be subsequently needed to lead an independent life. This concept, like IQ testing, had its roots in positive concepts but ultimately became an expression of how much below and above-average students would cost society, how much they could be expected to contribute and, therefore, how much investment should be made to help them attain their anticipated level of achievement. In addition to this problem, which considerably restricts individual opportunity in the most devious of ways, many anomalies can be found in these groupings, with little to no guidance on how to manage them. Children may bypass levels, return to levels, or remain well past expected time scales, clearly showing the flaws in a system that tries to systematise society.

Song Level Four: Who did all the baking?

Level Four songs use simple rhythms and the whole anhemitonic pentatonic scale, *la-so-mi-re-do*. This means that all the notes are at least a tone away from each other, so they are easier to sing and repeat successfully.

Who did all the baking, who did all the baking?
"I," said my mother, with your little baby brother
"It was I, it was I"

Figure 2.6 Song using la-so-mi-re-do notes

Table 2.6 Who did all the baking? rhythm table

⊓	⊓	I	I
Who did	all the	ba-	king
I I	⊓	I	I
Who did	all the	ba-	king?
I	⊓	⊓	⊓
"I,"	said my	mother,	"with your
⊓	⊓	⊓	⊓
Little	baby	brother	It was
I	⊓	I	-
I,	It was	I"	

We played this song with younger children and they sat opposite each other in two groups, and took turns playing instruments and singing. The first group sang and played the first two lines, then passed the instruments to the second group, who sang the rest of the song. With older children, we introduced them to simple line dancing. In parallel lines, the first group simply walked towards the second group and then back for the first two lines. The second group did a do-si-do, walking towards and around the opposite person, then back, while singing the longer second part of the song. Along with being a fun game, we found that it developed co-ordination, sensory and space awareness, as well as the skill of listening for and responding to cues.

Educators who focussed on child-centred pragmatism

Most often, the term "education" conjures thoughts of the wise and experienced teacher imparting knowledge to the naïve and inexperienced youth. As a result, ideas of basing education from the child's interests seem to be innovative and even rebellious. In fact, the idea of child-centred education is not new and was recommended centuries ago. Over time, it has been reintroduced as there is new evidence of benefits to both children and teachers. Pragmatism describes the real-world application of theory. Looking at the various theories and reasons behind child-centred pragmatism, it appears that basic human rights like respect and individual welfare are the motivating factors in contrast to the one-size-fits-all view of national curricula around the world. This clearly illustrates the dilemma of education provision: should education suit the state or the child?

John Amos Comenius on child-centred pragmatism

The Czech educational and religious leader, **John Amos Comenius (1592–1670)**, was one of the first teachers to include pictures in textbooks to show what he had described in words (Schwarz and Martin, 2012; Stroope, 2005). His rebellion did not end there. He also adopted a child-centred approach by teaching children in their native language instead of only using Latin, using the revolutionary approach of breaking ideas down to simple concepts from advanced theory. He encouraged students to develop skills in logical thinking instead of rote memorisation because he had been influenced by the scientists of his day, like Bacon and Descartes, who used theory that had practical and pragmatic application. Comenius is credited with being the first person to divide schools into the age groups found today, as well as providing equal opportunities to study, regardless of gender or financial status. Within music education, the use of pictures, child-friendly vocabulary (syllables) and logical problem-solving strategies are clear applications of Comenius' revolutionary teaching style.

Jean-Jacques Rousseau on child-centred pragmatism

Novels by Genevan philosopher Rousseau also demonstrate his child-centred approach by encouraging children to explore their own interests up to the age of 12 and then to learn a trade during adolescence (Bertram, 2010). His belief in the inherent goodness of children was based on his ideas that children were not intentionally manipulative or naughty, which was contrary to the prolific religious indoctrination of the day that insisted that human nature was inherently sinful and had to be actively forced out. Despite having levels of forward thinking, Rousseau has been criticised for not promoting gender equality in education and not basing his ideas on real childhood experience. Within both mainstream and music education, Rousseau's promotion of exploration may be applied using songs with engaging storylines and relatable characters for children, as well as musical exercises that are self-correcting.

Johann Heinrich Pestalozzi on child-centred pragmatism

The Swiss reformer Pestalozzi emphasised individual difference, sensory perception and active involvement, which were hallmarks of the successful schools he started (Bowers and Gehring, 2004). His teachings significantly impacted the development of language education and physical education, which he linked to general, moral and intellectual education, and were used in the school where Albert Einstein was educated. The latter valued the education he received, which was "based on free action and personal responsibility" (Isaacson, 2007). Within mainstream education, with the focus on conformity and uniformity, the lack of personal responsibility may in fact be a result of the lack of free action, so it may be useful to explore the possibilities of widening free action safely and responsibly. Within music education, opportunities to perform in real contexts (not only parent audience) provide the experience and demands the personal responsibility needed to value practising.

Friedrich Froebel on child-centred pragmatism

One of Pestalozzi's students, German **Friedrich Froebel (1782–1852)**, developed Pestalozzi's concept of individuality in play (Williams, 1954). His focus on active learning, "free work", movement games and self-directed play spread through the institutes that he founded, as well as the use of his specially invented play materials, which he called "Froebel gifts". With activities in his first "kindergarten" involving singing, dancing, gardening and self-directed play with the Froebel gifts, he is acknowledged for recognising the different needs and capabilities of children. Within education, Froebel's influence led to greater freedom in play, and in music education in particular this is seen through creating opportunities for children to investigate their environment/instruments at their own pace, and improvise or invent their own songs without intervention, with the recognition of their original songs being valuable in their own right.

John Dewey on child-centred pragmatism

American psychologist Dewey was known for wanting to use theory as a vehicle for change, not just as a representation of reality (Dewey, 1997). To this end, his idea of progressive education began with the child, involving experiential education, entre-preneurship, problem-solving, critical thinking, corporate work, co-operative learning, community service, identifying skills for future needs, and assessment by evaluation. His ideas on liberalism argued for introducing equality, social justice and a mixed economy through creating a social and interactive learning experience. In practice, this balanced curriculum theory with practical investigations into child-appropriate problems. Within music education, one practical application would be to use original composition to teach additional musical concepts.

Maria Montessori on child-centred pragmatism

Montessori developed her educational ideas and theories through, first, carefully observing children with disabilities, and afterwards mainstream children (Montessori, 1914). Controversially adapting furniture, tools, storage and materials for children's use, Montessori went on to develop activities specifically for children, from flower arrang-ing and cleaning to objective lessons and gymnastics. Even her class age divisions were organised based on peer teaching and focussed on individual interest and development. Her observations indicated that children who worked independently were both more autonomous and more self-motivated towards understanding. Thus, by treating them as individuals, children had freedom to move around and change activities as desired. Her success led to her method replacing many Froebel institutions in Switzerland and to developing new ones in America and subsequently all over the world. Within music education, Montessori's method is seen most closely in private tuition, where there is greater opportunity to follow the child's interests.

Édouard Séguin on child-centred pragmatism

French doctor **Édouard Séguin (1812–80)** is best known for his work with children with mental disabilities (Kraft, 1961). The schools that he started were focussed on develop-ing independence and autonomy for those with intellectual disabilities, which was done through a combination of physical and intellectual tasks. This was based on Séguin's belief that deficiency was caused by a weakness of the nervous system, which could be compensated for by motor and sensory training. His training included individualised instruction, sequenced tasks in increasing difficulty, developing sensory awareness, carefully arranging the child's environment, rewarding correct behaviour immediately, teaching self-sufficiency and productivity, and believing that every child should be educated as far as possible because every child can improve. Within music education, this motor and sensory training can be seen in the application of the Dalcroze technique, specifically eurhythmics, and in activities created for patients with Parkinson's.

William James on child-centred pragmatism

American psychologist and philosopher **William James (1842–1910)** was better known for his contribution to the start of psychology as a discipline than for contributions to education (James, 2013). However, James' thinking on functionalism helped to identify and break down mental activity by function rather than constituent parts. As a result, James radically promoted ideas on experience and empiricism in favour of metaphysical intellectualism. In music education, the same debate occurs frequently: whether it is better to teach concepts first or experience concepts first. Research to date suggests initial experience is more powerful before conceptual explanations.

Carl Rogers on child-centred pragmatism

The work done with troubled children by American psychologist Rogers helped him to develop his personality theory based on psychotherapy (Rogers and Dymond, 1954; Rogers and Koch, 1959). Developing 19 propositions of human existence and seven characteristics of personality development, Rogers applied his principles to person-centred therapy, cross-cultural relations and learner-centred teaching. A summary of his proposals included statements such as: people could not teach others but could only assist in learning; material should be personally relevant to students; people resist information leading to change; threats increase resistance to learning but freedom increases potential acceptance of new knowledge; interaction with students is essential. Within music education, the introduction of musical ideas (new) through songs that are already known, or known in another context, for example, as games, makes new knowledge more relevant and inviting.

The answer to whether education should suit the child or the state is, of course, that education should suit both the child and the state. The difficulty is in finding a way to suitably train teachers to be equipped not only with the knowledge that needs to be presented to educate citizens comprehensively and responsibly, but also with the skills to attract the interest and attention of the wide variety of individuals that teachers are expected to teach. To date, coercion, fear, distraction and control are the most popular ways that teachers use to manage large groups of children. These are shown countless times to be short term, ineffective and in fact, damaging solutions. Lessons we can learn from these great thinkers show that in order to learn effectively, various themes and principles keep coming up over and over again, including giving learning a practical application, increasing interaction with students, ensuring students experience concepts before explanations, giving students relevant problems to solve, and promoting independent thought and behaviour throughout learning.

Song Level Four: Bow wow wow

Level Four songs use simple rhythms and the whole anhemitonic pentatonic scale, *la-so-mi-re-do*. This means that all the notes are at least a tone away from each other, so they are easier to sing and repeat successfully.

Figure 2.7 Song using la-so-mi-re-do notes

Table 2.7 Bow wow wow rhythm table

I	I	I	-
Bow	wow	wow	
I	⊓	I	-
Whose	dog art	thou	
⊓	⊓	⊓	I
Little	Tommy	Tucker's	dog
I	I	I	-
Bow	wow	wow	

Bow wow wow
Whose dog art thou
Little Tommy Tucker's dog
Bow wow wow

We played this game with younger children by asking them to take turns at patting and passing around a toy dog for each line of the song, singing each child's name instead of "Tommy Tucker". Older children used this as a guessing game. One child sat at the front of the group with their back to the others. The teacher chose one child to sing the third line without the child at front knowing who was singing. The child in the front sang the first line, the group sang the second line, and the secret child sang the third line, while all of them sang the last line. The child at the front had to guess who sang the third line.

Applications of physical learning in education

Developing the concepts from the previous section, specifically experience, interaction, relevance and independence, all imply that physical movement should be involved in educational experience. Yet this is a concept that is becoming far removed from education at earlier and earlier levels in favour of teaching theory. This could be because explanations need few props, abstract descriptions need no physical experience, and discussion needs no practical time, which costs less in both human hours, and physical items to buy or make and then subsequently store. This was certainly the basis of post-industrialisation education, where officials tried to apply standardised systems and procedures to non-standardised human beings. Rote learning and neat handwriting were essential to knowing enough to get a job making straightforward calculations and communicating clearly. However, today, business has different requirements. Businesses now expect people to be able to personalise experiences to customers, develop new products or concepts that eliminate competitors, and solve problems that are not yet known. Skills that leading educators are finding develop through their teaching concepts, as listed above. It seems, then, that educators have been identifying the necessary skills to teach effectively for centuries: skills that business is now demanding. Nonetheless, now that the state has taken responsibility for education in order to make it more equitable, the challenge is to provide the necessary resources needed to give the necessary skills to the future workforce. But, what kind of physical involvement do education specialists recommend? And how could this be delivered through music education?

Johann Heinrich Pestalozzi on physical learning

The Swiss reformer, Pestalozzi founded his revolutionary system on child-centred methods based on recognising the importance of individual differences, sensory perception and active involvement (Bowers and Gehring, 2004). His teachings significantly impacted the development of language education and physical education. He focussed on these areas because he linked them to general, moral and intellectual education. Within both mainstream and music education, this active approach is nearly impossible for inexperienced teachers, and requires significant training opportunities. Practically, this includes creating as many sensory experiences as possible, free choice and interaction, which are most commonly found in private music teaching.

Jean Marc Gaspard Itard on physical learning

French doctor **Jean Marc Gaspard Itard (1774–1838)** specialised in research on the ear, which led him to devise new ways to educate and treat the deaf (Gaynor, 1973). After finding an abandoned child, seemingly wild, Gaynor committed to educating and socialising the child. From his descriptions, we know today that the child would have been identified with special needs, possibly the reason for abandonment, however, Itard's work meant that he was recognised as a founding father of special education. His introduction of sensory-motor training within the education programme greatly influenced the educational methods developed by both Séguin and Montessori. Within music education, the ideas of rehearsing using sensory-motor techniques are being explored further, with current research focussing on injuries sustained in young musicians through insufficient warming up, bad postural habits and extended hours of rehearsal. Within healthy music rehearsal, the Dalcroze approach, particularly Dalcroze eurhythmics, focuses on sensory-motor responses, with current research taking place on the concept of dynamic rehearsal. This method of visualisation and movement during rehearsal (e.g. bouncing on an inflatable ball at the piano at points of special emphasis), is a method of rehearsing, and memorising and accurately performing especially complicated pieces of music.

Friedrich Froebel on physical learning

Although German educator Froebel is acknowledged for recognising the different needs and capabilities of children, his focus on education in early childhood centred on active learning (Moore et al., 2010; Niland, 2009; Williams, 1954). Allowing children to freely choose their activities through "free work" and self-directed play, Froebel introduced movement games throughout the institutes that he founded, as well as his play materials (Froebel gifts). These concepts have been applied today, seen in the emphasis on free play. Within music education, there is a growing recognition in early years music for the child's need to explore instruments and invent their own music, known musically as improvisation. Found to be more meaningful than repetition of known songs, this concept still battles with recognition as real music: all too often, old-school thinking will criticise children's original songs for not being "real music".

87

Elizabeth Mayo on physical learning

British citizen **Elizabeth Mayo (1793–1865)** was recognised as a major influence and reformer of education of infant teachers in Britain, significantly inspired by her stay with Pestalozzi (C. Mayo and E. Mayo, 1849; E. Mayo, 1874). Her writings detailed how children learn through object lessons, and were considered revolutionary because they ignored the idea of rote learning. Mayo's focus on using real objects for object lessons was found to be useful, especially for children from deprived backgrounds. Her influence can be seen in the value that preschool education places on real experience. Within music education, various composers, notably Kodály, insisted on using the best and highest quality recordings for children, particularly valuing the experience of attending live music events.

John Dewey on physical learning

Dewey's ideas on educational pragmatism and liberalism led to his promotion of education through experience and interaction (Dewey, 1997). Through his motivation to develop people to serve the greater good, he recognised that limiting experience would result in limited ability in many areas, including decision-making. Promoting education as social and interactive experience through balancing the curriculum with free choice, Dewey's influence in education is often seen as free choice at the expense of curriculum, which was not his intention at all. Within music education, the greatest motivation for musical development is embodied in social and interactive experience through the opportunity to perform in an orchestra or band.

Margaret McMillan on physical learning

Socialist **Margaret McMillan (1860–1931)** worked with her sister Rachel (1859–1917) to reform childcare in deprived areas in London, introducing basic ideas like children's toilets and school meals (McMillan, 1896). Margaret was interested in play-based learning and outdoor play, and the first purpose-built outdoor centre was named after her. Through her reports and books on nursery education and health, she was instrumental in realising the 1906 Provision of School Meals Act, opening medical centres, nurseries and training centres. Despite turning her interests to nursing later in life, her influence can still be identified in modern education. Within music education, Margaret's concept of care being fit for purpose can be seen in the development of child-sized instruments, making music education more accessible to younger (smaller) children, as well as the concept of play-based learning seen in children's instrumental exploration and improvisation.

Édouard Séguin on physical learning

Séguin was known for his work with children with mental disabilities (Kraft, 1961) (see p. 83). The schools he started focussed on developing independence and autonomy through a combination of physical and intellectual tasks. He believed that deficiency was caused by a weakness of the nervous system which could be compensated for by motor and sensory training. Many of Séguin's ideas can easily be identified in both mainstream and music education today in activities focussed on physical development.

William James on physical learning

James contributed the idea of functionalism to education, where mental activity was identified by function rather than its constituent parts (James, 2013). This promoted the idea that activities needed purpose to be considered valid. In addition, James' ideas on pragmatism, or recognising practical consequences of actions, have been used significantly in educational and music educational research. Action research is a specific example of interventions being introduced and improved on, towards more effective learning. James' interest in experience and empiricism as opposed to metaphysical intellectualism made education a more valuable experience for both teacher and student.

Evidently, many specialists discovered that physical education helped children to learn more effectively. This appears to have been applied when one individual found an effective way of teaching and taught that method to a number of other teachers. The idea of physical learning was supported by Gardner (Gardner, 1983, 2003, 2013), who attempted to identify different ways in which people appeared to learn best, including linguistic, logic-mathematical, musical, spatial, bodily-kinaesthetic, interpersonal, intrapersonal and naturalistic, as well as existential and pedagogical. As with many other theories, this concept was extended to a practical application, resulting in teachers reducing the ways that lessons were presented in order to suit the immediate students' apparent learning styles. Instead, material should have been presented in the wide variety of learning styles represented, which research has shown is more effective, as the same material is presented in multiple ways. Another argument for the inclusion of physical learning is its effective use in the special education sector. Various researchers suggest that ability can be found on a spectrum in which we can all be placed. If this is the case, we would surely all benefit from this experience. Taking the theory that we learn most effectively from concrete to the abstract, this adds to the argument for teaching through physical learning before abstract application. This is best described by Kolb's (1983) theory on experiential learning, initially identified through adult- and business-based education. Kolb found that experience of a phenomenon followed by explanation leads to abstract understanding and, finally, the ability to apply the principle to new situations. Among the benefits of more effective teaching and learning, physical learning works towards developing independence.

Song Level Five: Rabbit run

Level Five songs include simple time and introduce the 6/8 timing, like rocking songs, with the notes limited to *so-fa-mi-re-do*.

Figure 2.8 Song using so-fa-mi-re-do notes

Table 2.8 Rabbit run rhythm table

⊓	⊓⊓	⊓		
Rabbit	run on the	frozen	ground
⊩⏐	⊩	⏐	-
Who told	you	so	
⊓	⊓⊓	⊓		
Rabbit	run on the	frozen	ground
⊩⏐	⊩	⏐	-
How do	you	know	
⊓⊓	⊓	⊓	-
I caught a	rabbit,	uh-huh	

♫	♫	♫	-
I caught a	rabbit,	uh-huh	
♫	♫	♫	-
I caught a	rabbit,	uh-huh	
♫	♫	I	-
I caught a	rabbit,	oh!	

Rabbit run on the frozen ground
Who told you so?
Rabbit run on the frozen ground
How do you know?
I caught a rabbit, ah ha!
I caught a rabbit, ah ha!
I caught a rabbit, ah ha!
I caught a rabbit, oh!

We played this game with younger children using a toy rabbit that they hopped on their knee for each phrase and then passed to the next child. With older children, we got them to hop around the room to the beat, trying to catch another child ("rabbit"). When caught, the children hopped together until the last line, when the rabbit escaped.

The development of independence and responsibility through education

Independence and responsibility are two of the most important skills that can be taught in education, partly because they are so highly sought after by business but mostly because of the high quality of life that they afford. Yet, in conventional education settings there are few opportunities for students to demonstrate independence or responsibility. While in theory all children should be given opportunities, teachers particularly will recognise that this is difficult to achieve in practice, partly due to time and partly due to personalities: the children that usually lead often do it well enough that they continue to lead, thus get better at it; while the children who do not usually lead become comfortable with stepping back and then actively forego these opportunities. Another reason for few leadership opportunities could be the way that the current education system requires group members to behave the same way, expecting all to gain the same level of knowledge according to what is presented to them (regardless of individual interest and ability), and then to be equipped more or less to compete for the same types of jobs. There is so much potential for this system to fail. If educators fail to predict the career skills needed by the time children graduate, it will result in an under-skilled workforce, or even worse, a frustrated, purposeless workforce resorting to illegal activity or even non-activity (state benefit dependent). Not all children will share the same interests – should children with alternative interests be considered failures for not achieving in the same way as their peers? Doing a job that you are good at, but that you do not enjoy, can create unbearable stress within individuals, leading to ill health. Further, within relationships it can lead to relationships breaking down and the additional fall-out effects of unstable family life and potential safeguarding issues. Unfortunately, the alternative – promoting independence and responsibility – is not easy, requiring highly skilled people management to cope with the consequences that free choice brings. There are specialists that deemed this possible.

Johann Heinrich Pestalozzi on independence and responsibility

The thinking behind the educational system devised by Pestalozzi used individual difference as a starting point to develop independence and responsibility in his students. His core principles of home and family, vocational and individual self-determination, state and nation and, finally, inner sense or education, aimed to result in inner peace. Pestalozzi managed to virtually eradicate illiteracy in Switzerland through his commitment to developing independence and responsibility in his students, which seem to be the aims of more successful educational methods. These findings were echoed within music education. Sosniak found that once musicians took personal responsibility for their practice and piece selection, they worked towards their next stages without relying on external encouragement, and were then more successful.

Jean Marc Gaspard Itard on independence and responsibility

Working with the deaf, Itard devised methods of sensory-motor training to develop the ability of the deaf to live independently and confidently (Gaynor, 1973). His work with children with special needs used physical training to further develop the idea of independent living. By providing opportunities for students to progress their own musical lifestyle, from rehearsals to performances, music educators are able to successfully promote and support independence in older students, while younger children may be encouraged through the freedom to choose their own level and style of participation.

Friedrich Froebel on independence and responsibility

Froebel also promoted independence through his recognition of children having different needs and capabilities (Williams, 1954). Self-directed play encouraged autonomy, which usually translates in music education as improvisation and original composition. Children who are actively taught to improvise and compose develop their imagination, and these findings suggest that there may be a correlation with independence too.

Maria Montessori on independence and responsibility

Montessori began her work with children with special needs using sensory-motor ideas inspired by Itard and Séguin (Montessori, 1914). Her motivation, like Itard and Froebel, was to equip them to live independently, creating child-sized materials and furniture so that they could look after themselves and their environment. By giving children freedom to choose their activities, Montessori observed that the youngest children were able to concentrate for hours at a time, making them more autonomous and self-motivated to find out more. Montessori's work with mainstream children was an extension of this work: her goal for education was to develop independent thinkers, while the teacher's role was to observe and direct children's psychological development. While more observation has been included in the early childhood curriculum, it appears to have become a box ticking exercise, more often than not managed by software. As with mainstream education, even music education is more about observing as a judgement of skill acquired, with both parents and children expecting the teacher to specifically direct children before they can show any real preference or interest.

Édouard Séguin on independence and responsibility

Séguin developed his ideas on independent living while working with children with mental disabilities (Kraft, 1961) (see p. 83). His schools developed independence and autonomy for those with intellectual disabilities, which was addressed through physical and intellectual tasks. His training included individualised instruction, sequenced tasks in increasing difficulty, developing sensory awareness, carefully arranging the child's environment, rewarding correct behaviour immediately, and teaching self-sufficiency and productivity. Prepared areas are classic teaching strategies in both mainstream and music education, where sensory concepts are also used, specifically in listening, despite the real reason being to comply to instructions.

Susan Isaacs on independence and responsibility

English psychologist and psychoanalyst **Susan Isaacs (1885–1948)** promoted the development of nursery schools and independence to support learning (Isaacs, 1930, 1933; Isaacs and Thouless, 1941). Training as a teacher for 5–7-year olds, Isaacs gained a degree in philosophy and then completed her master's degree in psychology. In addition to this, she trained as a psychoanalyst, developing her ideas on children's intellectual development and furthering these ideas in experimental schools, where children were supported in independent play, and teachers observed the children as research workers.

Her academic involvement promoted the role of psychodynamic theory in developmental psychology. Isaacs championed developing children's thinking skills and independence, prioritising parental involvement, and viewed play as "perpetual experiment". She challenged Piaget's set stages, not having found the same results in her real setting experience, and promoted strict parenting. Despite being diagnosed with cancer, Isaacs managed to lead the Cambridge Evacuation Survey, identifying the effects of wartime evacuation on families. Her influence in both education and music education has challenged Piaget's set stages and emphasised the role of parents in early childhood.

Mihalyi Csikszentmihalyi on independence and responsibility

Csikszentmihalyi identified the concept of "flow" in his studies on happiness and creativity, where flow referred to a state of intrinsic motivation based on having a sufficient balance of skill and challenge to be successful (Csikszentmihalyi, 2008). He identified nine characteristics of flow, as well as seven alternative states to flow (when tasks or skills are too easy or too difficult). Recently, his work has centred on motivation, challenge and success, and his argument that work orientation (achievement, endurance, cognitive structure, order, play and low impulsivity) is a better predictor of academic success and the ability to fulfil long-term goals than home or social influence. He is considered a world leader on positive psychology, promoting the idea that work should be freely chosen in order to be enjoyed successfully.

These great thinkers show that preparation from an early age is best practice for developing successful independent living later in life, regardless of ability, and this is clearly applicable to music education too. Research shows that successful learning can be achieved by educating through recognising and building on individual differences, sensorimotor training and self-directed play, which work together to develop a sense of responsibility and autonomy. The role that teachers are expected to play becomes significantly different to their current role. Instead of directing a prescribed curriculum, teachers are to use observation and provide training in skills as students require. As these are some of the skills that meet the requirements of business, the question is how this can be achieved through the current system.

Song Level Six: Over in the meadow

Level Six songs use more combined rhythms than before, extending the notes to *la-so-fa-mi-re-do.*

> *Over in the meadow*
> *In the sand, in the sun*
> *Lived an old mummy tiger*
> *And her little tiger one*

Figure 2.9 Song using la-so-fa-mi-re-do notes

Table 2.9 Over in the meadow rhythm table

♫	♫	♫	♫
Over	in the	meadow	in the
♩	♫	♩	♫
Sand	in the	sun	lived an
♩	♫	♫	♫
Old	mummy	tiger	and her
♫	♫	♩	-
Little	tiger	one	
♩	♫	♫	♩
"ROAR!"	said the	mummy,	"I
♩	♫	♩	♫
ROAR!"	said the	one,	so they
♩	♫	♩	♫
Roared	and they	snored	in the
♩	♫	♩	-
Sand	in the	sun!	

"ROAR!" said the mummy
"I ROAR!" said the one
So they roared and they roared
In the sand, in the sun

Over in the meadow
Where the streams run so blue
Lived an elephant mummy
And her little calves two
"STOMP!" said the mummy
"WE STOMP!" said the two
So they stomped and they stomped
Where the stream runs so blue

Over in the meadow
In the sky near a tree
Flew an old mummy bluebird
And her little bluebirds three
"FLY!" said the mummy
"WE FLY!" said the three
So they flew and they flew
In the sky near the tree

Over in the meadow
In a hive near the door
Lived an old honey bee
And her little bees four
"BUZZ!" said the mother
"WE BUZZ!" said the four
So they buzzed and they buzzed
In the hive near the door

Over in the meadow
In a warren so nice
Lived an old mother rabbit
And her little rabbit five
"HOP!" said the mother
"WE HOP!" said the five
So they hopped and they hopped
In their warren so nice

We used this song in animal themes and, while we used soft toys or pictures with younger children, older children pretended to be the animals as they skipped to the beat following the actions. As the song involves one additional animal in each verse, we extended the song using pictures with the additional animals.

Focus on universal education and citizenship

A significant number of educators and education thinkers held an underlying agenda in devising their ideas: helping students to see the value of good citizenship by making education universally available. Incredibly, universal education is still not a concept that can be taken for granted throughout the world, which is the reason so many organisations still exist to promote increased education opportunities for women. Along with the practical benefits of increasing income, higher levels of maternal education have been correlated to lower infant death and illness, lowering the national medical burden. In terms of citizenship, a number of its concepts came from theorists' direct experience with war-torn situations, either having personally narrowly escaped death or in helping others escape certain death. The extent to which thinkers wrote about their experiences shows the length of time that countries have battled to live in peace. Thanks to social media coverage as well as traditional media sources, we are more aware of the constant threats to different countries and people groups internationally through different forms of extremism. Perhaps, instead of National Curriculum quick fixes involving wall displays of British Values, it would be more effective to identify long-term principles taken directly from educators working towards the same purpose: world peace.

John Amos Comenius on universal education and citizenship

Comenius strongly promoted universal education, devising ways in which to teach children more effectively (Schwarz and Martin, 2012; Stroope, 2005). Coming from a background where both parents and siblings had died, Comenius could only start his schooling at 16 years old. From his revolutionary textbooks with pictures, use of children's native language, and teaching progression from the simple to advanced, his method of teaching logical thinking instead of rote memorisation helped him to promote equal educational opportunities regardless of wealth or gender. Influenced by scientists of the day (e.g. Bacon, Descartes), Comenius applied their analytical, pragmatic approach to the process of education. In most Western countries, girls are able to choose to study any subject, yet with boys and girls there is still a great divide in interest between the sciences and the creative subjects. Potential reasons include the way the subjects are taught, available job opportunities, parental support or gender perception. Within the early years, music education is enjoyed equally by both boys and girls, but this is known to change as boys become more aware of the cultural expectations of their behaviour and interests.

Jean-Jacques Rousseau on universal education and citizenship

Among the multiple works of Rousseau, he wrote one book, *Emile*, based on educating children for citizenship (Bertram, 2010). Having been abandoned by his own family at a young age, and giving his own children up for adoption in the hope of them having a better future, Rousseau was later criticised for his lack of life experience. Against the religious culture of the day, he promoted his belief that children were inherently good, not intentionally manipulative or naughty, and that they should be free to experience life in safety, without deliberate guidance or punishment except for natural consequences of actions. However, unlike other philosophers, Rousseau did not support gender equality. Today, popular views are mixed despite science supporting the view that infants are incapable of manipulation. Within both mainstream and music education, this view is supported by the notion that not only should all children have access to music education, universally, but also that all children are inherently musical, a notion that is also supported by science. In fact, science has shown that children are born with perfect pitch, and that they are also born with perfect rhythm (Bergeson and Trehub, 2002; Kessen et al., 1979; Saffran and Griepentrog, 2001). Both of these, if consistently developed, become evident once children are able to clearly express themselves and their abilities.

Elizabeth Mayo on universal education and citizenship

British educator Mayo was recognised as a major influence and reformer of education of infant teachers, influenced by Pestalozzi (C. Mayo and E. Mayo, 1849; E. Mayo, 1874; Sengupta, 2003). Her writings focussed on how children learn through object lessons, and were considered revolutionary because they ignored the idea of rote learning. While Mayo was also greatly influenced by religion, her focus on using real objects for object lessons was considered useful for underprivileged children, promoting the concept of universal education. Today, there is still a mixture of opinion on whether real objects are necessary to create real experiences in both mainstream and music education, mainly as a result of financial restrictions.

John Dewey on universal education and citizenship

Dewey had a clear basis for his progressive views: he saw education as a social and interactive experience in which students would learn effectively through interaction and independent decision (Dewey, 1997). His purpose for education was for each individual to gain the skills needed to serve the greater good. However, along with the concept of national curricula came the patriarchal view that government should take responsibility for providing business with a suitably skilled workforce. Whether this was due to pressure from business or because of the great disparity of teaching ability and an inability of the teaching board to guarantee qualification, it remains that teachers are currently unable to teach to Dewey's standards because of the increasing pressures to teach specific curriculum elements. Music education can also experience an external control of levels, nevertheless, with a little more leeway, different exam boards are now available so that most major influences are recognised, from classical to jazz, pop to metal.

Margaret McMillan on universal education and citizenship

American-British McMillan had socialist ideas for education, ultimately benefiting all children by specifically reforming childcare for deprived children in London (McMillan, 1896). Introducing basic ideas like children's toilets and school meals, McMillan was interested in play-based learning and outdoor play, and was instrumental in the 1906 Provision of School Meals Act. These are now considered basic requirements that are not even questioned, which shows the influence she has had on British education.

Édouard Séguin on universal education and citizenship

Séguin worked with children with mental disabilities, developing independence and autonomy through physical and intellectual tasks (Kraft, 1961) (see p. 83). His sentiment that every child should be educated because every child can improve has been used in many government policies as well as in special needs materials. Within music education, there is still a division in opinion on whether musical skill is in-built or can be improved. This is despite science proving that there are very few people truly tone deaf, and that the brain continues to learn throughout the lifetime. Most modern music teachers support this opinion, with some claiming that every person has musical potential.

Paulo Freire on universal education and citizenship

Brazilian educator **Paulo Freire (1921–97)** was best known for establishing critical education through his educational work with the poor (Freire, 1996). His personal experience of a late education due to poverty provided an insight into the imbalance of educational opportunities for the poor. This led him to develop a revolutionary 45-day adult literacy programme, motivated by his desire to create greater equity in education. Despite poor schooling due to poverty, as an adult Freire studied law, philosophy and psychology of language, starting as a secondary language teacher, then later becoming director of the department of education and culture of the social services of his area. He was offered a visiting professorship at Harvard based on his writings, and then became special education advisor to the world council of churches, and the national secretary of education. Freire's philosophy was founded on education for all, based on the modern and cultural knowledge of an individual's own humanity, starting from the culture from which the individual originates. He believed that education was necessary because it taught people that they can change their own circumstances by being aware of both what they know and what they do not know, including an awareness of the political agenda of those that teach. He criticised the "empty vessel" approach to students, as followed by Rousseau and Dewey, and argued that in having a dominant culture, a culture of silence was created that caused dominant people to ignore the situation of dominated people, who in turn kept silent about their domination. Through his book, *Pedagogy of the Oppressed* (1968), Freire introduced concepts that challenged areas within education, including the curriculum, teaching styles, the role of the state, influence of corporate power, the "hidden curriculum", cultural and individual identity. Within music education, the implications are that the awareness of a dominant culture implies that other subdominant cultures are in fact oppressed, and need to be empowered to return their human value.

Experience of adversity, it seems, is the main factor that has pushed these educators not only to fight for every child's right to free and unbiased education, but also to challenge and develop the discipline of education. Both Comenius and Rousseau lost their parents during their formative years; Mayo worked with underprivileged children; Séguin worked with children with disabilities; Freire rose from abject poverty to significantly powerful positions. In fact, many more educators mentioned in this chapter used life experience to guide their interest. Recognising the benefits that came from belonging to a group, and the significant difficulties experienced outside of groups, these educators specifically worked towards universal education and citizenship. Within most Westernised cultures, universal education is well on its way to being achieved and is considered a sign of a developed society. Taking Freire's views of limited opportunity as oppression, the corollary of this is that universally educated citizens are equal. Presumably, the expectation is that equal citizens would have no need for crime, thus leading to a peaceful society and peaceful world. Looking closely at the life events of some of these philosophers, it is clear to see why they saw this as the most worthy of ambitions.

Song Level Seven: **Skip to my Lou**

Level Seven songs use more combined rhythms than the Levels One–Six songs and the full range of notes, *ti-la-so-fa-mi-re-do*.

Figure 2.10 Song using ti-la-so-fa-mi-re-do notes

Table 2.10 Skip to my Lou rhythm table

⊓⊓	⊓⊓	⊓	Ⅰ
Fly in the	buttermilk,	shoo fly,	shoo
⊓⊓	⊓⊓	⊓	Ⅰ
Fly in the	buttermilk,	shoo fly,	shoo
⊓⊓	⊓⊓	⊓	Ⅰ
Fly in the	buttermilk,	shoo fly,	shoo
⊓⊓	⊓	Ⅰ	Ⅰ
Skip to my	Lou, my	dar-	ling
Ⅰ	Ⅰ	⊓⊓	Ⅰ
Skip,	skip,	skip to my	Lou
Ⅰ	Ⅰ	⊓⊓	Ⅰ
Skip,	skip,	skip to my	Lou
Ⅰ	Ⅰ	⊓⊓	Ⅰ
Skip,	skip,	skip to my	Lou
⊓⊓	⊓	Ⅰ	Ⅰ
Skip to my	Lou, my	dar-	ling!

Fly in the buttermilk, shoo fly shoo
Fly in the buttermilk, shoo fly shoo
Fly in the buttermilk, shoo fly shoo
Skip to my Lou, my darling

Skip, skip, skip to my Lou
Skip, skip, skip to my Lou
Skip, skip, skip to my Lou
Skip to my Lou, my darling

With younger children, we used instruments that we passed around, developing ideas of turn-taking, and focussing on either using metals or woods. With older children, they held hands in pairs and walked around the space while one child skipped around the pairs. On the last line, everybody left their partner and skipped to find a new one, including the person left out. The new left out person then skipped around the new pairs until the last line of the next verse, when they all let go again, and skipped to find a new partner. Along with developing concentration and planning skills, this gave children the opportunity to play with different children outside their usual group.

The essence of play

Play is finally being recognised as a major factor in learning, with departments of play now being set up in leading universities. Once considered irrelevant and a waste of time, presumably because there was no immediate commercial value to be made from play, the leading popular view is that play is the child's work. As educators observed in more detail what was involved in various aspects of play, they recognised the life preparation that it involved. This, along with other research reports, has led to countries increasing the length and frequency of play allocation during the school day, and crediting their success on international education league tables to this.

Friedrich Froebel on play

Froebel focussed his activities on active learning, "free work", movement games and self-directed play (Niland, 2009; Williams, 1954). These principles spread through the institutes that he founded, as well as his play materials (Froebel gifts). The activities in his first "kindergarten" involved singing, dancing, gardening and self-directed play with the Froebel gifts. This focus on play has been shown to increase student motivation, improve test scores and classroom behaviour, yet is still being measured by some according to traditional standards of submissive obedience. Music education specifically shows the benefit of play, with musical value being particularly evident in playing together in orchestra or bands.

Margaret McMillan on play

McMillan used her studies in psychology, physiology, languages and music, and political socialism to reform childcare in deprived areas in London (McMillan, 1896). She developed ideas in play-based learning, specifically in outdoor play. In recent years, outdoor play has been strongly promoted through initiatives like Forest School, where outdoor areas are minimally developed, creating space for children to play in natural environments. Educational philosophy is also exploring environment as a "third teacher", considering whether the overpowering, bright "child displays" are at all beneficial for effective learning. Within music, the consideration of the environment of play has always been a determining factor, especially when planning performances. This has led to specially designed rooms built to create optimal acoustic experiences, with musicians and composers acutely aware of the effect that the environment can have on the audience's musical experience.

Melanie Klein on play

Austrian psychoanalyst **Melanie Klein (1882–1960)** practised child psychology in England (Klein and Strachey, 1997). Despite having no degree, she trained in psychoanalysis, after which she came to England where she was the first person to use psychoanalysis on children. Klein used innovative techniques that involved interpreting child play with toys, leading to the development of object relations theory. Her greatest contribution to psychoanalysis is considered to be her identification of the "depressive position", or state of positive behaviour, as opposed to a negative "aggressive position". This led to a disagreement with Anna Freud (Sigmund Freud's daughter) who also worked with children, which was significant enough to result in a split within the British Psychoanalytical Society. The effects of this fall-out can still be seen in the difference in emphasis between American and European psychoanalysis. Klein's theory led to the development of various therapies used for children who have experienced significant life events that may have the potential to affect their future development. Recognised by the Health and Care Professions Council (HCPC), specific job titles are protected and may only be used by licensed professionals, including Play therapists, Drama therapists, Art therapists and Music therapists. Often requiring significant personal experiences of therapy as well as study into interpretation, these professions require high levels of artistic competence in addition to the required study and personal therapy.

Susan Isaacs on play

Isaacs advocated nursery schools and independence to develop learning (Isaacs, 1930, 1933; Isaacs et al., 1941). After gaining qualifications in philosophy and psychology, Isaacs trained in psychoanalysis, where she developed her ideas on children's intellectual development. She started experimental schools, where children were supported in independent play with teachers as observers. Promoting psychodynamic theory in developmental psychology, Isaacs viewed play as "perpetual experiment" and identified the importance of imaginative play in developing experience because it released feelings and developed reasoning. Having found different results to Piaget's set stages, Isaacs has impacted both mainstream and music education views on Piaget's ideas, showing that stages were not fixed and that they relate to parenting experience.

Mihalyi Csikszentmihalyi on play

Csikszentmihalyi coined the concept of "flow" in his studies on happiness and creativity. Here, "flow" refers to a state of intrinsic motivation based on having sufficient skill and challenge to be successful (1996; Csikszentmihalyi and LeFevre, 1989; see also p. 94). Additional work by music researchers has identified that reduced play opportunity reduces the creativity of children, specifically school-age children, leading to questions of academic priorities.

Song Level Seven: Aiken Drum

Level Seven songs use more combined rhythms than the Levels One–Six songs and the full range of notes, *ti-la-so-fa-mi-re-do*.

> *There was a man lived in the moon*
> *Lived in the moon, lived in the moon*
> *There was a man lived in the moon*
> *And his name was Aiken Drum*
>
> *And he played upon a ladle*
> *A ladle, a ladle*
> *And he played upon a ladle*
> *And his name was Aiken Drum*

With younger children, we used drums or each took a turn with a special drum that we played and passed. This was as preparation for the game played with the older children. With older children, we used this game to introduce the idea of the moon travelling

Figure 2.11 Song using ti-la-so-fa-mi-re-do notes

Table 2.11 Aiken Drum rhythm table

⊓ ⊓	⊓	⊓	⊓
(There) was a	man, lived	in the	moon, lived
⊓	⊓	⊓	⊓⊓
In the	moon, lived	in the	moon, there
⊓	⊓	⊓	⊓⊓
Was a	man lived	in the	moon and his
⊓	⊓		⊓
Name was	Aiken	Drum	And he
⊓	⊓		⊓
Played u-	pon a	la-	dle a
	⊓		⊓⊓
La-	dle a	la-	dle and he
⊓	⊓		⊓⊓
Played u-	pon a	la-	dle and his
⊓	⊓		-
Name was	Aiken	Drum!	

around the earth, with the children in two groups. Half of the group sat in the middle while playing drums, with the other half walking around the drumming group. After the first four lines, the groups swap for the last four lines.

Summary

Using the ideas and experiences of over 40 educational thinkers, from philosophers to psychologists, doctors to government ministers, the nine common themes covered in this chapter can be found throughout their writings, running like threads through the fabric of child development theory. Relationship was identified by the theorists as the most important theme based on the regularity, emphasis and impact that it has on development. Overall, these educational thinkers recognised the unsurpassable benefit of parental support and care. Within the education system, this theme is applied through the introduction of early childhood key workers, primary class teachers and secondary form tutors, so that students have specific individuals to access with concerns or request advice from. Various universities have this idea in place too, with the Oxbridge universities appointing both academic and non-academic (residential/college) tutors per student. Internal motivation was the second highest identified theme, with the majority of specialists recognising the unsurpassed achievement that results from personal choice. Regardless of previous achievement or experience, internal motivation not only led these specialists to their various contributions to the development of educational theory, but also determined their behaviour, an important point for teachers and those working with others: what you truly believe will be evident through your behaviour and the way you treat others, and will often be reflected back at you.

The third most common theme was identified as external motivation, which can be a powerful source of motivation combined with relationship. Often used in situations requiring a clear winner or coercive obedience, external motivation is partly a result of behaviourism training, and this can be enhanced through relationship. In this chapter, external motivation also refers to environmental factors that impact the individual which are not always recognised or acknowledged. Environment has been shown to be so effective in social situations that some European countries are trialling a new form of prison. By providing offenders with independent, self-sufficient living, they reside in an environment where they learn the independent living skills needed to thrive so that, once released, they can live successfully. Another example of addressing environment is ensuring a national minimum income or guaranteed provision of housing for all. These options, much like music, all return respect and humanity to individuals, and so it is certainly appropriate that these principles are developed from birth.

Stage development theory was the fourth highly identified theme. Clearly there are expected sequences of development, for example, crawling before walking, walking before running, but many people know of exceptions to these "rules", for example, children who progress from sitting to walking without crawling, infants weaned early through lack of maternal milk or suitable substitutes. Interestingly, the idea of following individual interest and development has been identified for centuries as the most effective way to educate, which explains why parents as first teachers are so effective – education is automatically personalised to each child. This is one reason why so many music teachers choose to teach privately – to individualise a child's musical journey, working towards greater success.

Child-centred pragmatism was the fifth theme identified by at least a quarter of the theorists considered. This is based on the idea that learning that begins with the child will automatically follow that child's interest. In contrast, the concept of presuming that an entire group of children will share the same interest is a short-term solution and is as ill-conceived as providing only one option for the adult population. Allowing children to choose to participate in a topic has been shown to make a significant difference in student achievement as well as classroom behaviour.

The sixth commonly found theme was in kinaesthetic learning, or learning through movement. Found to be exceptionally effective for people with learning difficulties and people from deprived backgrounds, physical training in effective movement and potential responses was shown to help people live independently despite having severe limitations. With children, this type of learning appeared to facilitate the development of theoretical learning by providing a practical basis of knowledge. Backed by so many thinkers, the idea of participation before explanation is a common methodology used by private music teachers precisely because it is so effective.

The seventh theme, developing independence and a sense of responsibility, was addressed by approximately half of the identified theorists. This is a concept that is literally centuries old, yet is now considered revolutionary because it is so different from traditional teaching. Recognising student autonomy by giving students choices from the earliest years is shown to result in increased engagement and successful learning, but requires the teacher to be confident in child engagement. This confidence comes from relationship, and this approach has such different priorities to those by which teachers are measured by OFSTED, that it would require a complete overhaul of the system.

Sadly, one of the ideas that theorists referred to less frequently was that of universal education, the eighth theme. Most often, equal educational opportunities were mentioned by those who had lost parents, came from poverty, witnessed the effects of war, or missed out on opportunity for unfortunate reasons. In one sense, the fact that these theorists wrote books, articles or pamphlets meant that they all intended for their theory to be used in multiple settings to the benefit of all children. In addition, these theorists specifically mentioned that their ultimate intention through developing their theories was to promote the importance of universal education to national governments. They viewed the long-term benefits of an education without agenda, to be freely accessed by all, as essential to good citizenship. From providing equal career opportunities to understanding the reasons for the way that services are organised, the theorists felt that knowledge would reduce the potential of the majority to support destructive powers, with the assumption that all people wanted to live in free and fair societies. As this needs to be a deliberate intention, it is based on clear modelling, an essential skill found in both mainstream and private music teaching.

Finally, the ninth theme, the importance of play, was also a concept mentioned by comparatively few of the theorists. However, this may be because the older theorists took free play for granted as a concept based on the social norms of their day. Regardless, the power of play as preparation, explanation, therapy, invention and intervention is agreed to potentially hold the keys for many current unexplained ideas, illnesses and unresolved conflicts.

Putting these themes together, the ideal education would begin with supportive and interested parents who allow only trusted individuals into their children's lives: this focussed interest would develop the child's own internal motivation and relational model. Creating an environment conducive to independence, interest, creativity and responsibility would set children up for successful living later in life – learning that is personalised according to individual interest, with a basis in physical experience of theoretical concepts. Physical experience would build students' personal confidence and independence, and universal education would ensure that all children receiving the same education opportunities would understanding the importance of becoming responsible citizens. Students who were free to play in such a supportive environment would then have any and every opportunity open to them, including the freedom to both fail and succeed.

References

Addessi, A. R. (2009). The musical dimension of daily routines with under-four children during diaper change, bedtime and free-play. *Early Child Development and Care, 179*(6), 747–768. https://doi.org/10.1080/03004430902944122 (Accessed 6 April 2017).

Adelman, C. (1993). Kurt Lewin and the origins of action research. *Educational Action Research, 1*(1), 7–24.

Ainsworth, M. D. S. (1967). Infancy in Uganda: Infant care and the growth of love. http://psycnet.apa.org/psycinfo/1967-35025-000 (Accessed 7 July 2016).

Ainsworth, M. D. S. (1979). Infant–mother attachment. *American Psychologist, 34*(10), 932–937.

Ainsworth, M. D. S. and Bell, S. M. (1970). Attachment, exploration, and separation: Illustrated by the behavior of one-year-olds in a strange situation. *Child Development, 41*(1), 49–67.

Ainsworth, M. D. S. and Bowlby, J. (1991). An ethological approach to personality development. *American Psychologist, 46*(4), 333–341.

Barrett, M. S. (1997). Invented notations: A view of young children's musical thinking. *Research Studies in Music Education, 8*(1), 2–14. https://doi.org/10.1177/1321103X9700800102 (Accessed 6 April 2017).

Barrett, M. S. (2006). Inventing songs, inventing worlds: The "genesis" of creative thought and activity in young children's lives. *International Journal of Early Years Education, 14*(3), 201–220.

Barrett, M. S. (2011). Musical narratives: A study of a young child's identity work in and through music-making. *Psychology of Music, 39*(4), 403–423. https://doi.org/10.1177/0305735610373054 (Accessed 6 April 2017).

Barrett, M. S. (2012). Preparing the mind for musical creativity: Early music learning and engagement. In O. Odena (Ed.), *Musical Creativity: Insights from Music Education Research*. Burlington, VT: Ashgate Publishing Ltd.

Bell, S. M. and Ainsworth, M. D. S. (1972). Infant crying and maternal responsiveness. *Child Development, 43*(4), 1171–1190.

Berger, A. A. and Cooper, S. (2003). Musical play: A case study of preschool children and parents. *Journal of Research in Music Education, 51*(2), 151–165. https://doi.org/10.2307/3345848 (Accessed 6 April 2017).

Bergeson, T. R. and Trehub, S. E. (2002). Absolute pitch and tempo in mothers' songs to infants. *Psychological Science, 13*(1), 72–75.

Bertram, C. (2010). *Jean Jacques Rousseau*. http://stanford.library.usyd.edu.au/entries/rousseau/ (Accessed 12 June 2016).

Bilhartz, T. D., Bruhn, R. A. and Olson, J. E. (1999). The effect of early music training on child cognitive development. *Journal of Applied Developmental Psychology, 20*(4), 615–636. https://doi.org/10.1016/S0193-3973(99)00033-7 (Accessed 6 April 2017).

Bowers, F. B. and Gehring, T. (2004). Johann Heinrich Pestalozzi: 18th century Swiss educator and correctional reformer. *Journal of Correctional Education, 55*(4), 306–319.

Bowlby, J. (1958). The nature of the child's tie to his mother. *The International Journal of Psycho-Analysis, 39*, 350.

Bowlby, J. (1977). The making and breaking of affectional bonds. I. Aetiology and psychopathology in the light of attachment theory. An expanded version of the Fiftieth Maudsley Lecture, delivered before the Royal College of Psychiatrists, 19 November 1976. *The British Journal of Psychiatry, 130*(3), 201–210.

Britzman, D. (2015). Reading Freud today for the destiny of a psychology of education. *Knowledge Cultures, 3*(2), 82–97.

Bronfenbrenner, U. (1977). Toward an experimental ecology of human development. *American Psychologist, 32*(7), 513–531.

Bronfenbrenner, U. (1986). Ecology of the family as a context for human development: Research perspectives. *Developmental Psychology, 22*(6), 723–742.

Bronfenbrenner, U. and Condry Jr, J. C. (1970). Two worlds of childhood: U.S. and U.S.S.R. http://eric.ed.gov/?id=ED053013 (Accessed 6 April 2017).

Bronfenbrenner, U. and Morris, P. A. (1998). The ecology of developmental processes. http://psycnet.apa.org/psycinfo/2005-01926-019 (Accessed 6 April 2017).

Bruner, J. S. (1957). On perceptual readiness. *Psychological Review, 64*(2), 123–152.

Bruner, J. S. (1966). *Toward a Theory of Instruction*. Cambridge MA: Harvard University Press.

Bruner, J. S (1991). The narrative construction of reality. *Critical Inquiry, 18*(1), 1–21.

Bruner, J. S., Postman, L. (1949). On the perception of incongruity: A paradigm. *Journal of Personality, 18*(2), 206–223.

Campbell, P. S. (1991). Rhythmic movement and public school music education: Conservative and progressive views of the formative years. *Journal of Research in Music Education, 39*(1), 12–22. https://doi.org/10.2307/3344605 (Accessed 6 April 2017).

Cooper, S. and Cardany, A. B. (2011). The importance of parents in early childhood music program evaluation. In S. L. Burton and C. C. Taggart (Eds.), *Learning from Young Children: Research in Early Childhood Music*. Lanham, MD: R&L Education.

Csikszentmihalyi, M. (1996). *Flow and the Psychology of Discovery and Invention*. New York: Harper Collins. www.bioenterprise.ca/docs/creativity-by-mihaly-csikszentmihalyi.pdf (Accessed 6 April 2017).

Csikszentmihalyi, M. (2008). *Flow, the Secret to Happiness*. www.ted.com/talks/mihaly_csikszentmihalyi_on_flow.html (Accessed 6 April 2017).

Csikszentmihalyi, M., Khosla, S. and Nakamura, J. (2017). Flow at work. In L. G. Oades, M. Steger, A. Delle Fave and J. Passmore (Eds.), *The Wiley Blackwell Handbook of the Psychology of Positivity and Strengths-Based Approaches at Work* (pp. 99–109). Malden, MA, and Oxford: Wiley-Blackwell.

Csikszentmihalyi, M., and LeFevre, J. (1989). Optimal experience in work and leisure. *Journal of Personality and Social Psychology, 56*(5), 815–822.

Dewey, J. (1997). *Experience and Education*. New York: Simon & Schuster.

Dewey, J. (2013). *The School and Society and the Child and the Curriculum*. Chicago, IL: University of Chicago Press.

Duckworth, A. L., Peterson, C., Matthews, M. D. and Kelly, D. R. (2007). Grit: Perseverance and passion for long-term goals. *Journal of Personality and Social Psychology, 92*(6), 1087–1101. https://doi.org/10.1037/0022-3514.92.6.1087

Erikson, E. H. (1956). The problem of ego identity. *Journal of the American Psychoanalytic Association, 4,* 56–121. http://psycnet.apa.org/psycinfo/1957-02625-001 (Accessed 7 July 2016).

Erikson, E. H. (1959). Identity and the life cycle: Selected papers. *Psychological Issues, 1,* 1–171. http://psycnet.apa.org/psycinfo/1960-02756-001 (Accessed 6 April 2017).

Ferster, C. B. and Skinner, B. F. (1957). *Schedules of Reinforcement*. East Norwalk, CT: Appleton-Century-Crofts. http://psycnet.apa.org/psycinfo/2004-21805-000/ (Accessed 6 April 2017).

Freire, P. (1996). *Pedagogy of the Oppressed*. London: Penguin Books.

Freud, S. (1905). *Three Essays on the Theory of Sexuality*. Martino Publishing.

Gardner, H. (1983). *Frames of Mind: The Theory of Multiple Intelligences*. New York: Basic Books.

Gardner, H. (2003). Multiple intelligences after twenty years. Paper presented at the American Educational Research Association, Chicago, Il, 21 April. www.kvccdocs.com/FYE125/lesson-resources/Gardiner-MI-Article.pdf (Accessed 6 April 2017).

Gardner, H. (2013). The theory of multiple intelligences. In B. Moon and A. S. Mayes (Eds.) *Teaching and Learning in the Secondary School*. Oxford: Routledge Falmer.

Gardner, H. and Hatch, T. (1989). Educational implications of the theory of multiple intelligences. *Educational Researcher, 18*(8), 4–10.

Gaynor, J. F. (1973). The "failure" of JMG Itard. *The Journal of Special Education, 7*(4), 439–445. http://psycnet.apa.org/psycinfo/1974-28672-001 (Accessed 6 April 2017).

Green, L. (2002). *How Popular Musicians Learn: A Way Ahead for Music Education*. Aldershot: Ashgate Publishing Ltd. https://books.google.co.uk/books?hl=en&lr=&id=vr-v4sY7MMYC&oi=fnd&pg=PP1&ots=R5gKGLj0qy&sig=SZYTGDFTQLaIoXDSZRSf55NIf04 (Accessed 6 April 2017).

Green, L. (2008). Group cooperation, inclusion and disaffected pupils: Some responses to informal learning in the music classroom. Presented at the RIME Conference 2007, Exeter, UK. *Music Education Research, 10*(2), 177–192.

Green, L. (2010). Musical "learning styles" and "learning strategies" in the instrumental lesson: Some emergent findings from a pilot study. *Psychology of Music*. https://doi.org/10.1177/0305735610385510 (Accessed 6 April 2017).

Harlow, H. F. (1958). The nature of love. *American Psychologist, 13*(12), 673–685.

Harlow, H. F., Harlow, M. K. and Meyer, D. R. (1950). Learning motivated by a manipulation drive. *Journal of Experimental Psychology, 40*(2), 228–234.

Isaacs, S. (1930). *Intellectual Growth in Young Children*. Oxford: Harcourt, Brace. http://psycnet.apa.org/psycinfo/1931-02002-000 (Accessed 6 April 2017).

Isaacs, S. (1933). Social development in young children. *British Journal of Educational Psychology, 3*(3), 291–294.

Isaacs, S., Brown, S. C. and Thouless, R. H. (1941). *The Cambridge Evacuation Survey*. New York: Methuen. http://psycnet.apa.org/psycinfo/1942-02107-000 (Accessed 6 April 2017).

Isaacson, W. (2007). *Einstein: His Life and Universe*. New York: Simon & Schuster.

James, W. (2013). *The Principles of Psychology*. Redditch: Read Books Ltd. https://books.google.co.uk/books?hl=en&lr=&id=sah8CgAAQBAJ&oi=fnd&pg=PT8&dq=william+james&ots=ELvIIgijm5&sig=B5zcmcYb-1j1Dp47TPm2J7yKL28 (Accessed 6 April 2017).

Kagan, J. (1966). Reflection-impulsivity: The generality and dynamics of conceptual tempo. *Journal of Abnormal Psychology, 71*(1), 17–24.

Kagan, J., Reznick, J. S. and Snidman, N. (1987). The physiology and psychology of behavioral inhibition in children. *Child Development, 58*(6), 1459–1473.

Kagan, J., Reznick, S. and Snidman, N. (1988). Biological bases of childhood shyness. *Science, 240*(4849), 167–171.

Kagan, J., Rosman, B. L., Day, D., Albert, J. and Phillips, W. (1964). Information processing in the child: Significance of analytic and reflective attitudes. *Psychological Monographs: General and Applied, 78*(1), 1–37. https://doi.org/10.1037/h0093830 (Accessed 6 April 2017).

Kaviani, H., Mirbaha, H., Pournaseh, M. and Sagan, O. (2014). Can music lessons increase the performance of preschool children in IQ tests? *Cognitive Processing, 15*(1), 77–84. https://doi.org/10.1007/s10339-013-0574-0 (Accessed 6 April 2017).

Kessen, W., Levine, J. and Wendrich, K. A. (1979). The imitation of pitch in infants. *Infant Behavior and Development, 2*, 93–99. https://doi.org/10.1016/S0163-6383(79)80014-4 (Accessed 13 April 2017).

Klein, M. and Strachey, A. (1997). *The Psycho-analysis of Children*. London: Random House. https://books.google.co.uk/books?hl=en&lr=&id=b-WixrpvQzQC&oi=fnd&pg=PR8&dq=melanie+klein&ots=6XmJAfEpF6&sig=HSqxiPxREMgjpXGV7OQb1MkXnbc (Accessed 6 April 2017).

Kohlberg, L. (1963). The development of children's orientations toward a moral order. *Human Development, 6*(1–2), 11–33.

Kohlberg, L. (1964). Development of moral character and moral ideology. *Review of Child Development Research, 1*, 381–431.

Kohlberg, L., Levine, C. and Hewer, A. (1983). Moral stages: A current formulation and a response to critics, *Contributions to Human Development, 10*. http://psycnet.apa.org/psycinfo/1984-25459-001 (Accessed 7 July 2016).

Kolb, D. A. (1983). *Experiential Learning: Experience as the Source of Learning and Development* (1st edition). Upper Saddle River, NJ: Financial Times/ Prentice Hall.

Kraft, I. (1961). Edouard Seguin and 19th century moral treatment of idiots – ProQuest. *Bulletin of the History of Medicine, 35*, 393–418.

Lewin, K. (1946). Action research and minority problems. *Journal of Social Issues, 2*(4), 34–46.

Lewin, K. (1947). Frontiers in group dynamics II. Channels of group life; social planning and action research. *Human Relations, 1*(2), 143–153.

Lewin, K., Lippitt, R. and White, R. K. (1939). Patterns of aggressive behavior in experimentally created "social climates". *The Journal of Social Psychology, 10*(2), 269–299.

Maslow, A. H. (1943). A theory of human motivation. *Psychological Review, 50*(4), 370–396.

Maslow, A. H. (1959). *New Knowledge in Human Values*. Oxford: Harper. http://psycnet.apa.org/psycinfo/1961-03315-000 (Accessed 17 April 2017).

Mayo, C. and Mayo, E. (1849). *Practical Remarks on Infant Education: For the Use of Schools and Private Families*. London: Home and Colonial School Society. https://books.google.co.uk/books?hl=en&lr=&id=XfNBAQAAMAAJ&oi=fnd&pg=PR2&dq=lessons+on+objects+mayo&ots=KnYD7Abbl3&sig=7h5Nf-2w_6s57cJSKKB0c0DW320 (Accessed 6 April 2017).

Mayo, E. (1874). *Lessons on Objects: As Given to Children Between the Ages of Six and Eight, in Pestalozzian School, at Cheam, Surrey*. London: Seeley, Jackson, and Halliday. https://books.google.co.uk/books?hl=en&lr=&id=ljvbAAAAMAAJ&oi=fnd&pg=PA1&dq=lessons+on+objects+mayo&ots=LAV81OMEgL&sig=ikabyglcZv-CEc_EdgxGoQrTL8o (Accessed 6 April 2017).

McMillan, M. (1896). *Child Labour and the Half-time System*. London: "Clarion" Newspaper Company. www.jstor.org/stable/60218801 (Accessed 7 July 2016).

Miettinen, R. (2000). The concept of experiential learning and John Dewey's theory of reflective thought and action. *International Journal of Lifelong Education, 19*(1), 54–72.

Montessori, M. (1912). *The Montessori Method*. Radford, VA: Wilder Publications.

Montessori, M. (1914). *Dr. Montessori's Own Handbook*. New York: Knopf Doubleday Publishing Group.

Moore, M. R., Campos, D., Collazo, J., Maytum, A. F., Sampayo, V. and Sanchez, M. A. (2010). Inspiration to teach – Reflections on Friedrich Froebel and why he counts in early childhood education. *YC Young Children, 65*(6), 74–76.

Niland, A. (2009). The power of musical play: The value of play-based, child-centered curriculum in early childhood music education. *General Music Today, 23*(1), 17–21.

Peterson, J. (1924). Binet's early experiments on intelligence testing. *Peabody Journal of Education, 2*(2), 87–92.

Petryszak, N. G. (1981). Tabula rasa – its origins and implications. *Journal of the History of the Behavioral Sciences, 17*(1), 15–27. https://doi.org/10.1002/1520-6696(198101)17:1<15::AID-JHBS2300170104>3.0.CO;2-3 (Accessed 6 April 2017).

Piaget, J. (1951). *The Child's Conception of the World*. Lanham, MA: Rowman & Littlefield. https://books.google.co.uk/books?hl=en&lr=&id=hhDQeE8rWlUC&oi=fnd&pg=PA1&dq=jean+piaget&ots=L1u27M0-3c&sig=jTSdTILtGVhQBtZRh-d5Tdw1SuM (Accessed 6 April 2017).

Piaget, J. (1976). Piaget's theory. In *Piaget and his School* (pp. 11–23). Heidelberg: Springer. http://link.springer.com/chapter/10.1007/978-3-642-46323-5_2 (Accessed 6 April 2017).

Piaget, J (1997). *The Moral Judgement of the Child*. New York: Simon & Schuster. https://books.google.co.uk/books?hl=en&lr=&id=6tUVIaRG7TMC&oi=fnd&pg=PA4&dq=jean+piaget&ots=57CQ2Qqs03&sig=kxFsIXhZtOO_r1Vr4kVCXyBrwP8 (Accessed 6 April 2017).

Piaget, J. and Cook, M. (1952). *The Origins of Intelligence in Children* (Vol. 8). New York: International University Press. www.bxscience.edu/ourpages/auto/2014/11/16/50007779/Piaget %20When%20Thinking%20Begins10272012_0000.pdf (Accessed 6 April 2017).

Piaget, J., Inhelder, B. and Weaver, H. (1969). *The Psychology of the Child*. New York: Basic Books.

Rogers, A. (2014). PISA, power and policy: The emergence of global educational governance. *International Review of Education, 60*(4), 591–596. https://doi.org/10.1007/s11159-014-9429-x (Accessed 6 April 2017).

Rogers, C. R. and Dymond, R. F. (1954). *Psychotherapy and Personality Change*. Chicago, IL: University of Chicago Press. http://psycnet.apa.org/psycinfo/1955-04163-000 (Accessed 6 April 2017).

Rogers, C. R. and Koch, S. (1959). A theory of therapy, personality, and interpersonal relationships: As developed in the client-centered framework. In S. Koch (Ed.), *Psychology: A Study of a Science. Study 1, Volume 3: Formulations of the Person and the Social Context*. New York: McGraw Hill. http://bibliotecaparalapersona-epimeleia.com/greenstone/collect/ecritos2/index/assoc/HASH01a5/4583605e.dir/doc.pdf (Accessed 6 April 2017).

Saffran, J. R. and Griepentrog, G. J. (2001). Absolute pitch in infant auditory learning: Evidence for developmental reorganization. *Developmental Psychology*, *37*(1), 74–85. https://doi.org/10.1037/0012-1649.37.1.74 (Accessed 6 April 2017).

Sala, G. and Gobet, F. (2016). When the music's over. Does music skill transfer to children's and young adolescents' cognitive and academic skills? A meta-analysis. *Educational Research Review*, *20*, 55–67. www.sciencedirect.com/science/article/pii/S1747938X16300641 (Accessed 6 April 2017).

Sawyer, R. K. (1997). *Pretend Play as Improvisation: Conversation in the Preschool Classroom*. Hove: Psychology Press.

Schwarz, G. and Martin, J. (2012). Comenius: Dead white guy for twenty-first century education. *Christian Scholar's Review*, *42*(1), 43.

Sengupta, P. (2003). An object lesson in colonial pedagogy. *Comparative Studies in Society and History*, *45*(1), 96–121. https://doi.org/10.1017/S0010417503000057 (Accessed 6 April 2017).

Skinner, B. F. (1938). *The Behavior of Organisms: An Experimental Analysis*. Oxford: Appleton-Century-Crofts.

Sosniak, L. A. S. and Gabelko, N. H. (2008). *Every Child's Right: Academic Talent Development by Choice, Not Chance*. New York: Teachers College Press.

Spitz, R. A. (1946a). Hospitalism; A follow-up report on investigation described in Volume I, 1945. *The Psychoanalytic Study of the Child*, *2*, 113–117. http://doi.apa.org/psycinfo/1948-01143-001 (Accessed 6 April 2017).

Spitz, R. A. (1946b). The smiling response: A contribution to the ontogenesis of social relations. *Genetic Psychology Monographs*, *34*, 57–125. http://psycnet.apa.org/psycinfo/1947-00954-001 (Accessed 6 April 2017).

Spitz, R. A. (1950). Anxiety in infancy: A study of its manifestations in the first year of life. *The International Journal of Psycho-Analysis*, *31*, 138–143.

Spitz, R. A. and Wolf, K. M. (1946). Anaclitic depression; An inquiry into the genesis of psychiatric conditions in early childhood, II. *The Psychoanalytic Study of the Child*, *2*, 313–342. http://psycnet.apa.org/psycinfo/1948-01290-001 (Accessed 6 April 2017).

Steiner, R. (2013). *Stages of Higher Knowledge*. Redditch: Read Books Ltd.

Stroope, M. W. (2005). The legacy of John Amos Comenius. *International Bulletin of Missionary Research*, *29*(4), 204.

Von Culin, K. R., Tsukayama, E. and Duckworth, A. L. (2014). Unpacking grit: Motivational correlates of perseverance and passion for long-term goals. *The Journal of Positive Psychology*, *9*(4), 306–312. https://doi.org/10.1080/17439760.2014.898320 (Accessed 6 April 2017).

Vygotsky, L. S. (1967). Play and its role in the mental development of the child. *Soviet Psychology*, *5*(3), 6–18.

Vygotsky, L. S. (1978). Interaction between learning and development. *Readings on the Development of Children*, *23*(3), 34–41.

Vygotsky, L. S. (1979). Consciousness as a problem in the psychology of behavior. *Soviet Psychology*, *17*(4), 3–35.

Williams, L. P. (1954). Review of *Review of Friedrich Froebel and English Education*, by E. Lawrence. *Educational Research Bulletin*, *33*(3), 77.

Winner, E. (1982). *Invented Worlds: The Psychology of the Arts*. Cambridge, MA: Harvard University Press.

Wood, D., Bruner, J. S. and Ross, G. (1976). The role of tutoring in problem solving. *Journal of Child Psychology and Psychiatry*, *17*(2), 89–100.

A way forward for music education

Introduction

Since the mid-1980s, many interest groups have taken more notice of music provision for children under 7 years old. Music and education departments in universities across the UK have started to address this growing interest by offering specific training and conferences to better understand this phenomenon. Academics are divided between those seeking evidence that music education offers additional benefits, and those seeking to identify the multiple ways that music can be learnt and taught. As a consequence, researchers are dedicating a substantial level of time and energy to understanding what is involved in music education for children under 7 years old. In addition to academic interest, the benefits of musical inclusion are being debated within both the UK national and local governmental levels (Johnston, 2001; Kenny, 2011), where the effects of music on community behaviour have been considered within different countries. This indicates that political parties are recognising that musical involvement holds the attention of a significant proportion of the public, with potential benefits for the larger social issues that they face. Even business has been affected by the increased interest in music education. A growing subsection of entrepreneurs involves private music teaching for parents and preschool children (Gudmundsdottir and Gudmundsdottir, 2010), especially by musical parents of young children, giving a small sector of society an additional form of income. With the increasing interest in this growing industry, it would be useful to consider how music education has evolved over time to understand more about where it may be headed.

Song Level One: Where are you going?

Level One songs start with two notes, the ambulance ni-naw sound, *so-mi*.

Figure 3.1 Song using so-mi notes

Table 3.1 Where are you going? rhythm table

♫	♫	♫	❘
Where are you	going?	To the	woods
❘	♫	♫	❘
What	for? To	get some	wood
❘	♫	♫	♫
What	for? To	boil some	water
❘	♫	♫♫	♫
What	for? To	eat all of your	chickens!

Where are you going? To the woods
What for? To get some wood
What for? To boil some water
What for? To eat all of your chickens!

We played this with younger children as a call and response song, with the teacher calling first and the children responding. With the older group, we split into boys and girls and took turns calling and responding, standing opposite each other in parallel lines.

Music education in the early 21st century

Application of music education

Music as a subject was once considered essential to every good education curriculum, and although music education is still recommended within the British National Curriculum (in England, Wales and Northern Ireland), musical skill is no longer valued in the same way. At the turn of the 20th century, musical skill was considered a sign of a good and thorough education: a result of accomplishment and a high level of skilled training because of the additional skills that were often learnt alongside the musical training. This may be because it was taught within a package of subjects designed to give a specific social group the skills to lead the masses, particularly as industry began to value mass production and reproduction. By mid-century, the capitalistic concept of creating greater quantity at a lower cost was applied to more and more social situations within Westernised, democratic countries, including the education system. Education specialists identified the subjects that most careers would find useful, notably the three Rs of "reading, 'riting and 'rithmetic", and these were seen as more valuable for government funding and administration. This left music education to those who could afford it or who were interested.

Application of political investment in education

Each successive UK government has held broadly similar views on the relative importance of education to other national areas of interest, ensuring that while most of the funding was allocated to national security and social welfare, approximately 10–13 per cent of the national budget has been allocated to the national education system. Internationally, online UNESCO data for most countries is now available up to 2014 and shows that countries have allocated between 4.3 per cent of the national budget to education (South Sudan) and 30 per cent (Zimbabwe), while the UK allocated 13.6 per cent, similar to the USA (14.5 per cent in 2014). As international countries compared their economic value, they looked to improve their situation through considering the quality of their workforce and, in order to improve the quality of their workforce, they would need to address the workforce's training, that is, school education. Countries that score highest in educational tests had and still have a number of factors in common, including fewer citizens, smaller economic differences and a less multicultural society. In addition, these smaller countries based their education systems on their national culture, making the system more natural for teachers to adopt and promote. This makes it easier for students and parents to accept and embrace, particularly as their teachers are post-graduate qualified, well-paid professionals. In comparison, the UK population has a wide financial and multicultural spectrum, often undergraduate-qualified teachers that are poorly paid, and a system based on other countries' national cultures, for example, the American Head Start system adopted as the UK Sure Start;

the Asian-inspired focus on Science, Technology, Engineering and Mathematics (STEM) subjects and exam results. These difficulties have led to an attempt to focus on some subjects to the exclusion of others, and music has always been considered optional. For this reason, it may be more effective to identify a system of principles that surpass political agendas and embraces both national and international heritage.

Application of UK political educational priorities

Looking into where the education funding is actually used in the UK, the Department of Education was originally allocated a percentage of the national budget to distribute as it saw fit. This led to plenty of university investment to encourage the development of national patents and inventions, with the school sector "sharing" the rest between pre-school, primary and secondary. It is only relatively recently that the UK government has demanded a more transparent system where funding for different areas is ring-fenced, ensuring that a level of funding is assured to each educational level: tertiary, second-ary, primary and early childhood. Even now, the greatest levels of funding are allocated to tertiary institutions (universities) for the research they provide to the nation, then to secondary schools for the preparation they provide towards identifying suitable uni-versity candidates, then to primary schools with the remit to educate every child to a guaranteed minimum standard and, finally, the smallest percentage is allocated to early childhood. Research now shows that the level of care received early on has a significant impact on the later socio-economic achievement of the population.

Application of the national education curriculum

Since the randomised control trial method has been used to understand correlations between opportunities and behaviour, the UK government has become more specific about the content that educators teach in order to provide the opportunities deemed most benefi-cial for the future workforce. The last Labour UK government (1997–2010) took the step of categorising achievement and behaviours based on developmental findings, however, the current Conservative government (2015–) has replaced this with a curriculum that has sig-nificantly less detail for some areas or subjects. In one sense, this format can appear more open and flexible but, in another sense, with no clear goals and changing exam standards, it can leave teachers feeling insecure and unsure of their goals for each subject or session.

Application of music in the national education curriculum

The music curriculum is one of the subjects that has undergone this reduced transformation in the UK. As a result, the music curriculum for early years consists of a few paragraphs, and even the primary music curriculum is only a few pages of guidance as opposed to the comprehensive detail that has gone into the maths (numeracy) and English (literacy) curricula. Consequently, more often than not it is left to the public's individual interest to pursue music training, competition, performance and even career opportunities. This said, the increasing interest in the impact of early childhood music has resulted in more research being done on the various implications of music education. In turn, this has led to more and more research claims specifically linking music to academic skill development. Interestingly, this link has inspired new forms of employment and self-employment opportunities for those involved in music education. These include an increased interest in music therapists (requiring licensing and significant cost and training time), early childhood music session leaders and early childhood music session franchises (unregulated sector with no specific qualification requirements). Frequently, these career changers come from a level of formal or informal music education, with a passion for sharing their skills with children.

Application of career potential for the musically trained

Within formal music education training, those that study music usually go on to perform or teach – usually both. Within informal music education (e.g. rock bands, street or community musicians), performances are much less prescribed (although they can be equally or even more financially successful), while teaching is rare because so many skills have been self-taught. Despite these differences, both groups battle with one of the greatest concepts in music philosophy: the meaning of music. Creating a music-meaning continuum (Figure 3.2), one extreme supports musical education and development purely for the creative expression that it brings to humanity. At the other end of the continuum, musicians are interested in the secondary benefits of creativity. Admittedly, one of the main reasons for the interest in secondary benefits to music is the need to market music teaching to the general public, who enjoy music but have not necessarily had the opportunity or interest to pursue music lessons. However, there are those with a genuine scientific interest in trying to find a form of measurement for a skill that measures quality according to individual taste. These two groups can be found in both the formally and informally trained musician groups, and can become polarised in their argument.

At the extremes, supporters of music for the benefit of creative expression consider investigation into additional benefits of music unnecessarily apologetic, and deem any practical reason for music education to be an example of watering down a concept too complex to understand. Meanwhile, those that support the scientific investigation into the secondary benefits of music education see the purist view as short-sighted and unnecessarily divisive. As the focus of this chapter is on the use of music within early childhood,

Creative expression   Secondary benefits

Figure 3.2 Music-meaning continuum
Source: author

this book takes the position that it is useful to acknowledge and if necessary address the academic research that has gone into investigating the effects of music on early childhood development.

Application of investment importance in early childhood

Current academic research has already identified external contributing factors from early childhood that may predict outcomes later in life, including: environment (Martin et al., 2012); experience (Sawyer et al., 2014); and interactive opportunities (Arterberry et al., 2007). Looking more closely at these studies, these complex factors suggest a potential relationship between later outcomes and early developmental skills. Links have been identified to include: school readiness (Brown et al., 2010; Gordon et al., 2014; Moreno, Bialystok et al., 2011; Moreno, Friesen and Bialystok, 2011; Tierney and Kraus, 2013); social development (Hallam, 2010); physical development; academic development (Miendlarzewska and Trost, 2014); creative development (Welch, 2005); and emotional development (Barrett, 1997, 2006, 2011, 2012; Rabinowitch et al., 2013) – simultaneously developing skills in all these areas. Understandably, these links have attracted the attention of a number of parties with vested interests, including: national governments, as they work to include the latest and greatest developments in creating leading educational policy; the general public, as parents work to provide their children with leading opportunities and resources for successful development; and industry, as private instrumental teachers, musical nursery teachers and musical parents start businesses to provide leading specialist musical training for settings like nursery schools, toddler groups and private small-group sessions. This chapter suggests a way forward in the provision of music education for each of these three groups.

Song Level Two: Teddy bear

Level Two songs use simple rhythms and three notes that are far enough apart to hear the difference clearly, so-mi-do.

> Teddy bear, teddy bear, turn around
> Teddy bear, teddy bear, touch the ground
> Teddy bear, teddy bear, tie your shoe
> Teddy bear, teddy bear, I love you
>
> Teddy bear, teddy bear, climb the stairs
> Teddy bear, teddy bear, say your prayers
> Teddy bear, teddy bear, turn off the light
> Teddy bear, teddy bear, kiss goodnight

We simply played this song by following the directions with both age groups.

Figure 3.3 Song using so-mi-do notes

Table 3.2 Teddy bear rhythm table

Π	I	Π	I
Teddy	bear,	teddy	bear
I	I	I	I
Turn	a-	rou-	nd
Π	I	Π	I
Teddy	bear,	teddy	bear
I	I	I	-
Touch	the	ground	
Π	I	Π	I
Teddy	bear,	teddy	bear
I	I	I	I
Tie	your	sho-	e
Π	I	Π	i
Teddy	bear,	teddy	bear
I	I	I	-
I	love	you	

Current delivery arrangements

Interested user groups

National governments have a specific agenda – to use minimal resources to ensure maximum national economic results. Economic results involve training the general public to suitable standards that helps employers to generate a healthy business that supports the country. Training the general public involves creating an educational system that develops the necessary skills required to support business. With so many facets of business today, from retail to manufacture, production to finance, a wide variety of skills is needed, and with the advances in science, technology and AI (artificial intelligence), it is understand-able that more emphasis has been placed on encouraging the subjects involved, including STEM. This has led to an increase in UK government funding to support these areas while the humanities and arts have been reduced. Ironically, it is the additional skills gained from study in the humanities and arts that are now attracting the interest of the leading technology companies. Skills including creativity, research, forecasting, communication, innovation and switching focus are being used to disrupt (reinvent and even invalidate entire industries), so these are skills that business is now pursuing. Unfortunately, govern-ments take a significant amount of time to catch up to the demands of business, mainly because of the level of investment that new initiatives require at a national level. Thus, since the UK government spent the 1990s demanding evidence for the need of scientific skills, it is only in the 2010s that it has begun to focus on these skills at state schools, despite business having moved on. Private schools that are not subject to the government agenda will no doubt be more successful at meeting the demand.

Parents, too, have a specific agenda: their children's long-term success. Regardless of cultural class, parents will be aware that specific skills lead to different forms of success, and they will do all they can to ensure this success. Regrettably, they are also a group easily scared into action through pressure, both from the child and society. As a result, substantial marketing messages are geared at children, with savvy advertisers fully aware that parental fears have the power to influence financial decisions. Convincing parents that specific skills or activities will improve the chances of their children getting into elite schools or groups is a big part of marketing to children, and this has been achieved successfully by church schools that specifically allocate places to children whose fami-lies attend church regularly, or grammar schools where children with higher academic training (and incomes) are encouraged. Other examples are specialist music, sports and art schools, which can generate secondary business demands in private coaching.

The agenda of private instrumental teachers and musical nursery teachers is usually a lot more straightforward than government and parent expectations: they just want to make a living doing what they love. However, with the UK government still diverting focus and funding from the arts, even fewer existing jobs are available and so these teachers have created their own industry of early childhood music specialists. As they are so alike in purpose and practice, it is not surprising that many early childhood music specialists also use similar marketing tactics, such as part-quoting generalised research findings of the benefits of music correlated with different skills. The problem with part-quotes is that the original articles have usually not been entirely addressed, so significant detail has been overlooked or even excluded. This potentially leads to misquoted or misdirected results. Grand claims of across-the-board, long-term benefits of using certain systems, despite the fact that they have not been rigorously tested, have used biased personal reports from supporters and cannot be substantiated any other way. Due to the notorious difficulties in quantitatively and rigorously testing children in general, and music education in particular, much marketing is just that. It falls to the educator to determine whether specialists have the skills to pass on to nursery settings, whether they have educational planning behind sessions, or whether they are children's entertainment, someone able to hold a tune. This chapter aims to address inaccurate claims by analysing appropriate research, identifying common themes, and devising a principle-led curriculum suitable for any early childhood setting.

Music education teacher training for early childhood music specialists

In terms of music education teacher training, currently the remit of music education research is found between higher education music departments and education departments, depending on the interests of their leadership. With the specified age delimitation, early childhood music education research more often than not falls under the remit of education departments, potentially creating a disconnect between "informal" and "formal" music education. In addition, umbrella organisations that support the training and development of early childhood music educators have split foci. As a consequence of this unclear responsibility, the early childhood music education industry has no single governing body in the UK. Unlike recognised sectors like the arts therapies, which are based on psychotherapeutic training combined with one of the arts, or Early Years Professional Status (EYPS) based on the effective application of educational theory in practice, music educators have a variety of influences, from musical through academic to social, emotional and therapeutic. Commercially, this new attention to the under-7s music industry has led to different styles of sessions based on group priorities, without a single, agreed standard for this industry. This results in differing quality provision, broadly differentiated according to their associated representational bodies; that is, trained musicians appear to value formal music training (e.g. Incorporated Society of Musicians, www.ism.org), community musicians prioritise informal "musicking" (e.g. Sound Sense, www.soundsense.org), child development experts emphasise socio-emotional development (e.g. Earlyarts, www.earlyarts.co.uk), while educators concentrate on school readiness (e.g. Pre-school Learning Alliance, www.pre-school.org.uk).

Informal conversation with a number of diverse early childhood specialists suggests a prevailing view of a lack of music teaching material for under-7s. This is unfortunate as within the last century a few, admittedly situated, theories of music education were developed using the scientific and psychological discoveries of the age – ideas which are still finding success in many parts of the world. Informal conversations with practitioners attending courses on the major music education approaches of Dalcroze, Orff and Kodály indicate a renewed interest in the practical principles that these composer-educators proposed in music education, yet many practitioners expressed a reluctance to commit to a single approach, instead preferring to focus on the most appropriate approach for the student. A comparative analysis of these approaches may work towards providing music teaching principles for this disparate, yet growing sector.

Looking more closely at the leading music education theories, a theoretical appraisal of the principles used in the major music education approaches can help to identify ways to apply these ideas to early childhood educational developmental theory. To compare them, the theories were focussed on the three prevailing UK age groupings found within the general age grouping in national early childhood education (usually 0–8 years): 0–2 years; 2–4 years; 4–7 years. Then, I applied a thematic analysis to identify common principles. This resulted in identifying the musical skills to be developed and the approximate ages and/or levels along the lines of a stage development theory.

Song Level Three: No one in the house

Level Three songs use simple rhythms and four notes that are closer together than the Level One and Two songs, *so-mi-re-do.*

> *No one in the house but Dinah, Dinah*
> *No one in the house but me, I know*
> *No one in the house but Dinah, Dinah*
> *Strumming on the old banjo*

With younger children, we used this song as an opportunity to have a turn to play and pass a ukulele. With older children, the group stood in a semicircle, leaving a big gap – this created a "house" of walls with a "doorway". Children took turns walking around the inside

Figure 3.4 Song using so-mi-re-do notes

Table 3.3 No one in the house rhythm table

Π	Π				
No-one	in the	house	but
Di-	nah	Di-	nah
Π	Π				
No-one	in the	house	but
					-
Me		know	
Π	Π				
No-one	in the	house	but
Di-	nah	Di-	nah
Π	Π				
Strumming	on the	old	ban-
jo			

of the circle with their eyes closed, listening to the singing "walls". When they did not hear the wall singing, they were able to leave the "house" through the open "doorway".

Current theory in practice

Interactive child development learning theories

Maria Montessori on interactive child development learning theories

Demonstration and self-directed activity defined the programme by Maria Montessori (1870–1952), the first female Italian doctor who is best known for the principle of developing independence in education, particularly for under-7s (Montessori, 1912, 1914). Originally designed to help children with mental disabilities, and then children from low-income families in Italy, Montessori's programme compensated for the lack of adult care. Teaching the children empowering skills for living and learning independently, she observed common stages in child development. She noted that children thrived in multi-age, semi-autonomous settings, and that they had the ability to concentrate for hours from very early on. Developing a range of children's furniture and self-correcting "toys", Montessori based her music theory on listening and imitating, in keeping with her philosophy of demonstrating activities beforehand.

Jean Piaget on interactive child development learning theories

Sequential stages of development were described in the theory of cognitive development, developed by Jean Piaget (1896–1980), and described age-related changing views of reality (Piaget et al., 1969). Piaget's stages included: sensorimotor (involving reflexes and reactions); pre-operational (involving speech and logic development); concrete operational (involving reduced egocentricism and increased logic); and formal operational (involving abstract thought and metacognition). He viewed learning as an irreversible process that could be measured by observing the effects of varying actions in naturalistic settings; this revolutionised the way that child development research was conducted. Despite criticisms of the strict sequential adherence and specific results being situated within cultural contexts, conceptually this theory plays a pivotal role in recognising the progression of physical knowledge to theoretical concepts.

David Kolb on interactive child development learning theories

The model of experiential learning by David Kolb (1939–) identified four separate stages in learning based on his observations. Kolb described concrete experience as physical involvement in the skill to be learnt, observation as a time when the skill was watched; reflection as a process of creating an abstract theory or rational explanation; and testing as a trial of using the newly-acquired knowledge in new situations (Kolb, 1983). Developing this model into a "learning style inventory", it has primarily been

Montessori Theory	Piagnet Theory	Kolb Theory
Demonstration	Sensorimotor: reflexes, reaction	Concrete experience
Imitation	Pre-operational: speech and logic	Observation
Self-directed activity	Concrete operational: increase awareness, logic	Reflection
Semi-autonomy	Formal operational: abstract, metacognition	Testing

Figure 3.5 Summary of major interactive learning theories

used in business and management scenarios. Yet, in observing early childhood development, it appears to describe skill acquisition remarkably accurately. These combined developmental principles of demonstration and independence, stage development and experiential learning act as the conceptual framework to this musical progression skills guide presented in this book (Figures 3.5 and 3.9).

Major music education approaches

Émile Jacques-Dalcroze on music education

The concept of learning through associating specific movements to music is formally attributed to Swiss-born Émile Jaques-Dalcroze (1865–1950), professor of Solfege at the Geneva Conservatoire (1892). Realising that his technically proficient students lacked basic musical understanding, he devised training to finely tune the body to physically express a piece of music with musical accuracy (Bachmann, 1991; Gell, 2005; Seitz, 2005). Using rhythm, pitch and dynamics, Jacques-Dalcroze found that this movement enhanced his students' instrumental performances. This method is used by the Junior Strings Programmes at the Royal Northern College of Manchester (RNCM) and Junior Guildhall, London, as well as in music training for RNCM students. As movement is an infant's natural response on hearing music (Amini et al., 2013; Ilari, 2015; Loewy et al., 2013; Standley, 1998, 2000; Tafuri and Welch, 2008), this suggests that it may be an effective teaching principle (Custodero, 2005).

Zoltán Kodály on music education

Singing before playing was the basis of Hungarian Zoltán Kodály's (1882–1967) approach to music education. Various accounts state that Kodály grew up with little formal music training until university, where he played the violin and sang in the choir. During his studies, he began collecting folk music and developed his own musical career to become professor at the Academy of Music in Budapest. Kodály was known for his own compositions and for informing children's music education (Choksy, 1999). His principles for music education include inner hearing, reading/writing music by recognising intervals, and the 'movable doh', easily transposing music using sol-fa (doh-re-mi . . .) based on the hand sign techniques of English clergyman John Curwen. As singing is foundational to music education in under-7s, and research shows that using gesture is an effective way of singing accurately (Liao, 2002, 2008; Liao and Davidson, 2007), this is another principle that may affect later skill development.

Carl Orff on music education

Maintaining rhythm and the ability to improvise was essential to the programme developed by German-born Carl Orff (1895–1982). He began formal music lessons at

Dalcroze Theory	Kodály Theory	Orff Theory
Move	Prepare: chants, songs, dances	Sing
Sing	Present: clarify skills	Play
Play (instruments)	Practise: use skills in new ways	Create
Improvise		Explore

Figure 3.6 Summary of major music education approaches

5-years-old, but progressed to composing music using the different musical instruments in which he had been trained (Keetman, 1954; Thresher, 1964). Best known for his composition *Carmina Burana*, Orff later started a school for gymnastics, music and dance in Munich, developing his *Schulwerk* manual that combined movement, singing, playing and improvisation. His approach is known for its use of body percussion, untuned percussion and chimed instruments, as well as movement and improvisation. Percussion, or keeping a rhythmic beat, is the natural inclination of a child able to grasp and move, as is clapping, tapping and stamping, so this principle works to extend a child's natural ability.

The idea of combining or uniting methodologies is not new, and while most papers unite the Kodály and Orff approaches (Barton and Hartwig, 2012; Benedict, 2009; Coppola, 2009; Gault, 2005), few seem to include the Dalcroze approach. This is found particularly where methodological focus is prioritised ahead of musical creativity (Benedict, 2009). However, finding the commonalities within these ideas appears to be a reasonable starting point in identifying concepts leading to successful, creative musical education for children under 7 (Figure 3.6). The need to include the Dalcroze approach for children under 7 appears particularly relevant in an age group where concrete experience supersedes theory (Kolb, 1983; Piaget et al., 1969; Swanwick and Tillman, 1986).

Comparative summary of music education approaches

Table 3.4 summarises the different levels involved based on the music education approaches described above. Detail has been taken from specialist music training as well as the original texts of Kodály (Choksy, 1999), an Orff-Kodály comparative document (Casarow, 2012) and original texts of Dalcroze (Findlay, 1971; Jaques-Dalcroze, 1912). Each of the principles can be separated into three progressive levels, and these include the main principles in each approach (beginner, intermediate, advanced). Looking closely, it seems that the

Table 3.4 Summary of the Dalcroze, Kodály and Orff approaches by level

Level	Kodály	Orff	Dalcroze
Beginner	• In-tune singing • Steady beat • Simple duple, triple and quadruple metre • Form, dynamics, notation (crotchets, quavers, rests)	• Establish beat, in-tune singing • Chanting, clapping, moving, playing, singing • Hear and make music before reading and writing • Fold and traditional song repertoire	• Developing the muscular and nervous system through training in time, energy and space • Social integration into a productive group ensemble • Developing co-ordination to perform similar and dissimilar acts simultaneously
Intermediate	• Major trichord • Pentatonic scale, major pentachord, hexachord • Absolute letter names • Notation (minim, semibreve, dotted quaver, semiquaver)	• Body percussion, non-pitched percussion, barred instruments • Chant-rhythm-body percussion instruments • Emphasis on music-making process • Known song for new concepts	• Train reactions to inhibit (slow) or excite (energise) on visual or auditory stimulus • Develop concentration to reproduce more bars accurately from memory • Developing the body technique of balance to physically start and stop moving in equilibrium
Advanced	• Syncopation, compound metre • Minor scale, modes • Dotted quaver, semiquaver • Minor hexachord, pentachord scales	• Age-appropriate songs and activities • Notating and performing improvisations • Improvisations and composition lead to lifetime love of music • Reward of music making is the pleasure of making music with others	• Understanding and awareness of the left and right sides of the body • Timing breathing adequately to ensure flow • Developing awareness of spatial orientation in relation to people and props

Kodály approach contains the most comprehensive detail, but they all contain such similar activities that it makes sense to unite them. They all follow a similar sequence:

- in-tune singing (beginner)
- steady beat and notation
- introducing the major trichord (intermediate)
- pentatonic scale
- expanding rhythmic notation
- syncopation (advanced)
- compound metre
- major and minor scales.

While the Kodály approach uses a variety of songs, rhythmic and interval exercises to develop these concepts, the Orff approach uses rhythm-keeping devices (body and untuned percussion) and a focus on improvisation or composition as a final "product". The Dalcroze approach appears to develop the body percussion, rhythmic focus of the Orff approach by specialising in movement training as the most effective way to experience, perform and ultimately improvise or compose music. These ideas are summarised in Table 3.4.

Song Level Four: **Here comes a bluebird**

Level Four songs use simple rhythms and the whole anhemitonic pentatonic scale, *la-so-mi-re-do*. This means that all the notes are at least a tone away from each other, so they are easier to sing and repeat successfully.

Figure 3.7 Song using la-so-mi-re-do notes

Table 3.5 Here comes a bluebird *rhythm table*

I	П	I	I
Here	comes a	blue	bird
I	П	I	I
in	through my	win-	dow
I	-	П	П
Hey,		diddle	dum-a
I	I	I	-
day,	day,	day	
П	П	I	П
Take a	little	part-	ner and
I	П	I	I
jump	in the	gar-	den
I	-	П	П
Hey		diddle	dum-a
I	I	I	-
day,	day,	day	

Here comes a bluebird in through my window
Hey, diddle dum a day, day, day
Take a little partner and jump in the garden
Hey diddle dum a day, day, day

With younger children, we organised one adult per child standing in a circle. Each pair had a turn to weave in and out of the circle, until choosing the next pair. With older children, we followed a similar pattern of standing and each child weaving in and out. Children all held their hands raised in arches to allow the "bluebird" to fly through the "windows". On the last line, the bluebird chose the person they were nearest, went to the centre of the circle, and held hands while jumping up and down.

Music education with child development

The study of music education for early childhood began in earnest in the 1970s with studies on infant perception and the recognition that babies can tell the difference between changes in pitch and timing. In the 1980s, researchers found that infants could recognise melodic contour, where music goes higher and lower, and that they were able to process pitching and timing like adults. By the 1990s, researchers found that infants could identify scales and intervals even more accurately than adults and, in the 2000s, researchers have found a way to show that infants retain a long-term memory for music (Vongpaisal et al., 2010). Together, this shows that not only are infants far from the blank tablets they were assumed to be not so long ago, they show considerably advanced thinking processes. Through studies involving non-invasive scanning procedures such as magnetic resonance imaging (MRI) and positron emission tomography (PET), we now know that the brain records memories of experience, and that the more times the same experience is recorded, the easier it is for the brain to access that memory, and even turn it into an automatic response. This has significant implications for the way we interact with babies, the behaviour they get used to as being normal, and the way that they will, in turn, behave in the future. In terms of music education, this evidence shows that the earlier that infants are exposed to music, the earlier they begin to learn how music works, much like body language, behaviour and relationships.

As a result of the subliminal way that music works, psychologists have begun to research other areas of learning that may be affected after musical training. Usually, this additional musical training is over a considerable length of time, over 12 months. Most studies operate in a fairly standard way in order to show that there has been a significant change. First of all, children or their parents are given a test or interview to set a baseline standard. Quite a large group needs to be chosen because it is meant to represent the variety of people that makes up society, known as a "sample". As psychologists recognise that the nature of childhood is to develop and learn, they know that children will be capable of significantly more in 12 months' time, so they identify another group or sample of children that are similar in specific respects. Some studies consider age, gender and socio-economic status as important predictors of achievement. Other studies consider age and mother's education level as more important because daily input makes such a big impact. Other factors could involve geography (urban/rural), parental jobs (manual/professional) or cultural influences (Western, Eastern, African, etc.). These are important descriptors in terms of whether the results of the sample accurately represent society or whether they represent a small anomaly town that happens to have a greater proportion of a specific type of population. Compared to national government studies, many of the studies mentioned in this section are regional-specific, with sample numbers in the 20s ranging to samples of 150–200. Consequently, the findings do not necessarily represent the world population, but the implication is that if any researcher follows the same procedure, they are more than likely going to find similar results.

Music and maths

For years, people have related musical ability to mathematical skill, but you do not need to look too far to see that all mathematicians do not play musical instruments and not all musicians are brilliant mathematicians. To date, the reasons for this cannot be explained except for generalisations such as personal choice or environmental opportunity/exposure. Relationships can be seen between music and different areas of mathematics, the most obvious one being fractions, as most rhythms are usually made up by dividing or multiplying by two or three, and this is one of the clearest ways to show how music complements mathematics. Even before Jerome Bruner developed his mathematics course (Bruner, 1966), people have been trying to identify the impact that music instruction has on mathematical skill.

National goals of mathematical education first appeared in the UK National Curriculum in 1988, after which the School Curriculum and Assessment Authority (SCAA) took the first steps in summarising the educational goals of an early childhood educator for children to achieve by their fifth birthdays, which included mathematical abilities (SCAA, 1996). This was superseded by the National Curriculum Early Years Foundation Stage (EYFS), and researchers have identified a particular skill set as a predictor of children's mathematical ability (Bull and Scerif, 2001).

Skills correlated to successful, independent citizenship were collectively named executive function. While a comprehensive list has not yet been agreed, some of the skills involved in executive functioning have been correlated with experience in different areas. When testing these skills before and after mathematics training, researchers found significant improvements in specific skills including inhibition, flexibility (the ability to switch and evaluate new strategies), and working (short-term) memory (Bull and Scerif, 2001), which are also skills developed through music education. Specifically, music involves producing sounds at specific moments (requiring inhibition), finding ways to respond physically on the instrument (choosing appropriate fingers, arms or legs to produce specific sounds, requiring the ability to switch and evaluate new strategies), and associating different pitches and lengths of notes with the appropriate keys or strings (working memory). In this way, it has been scientifically shown that music training may impact mathematical skill.

Research into the results of standardised testing also shows that music impacts mathematics. Groups of students were given opportunities to either attend musical training or alternative visual arts, and researchers found that the students who had received musical instruction outperformed the visual arts students (King, 2016). A study on teachers' views indicated that they were able to identify higher levels of reasoning from children who played musical instruments (Tezer et al., 2016), and an even more direct study, using music to learn mathematics, showed a significant difference in musical students' results (Kocabaa, 2009). These findings may be partly explained by Shlaug's research (Schlaug et al., 2005), identifying ways in which the musician's brain structure (the size of different parts of the brain) and function (the way it works) were different to non-musicians'. The reason given for these changes is the complex variation of skills involved in playing music, from translating written notation to physical motor reactions, all the while controlling the instrument and being aware of additional feedback. While it appears that music does impact mathematical understanding, it is not yet fully understood how, indicating that more research is needed. One danger in completing more research is that music may be considered a shortcut for mathematical benefits, especially for schools committed to increasing national scores and levels. This should not detract from music research, as all findings work together to try to explain the multiple levels in which music evokes the human response.

Music and executive function

Executive function, mentioned above, has been shown to predict socio-economic success with far greater accuracy than its predecessor, IQ (intelligence quotient) testing. IQ tests are known for the abstract pictures and patterns that are used, and the people who score within the top 5 per cent have the prestige of being part of a select group. It has also been found that this select group of people come from all walks of life, and that these people are just as likely to be socio-economically successful as not, indicating that in fact IQ scores simply identify people who think similarly.

Executive function covers a range of skills, with the most commonly agreed skills including attention, flexibility, working memory, planning, reasoning, self-control, task initiation and problem-solving. IQ tests are still useful in identifying specific executive function skill increases after interventions. One example is that verbal reasoning and short-term memory improved after 12 weeks of musical intervention, whereas numerical and abstract reasoning did not show any change (Kaviani et al., 2014).

This finding is supported by Miendlarzewska and Trost (2014), who used executive function testing to discover that children with musical training had a higher score in verbal memory, pronunciation in second languages, and reading ability. They also found that these skills increased with the amount of practice time, the intensity of the practice (improving the accuracy and timing in note-playing), and the younger they were when they started playing the instrument. Musical links with bilingualism were also found by Bialystok and DePape (2009).

This is an extremely relevant topic to education today, as executive function is being correlated to "school readiness skills", a term that has been devised to describe a child sufficiently equipped to learn successfully (Biermanet al., 2008). In fact, music may be used as a predictor in identifying executive dysfunction (Lesiuk, 2014), as a study on the role of executive function in music explored. Significant differences were found between typically and atypically developing children in relation to note duration and rhythmic patterns (no difference in pitch and melody), with the atypically developing children performing poorly in comparison. As children with executive dysfunction also perform poorly in working memory tasks, this study suggests that music-based activities may improve working memory, which may be evident in improved rhythmic ability.

A study comparing music lessons and intelligence (Degg et al., 2011) identified a clear link between increased music lessons and five specific executive functions. Links were strongest in selective attention and inhibition, and less so in planning, fluency and activity switching. However, Slevc et al. (2016) found that musical ability predicted better auditory and visual task scores, but did not appear to affect the abilities of self-control and activity switching. With research studies, these types of discrepancies may be due to sample sizes, specific tests or tasks used, or the individual music teaching approaches. Sample sizes, although small, are more or less standard within this sector, as are the types of tests and tasks used. My personal experience, however, in both learning and teaching music has identified that there is a distinct difference in how students understand the way that music works and the way that they use expression in performing pieces, and this seems to depend on whether they were taught using traditional or non-traditional music teaching approaches.

Music and the senses

In adults, long-term musical training has been found to improve the visual attention of musicians (Rodrigues et al., 2013), while fewer age-related auditory processing problems were found in musicians (Zendel and Alain, 2012). In children, an initial longitudinal study indicated that musical training in early childhood enhanced neural coding in speech (Strait et al., 2013), while the long-term group interactions positively influenced children's ability to empathise (Rabinowitch et al., 2013). Interactively, music offered as a reinforcement was found to be more effective than non-musical reinforcements with older and younger participants than with teenagers, reducing the effects of pain, crying, improving strength, posture, behaviour, listening, endurance and even sports accuracy (Standley, 1996). Daily routines appear to be enhanced by music, improving the transition of potentially difficult situations such as nappy changes, bath times and bed times (Addessi, 2009), and children respond better to adults who participate in songs as opposed to adults observing children (Berger and Cooper, 2003). Opportunities to play or improvise (make up music) have been identified as activities leading to independence or child agency (Barrett, 2011), while common play behaviours like musical stories, tapping the beat to pictures, playing musical games and moving to musical songs were found to encourage musical development, particularly when parents were involved (Cooper and Cardany, 2011).

Music has numerous benefits for other skills, and at this stage in research it is unclear whether music improves the extraneous senses of musicians or whether musicians acquire skills that make music more easily achievable. Research currently shows that music behaves like a language, acquired through modelling and interaction. Musical interaction can be used as a transition and reward because it is empowering and enjoyable. Whether it is enjoyable because it is empowering or whether it is empowering because it is enjoyable is not yet clear.

Music and pitch

Through non-invasive scans, researchers have begun to identify exactly which types of music babies prefer, most often based on Western cultures and mostly North American. Despite Michel initially stating that as 0–6-month-old children learn to hear and distinguish pitch (tune) and timbre (instrument voice), they can recognise all pitches and modes given suitable practice (Michel, 1973a), infants have been shown to prefer high pitch play songs but low pitch lullabies (Tsang and Conrad, 2010). Even more specifically, infants can recognise the perfect fourth (e.g. C–F) and perfect fifth (e.g. C–G) more accurately than a tritone (e.g. C–F#), which used to be called the devil's chord, and a major 6th (e.g. C–A) (Schellenberg and Trehub, 1996). These findings are useful in identifying the types of songs that will reassure infants (easily recognised) or encourage them to pay attention (cause them to look in surprise). Additional studies indicate that 3–5-year-old children become more accurate singers when group singing and individual instruction are combined (Rutkowski, 1990), while children as young as 5 years old are able to recognise the notes in one key, and 7-year-olds are able to recognise notes in harmony (Trainor and Trehub, 1994). This indicates that children's singing abilities are much more advanced than previously thought, with the implication that these additional skills could and possibly even should be taught earlier than they are. Additional implications are that sensitive periods in music education may exist, and that music teachers should potentially rethink their minimum student age, particularly in the UK where students are generally accepted at over 8 years old.

Music and movement

Research on musical characteristics recognised that musical development begins with the perception of volume, then pitch, then rhythm and finally harmony, suggesting that musical education should begin with activities developing rhythmic and melodic perception (Zimmerman, 1971). Research on the effects of spontaneous movement to music began through identifying 6-month-old infants swaying and bouncing to music, 2-year-olds rocking, bouncing and waving, 3–4-year-olds practising moves that they had been taught, and 4-year-olds imitating dance moves (Moog, 1976a). Four-year-olds were found to be capable of hopping, galloping, jumping, sliding, whirling and skipping (Scott-Kassner, 1993), and further research demonstrated that basic motor development was established before the age of 5, after which motor skills were stabilised (Gilbert, 1980). Similar studies on the effect of movement encoding rhythm in infants (Phillips-Silver and Trainor, 2005) and adults (Phillips-Silver and Trainor, 2007) showed a link between feeling rhythm and movement and indicating that experience is more vital than observation/modelling, certainly in infancy. The adult study confirmed that visual information was insufficient to recognise/remember rhythm, and body movement was critical. A further study (Phillips-Silver and Trainor, 2008) confirmed that movement of the legs alone did not impact rhythm recognition, but movement of the head with the legs (e.g. gross motor movement) or even head alone was sufficient to metrically encode the rhythm heard. This suggests that the balancing, vestibular system is integrally involved in the ability to recognise or reproduce a rhythm. This leads to the concept of entrainment: the ability to synchronise body movements to an external beat (Wilson and Cook, 2016), observable in studies on musical movement where preschool, primary and pre-service teachers physically responded to the style of music through movement (Sims, 1988).

Music and rhythm

As rhythm is considered so integral to music, it is no surprise that this has featured in early studies. Children between 3 to 5 years old were found to chant in time more accurately than they could clap in time or even use gross motor movement like walking (Frega, 1979). Another study on 3–4-year-old children found that they were able to maintain rhythms with simple instruments and chanting, finding that accuracy improved with age and, presumably, maturity (Rainbow and Owen, 1979). By the end of this study it was found that 3–4-year-old children were able to match vocal rhythms (chanting) but were unable to march and clap accurately to the beat (Rainbow, 1981). A later study demonstrated that 6–7-year-olds clap more accurately to the beat but step most accurately (Schleuter and Schleuter, 1985), while musical intervention was shown to accelerate rhythmic ability/ acculturation by holding regular sessions (Gerry et al., 2010). Therapeutically, rhythmic musical training has been shown to improve the posture and gait in the elderly (Maclean et al., 2014), which may have implications for toddlers learning to walk. Educationally, rhythm tests may indicate low achievers, with the intervention of increasing rhythm exercises to improve achievement (Lesiuk, 2014), and musical intervention has been shown to improve the mental process of rhythm in speech (Zhao and Kuhl, 2016).

Music education philosophy

Philosophers develop theories and explanations for events or occurrences common to people in the hope of improving social situations. They intend to improve the quality of life by helping people to recognise the impact of their individual or personal actions. By looking at the big picture, philosophers search for patterns of behaviour, linking smaller, "everyday" actions to larger social or global issues. For centuries, people have worked to identify the purpose of music, with suggestions of intrinsic and extrinsic motivation ranging from environmental influence to biological "hardwiring". The following philosophers and psychologists have specifically included mentions of music within their overarching philosophies, impacting the field of music education.

Bennett Reimer on music education philosophy

Aesthetic music education (i.e. meaning-filled) was proposed by Bennett Reimer (2005, 2007), who supported the notion of "good" music created by those able to both read and perform from notation. He saw music as a direct representation of emotion and feeling, with the implication that music that did not evoke feeling could not be considered "good", which he believed was a universal trait of "good" music, regardless of culture.

Musical knowledge came from an understanding of the different areas of music, leading to personal fulfilment, where the purpose was to teach feelings. Reimer unified the processes of listening and making music, and based teaching success on the clarity of the curriculum. He saw music as part of the arts and thought that it should be recognised as a subject in its own right, not recognised or used for its beneficial effects on other areas; for example, academic or rehabilitative.

David J. Elliott on music education philosophy

Praxial music education (i.e. actively creating) was proposed by David J. Elliot (1995, 2005) as he viewed music as a practice unique to humans who developed from novice to expert. He challenged the idea of music itself making people feel, arguing instead that music triggered memories, and that music was culturally specific, only creating meaning and feeling for those familiar with the culture that was performing it or listening to it. Musical knowledge developed from making and listening to music, to self-knowledge and growth, with the purpose of personal development and enjoyment. Elliott separated listening from music making, and based teaching success on the teacher.

Keith Swanwick on music education philosophy

A spiral model of musical development was proposed by Keith Swanwick and June Tillman (Swanwick, 2010; Swanwick and Tillman, 1986), who collected numerous children's original compositions (made-up songs). Using this spiral model, independent judges could accurately identify the age of the children because Swanwick and Tillman had identified a sequence of common overlapping developmental stages. They found that children from 0–4 years old developed mastery by exploring sound through dynamics and timbre; 4–9-year-olds imitated known music as a form of self-expression; and 10–15-year-olds could use metacognition (an understanding of other's thinking) with a focus on values. Children who did not fall into these groups were found to have a more musical home life than others, so moved through the stages more quickly. This view considered development as a staged transformation in thinking, broadly following Piaget's concept of child development.

David Hargreaves on music education philosophy

The concept of phases of artistic development, devised by David Hargreaves and Maurice Galton (Hargreaves, 2008; Hargreaves and Lamont, 2017), contemplated creativity more broadly. Also following Piaget's concept of child development, it began with the sensorimotor, pre-symbolic phase, and analysed the development of drawing (scribbling), writing (symbolic), singing (babbling), musical representation (scribbling/ movement), melodic perception (melodic contours) and musical composition (sensory manipulation). Children of 2–5 years entered the figural (concrete) phase; 5–8-year-olds entered the schematic (realism) phase; 8–15-year-olds entered the rule systems (style sensitivity) phase; and children over 15 years old entered the megacognitive (independent) phase. As with all systems that identify behaviours, teachers should be able to plan more effective lessons by understanding the phase of development displayed by children.

Mary Louise Serafine on music education philosophy

Music as cognition, a way of thinking, was proposed by Mary Louise Serafine (Serafine, 1983, 2013). She heavily criticised the idea of music as a personality trait or inherent ability and considered the different ways that music was seen, for example, music as natural law, communication or behaviourism. Through a series of experiments, Serafine concluded that music should be viewed as a way of thinking or cognition because of the mental processes involved in understanding that music moves through time. In addition, she viewed the process of musical ability as developmental. Serafine's conclusions were: a child's understanding of musical timing, patterns, processes and sequences is complete by 10 years old; formal lessons cannot improve musical ability; musical ability had nothing to do with identifying pitches (notes); skills related to timing or other skills developed slightly differently. Again, this sounds Piagetian in terms of abilities being set and measured in terms of the ability to think.

Adam Ockelford on music education philosophy

The Sounds of Intent model, developed by Adam Ockelford (Ockelford and Welch, 2012; Welch et al., 2009), originated from his work with children with physical and learning disabilities and expanded to include young children's musical development. Ockelford's zygonic theory comes from the idea of musical development through imitation, and has been used in many theoretical and analytical ways, including predicting the development of musical skill. In this model, musical skill has been divided into three main areas of interaction with sound: encountering sound; making sound; and relating through sound, with the focus on matching musical skill to the individual or specific group (as opposed to stating blanket age-appropriate behaviours). This model can be used not only to identify musical development but also to identify next steps or opportunities of potential experience.

At first glance, these ideas may seem almost predictable and fairly obvious, but there will be some aspects within each view that we as individuals agree with and prioritise above others. The usefulness of philosophy and philosophers is that by being more aware and understanding of the views that exist, we become aware of our own prejudices or preconceptions, and therefore more effective at sharing our knowledge and skills with others, including our children.

Figure 3.8 Song using so-fa-mi-re-do notes

Table 3.6 Oranges and lemons rhythm table

| | |	| | ⊓	| | |	| | |
Oranges and	Lemons, say the	bells of Saint	Clement's, I
| | |	| | ⊓	| | |	| | -
owe you two	farthing, say the	bells of Saint	Martin's
| | |	| | ⊓	| | |	| | -
When will you	pay me, say the	bells of Old	Bailey
| | |	| - ⊓	| | |	| - -
When I grow	rich, say the	bells of Shore-	Ditch
| | |	| - ⊓	| | |	| - -
When will that	be, say the	bells of Step-	ney
| | |	| - ⊓	| | |	| - -
I do not	know, says the	Great bell of	Bow

Song Level Five: **Oranges and lemons**

Level Five songs include simple time and introduce the 6/8 timing, like rocking songs, with the notes limited to *do-re-mi-fa-so*.

> *Oranges and lemons, say the bells of Saint Clement's*
> *I owe you two farthings, say the bells of Saint Martin's*

When will you pay me, say the bells of Old Bailey
When I grow rich, say the bells of Shoreditch
When will that be, say the bells of Stepney
I do not know, says the great bell of Bow

We used this song to extend the idea of bridges with children. Younger non-walkers used this for baby massage or instrument play. Older children stood in a single line, while the first two children formed a bridge for the rest of the children to walk under. We extended this to allow more children to create bridges for the line to follow, like "dot-to-dot".

The way forward

This part of the chapter reflects on the past and present in order to consider the best way to move forward in music education. This has partly been done earlier in this book (Chapter 1) by looking at the ways in which people have documented music teaching in the last century, and then in this chapter, by considering the current research that has gone into both understanding the development of people and the development of music education. By combining this information, it should be possible to draw conclusions and derive principles that will be useful in learning music for all ages.

Despite music education not being a priority within the current UK government, there is still a fairly large section of society that sees value in a musical education. Naturally, this group is made up of people who have individually different views on the best ways to develop music education, helped in no part by the different aesthetic views that believe some types of music to be more valuable than others. The principle-based approach to music education presented in this section aims to recognise the value that these different views and styles hold by applying the research available on music education and child development. Through this, a working framework of a progression of musical activities may be identified in which potentially music of any genre may be used with any type of group of children from birth to 7 years, with the aim of providing a solid foundational understanding of both the beauty and the language of music.

In teaching music at any level, it is important to recognise the multi-dimensional nature of music. As mentioned earlier (p. 137), music is aesthetic, which means that any music will appeal to some but not all people. This is partly because music is reflective, a snapshot of personal experience, which suggests that criticism of any music is an extremely personal judgement. Music is also transformative, with the ability to change moods, feelings, intentions and behaviours, and this is used to great effect in films and social activities. Finally, music is not only communicative but also a form of communication. Just as writing allows ideas to travel, an understanding of a universal way in which to communicate music allows musical styles and skills to travel and be experienced at a larger scale. A framework that reduces music to only one or a few of these dimensions, limits not only the music that may be created, but also the person creating the music. At any level of music teaching, it is essential that the different dimensions of music are included, even though it cannot be guaranteed that they will all be overtly learnt or even acknowledged by the learner. The table of early childhood music skills progression aims to recognise all these points to work towards creating a balanced programme of early childhood music education delivery.

Musical framework: table of early childhood music skills progression

While external music education providers may hold sessions for 30–45 minutes, the framework presented here is in the form of continuous provision, so that familiar adults are able to offer regular sessions at shorter intervals. Both approaches are useful and should not be used as a replacement for the other but should work to support each other. Bringing in high-quality musicians exposes the children to live skill with which they may not otherwise engage, while making music with familiar child workers ensures that music becomes part of their everyday experience and skill development.

This framework is subdivided into age-specific abilities because of the rapid development experienced in childhood. Some skills require on-going repetition to solidify concepts, bridging multiple years through multiple experiences, while other skills develop more quickly. As a guide, this table not only gives the educator an indication of the ability that children may attain at certain ages, it also allows educators to personalise children's learning journeys by identifying the next musical steps for children who are more interested and perhaps more musically experienced or quicker to progress than the group.

This framework is also subdivided into specific musical activities, including movement through games and dances, language, recognising shapes, as well as musical skill such as listening, singing, and matching pulse, again demonstrating the multi-dimensional aspect of musical skill. Each skill will be addressed separately below.

Circle work

Sitting in a circle is the beginning of recognising the shape of the circle. Various psychologists have tried to explain the usefulness of the circle in terms of everybody being recognised as having equivalent importance, being able to see everybody at the same time, everybody having equal access to the centre with less opportunity to become distracted or unseen, and perhaps there is some truth in these ideas. On a practical level, there is always the tendency to fill the void, so it is useful to use the space as an area to gather and return instruments or materials. Getting children to learn to collect and return their instruments is useful because it demonstrates respect and responsibility for the items, the area and each other, with the recognition that instruments have a specific purpose (music) as opposed to being another toy, for example. As children develop, walking in a circle is a physical, gross motor introduction to writing as children physically trace circles with their bodies. One Montessori technique is to have a permanent circle painted in the play area for children, and occasionally to encourage the children to carefully follow the adult walking around the shape, giving them the opportunity to experience physically the continuous curve of the circular shape with their gross motor muscles before refining and reproducing the shape through fine motor actions in drawing and writing.

Circle work as spectators: 0–3 years

With young babies, sitting in a circle with a 1:1 or 1:2 ratio allows them the opportunity to participate equally, but larger ratios can be difficult. At this stage, babies often sit and sway to the pulse. Toddlers aged 1–2 years begin to learn spatial awareness and self-control as they are encouraged to sit in a circle to play instruments and use their energy by getting up to return and fetch their instruments. Circular activities without instruments can involve sitting and tapping their knees to the pulse. Children aged 2–3 years old are still mainly spectators but are able to hold hands with help and walk in a circle.

Circle work as participants: 3–7 years

Children aged 3–4 years interact more confidently with creative and imaginary ideas. Their desire to be independent can be directed through introducing circle games, which rely on self-control to be played successfully and enjoyably (through activities like turn-taking, responding to timing or wording). Children aged 4–5 years are more able to co-ordinate whole-group actions such as stepping forward and backward on given counts or words, while children aged 5–6 years are able to successfully create inner and outer circles relatively independently, even walking in opposite directions. In the final early childhood age grouping, children aged 6–7 years are able to perform simple dance moves in a circular pattern, interacting with an inner and outer circle as partners and then moving to new partners.

Listening work

Listening skills are essential for taking in information, informed decision-making, and responding to both familiar and unfamiliar situations. Music is the ideal vehicle to develop listening skills because listening is the greatest feature of music. Listening takes time, which helps children to develop their own internal sense of timing through experience as they begin to anticipate the repeated patterns (motifs) and sounds. The greatest skill in teaching listening skills is to create an overwhelming engagement that requires a response. The more familiar a piece of music, the better a child will be at anticipating the part that comes before or afterwards. Listening can be developed through associating sounds with activities and movements that interest the children, that they find familiar, or that they find interesting or enjoyable. Besides the clear and obvious benefit of simple and effective group behaviour control is the development of the longer term skill of self-control and the ability to focus for ever-increasing lengths of time.

Listening observers: 0–3 years

Infants aged 0–1 year enjoy following movement initially with their eyes and then, as they develop their gross motor skills, with their bodies. Children aged 1–2 years enjoy developing skills like sharing through passing instruments or toys. Examples of this include taking turns to hold or pat a song-related toy (e.g. patting a sheep to *Baa Baa Black Sheep*), taking turns playing and passing around a valuable instrument like a ukulele or, quite simply, rolling balls across a distance, experiencing the time it takes to arrive between one child and the next. Along with developing muscular skills in the eyes, spatial awareness and hand-eye co-ordination, these activities develop skills like patience and turn-taking, recognising the role that silence plays in music, the role that waiting plays in games, and the role that individuals play in teamwork, whether as contributions to a project or as contributions to an orchestra. Delayed responses to specific sounds can be introduced to children aged 2–3 years, and we naturally introduce this through associating actions with words such as *Twinkle, Twinkle*, by using gross motor actions as vocabulary reminders.

Listening participants: 3–7 years

Older children can start to associate listening with timing. From 3–4 years old, we can develop this idea through perhaps playing chiming instruments instead of "twinkling" in *Twinkle, Twinkle*, and then by playing the instruments on the first word of the first line, introducing children to the concept of the first beat in the bar, and playing together in time. Children aged 4–5 years enjoy interacting with a partner, playing simple hand clapping games, or walking down a line of children while singing a song, while children aged between 5–6 years can learn more complicated partner games to songs, learning specific movement sequences that match the rhythm or theme of each line of the song. Simple conducting can be introduced to children aged 6–7 years in 2/4 (up/down) timing, helping children to internalise the idea of an eternal, on-going beat or rhythm with the rest of the group. It is useful to teach this skill by initially asking children to feel the beat of the song by walking around a room while conducting the music (up and down), and then developing this idea by asking individuals to take turns conducting as the rest tap or shake simple percussion instruments, developing experience in confidence, performance, leadership and group communication.

Memory work

Many memory games involve the concept of location, which helps with locating lost items, but locating knowledge can be a little trickier. Mnemonics are often used to help to memorise difficult or unfamiliar information by using more familiar vocabulary, e.g. *Richard Of York Gave Battlie In Vain* as a mnemonic for the colours of the rainbow: Red, Orange, Yellow, Green, Blue, Indigo, Violet. It has been found that people generally tend to memorise the end of information first, most likely because it is the most recent information heard. Even small children tend to first join in with songs by finishing them together from the last line to the first. This concept is useful to remember and use with children in teaching rules, procedures and behaviours that involve specific sequences.

Memory work as observers: 0–3 years

Within the first few weeks from birth, infants become familiar with situations extremely quickly, and are able to recognise when situations end earlier than expected. From conversations to songs to games, babies aged 0–1 year will show surprise when their expectation is not met and, as they get older, they will find a way to fill in the missing space, from moving and wriggling to vocalising and deliberate eye movements. This is very much like the reaction most people experience to the rhythm (or tune): tap – tappy – tap – tap . . . most people naturally want to finish it with: tap – tap! Using this technique, as infants grow older, they move more expressively in response to the missing words, may even start to vocalise the last line, and are more likely to learn those words first. As their vocabulary develops, children around 2 years old will continue the song with a vocal accompaniment and, depending on their home music experience, will potentially sing both words and tune accurately.

Memory work as participants: 3–7 years

From 3 years old it is reasonable to expect inexperienced children to join in the last line of new songs most accurately, with more experienced children singing the entire song confidently from very early on. We know that early exposure to a wide variety of experiences develops coping skills, and this is one of the ways in which we can play an active role in helping children who may not have had the opportunities of others, whether through difficulties in background or health. Children aged 4–5 years will find the last two lines significantly easier to learn than the first few, whereas children aged 5–6 years would enjoy singing the missing line. Children aged 6–7 years could have this concept extended by clapping the rhythm of the words of the missing line, showing that they remember what is missing, and that they have internalised the music. Internalising music, the ability to imagine the tune (pitch) and timing (rhythm) of a song, is a deeper form of self-control useful in situations where groups rely on co-operation, most clearly seen in orchestras. From musicians and nurses to teaching assistants, sports teams and boardrooms, being able to understand the undercurrents and pacing of an activity ensures that you can play your instrument at the perfect time, provide life-saving medical support, know when to push and when to back off with a student, be in a position to score, and even have the upper hand in negotiation – purely based on subtle clues in the environment.

Instrument suitability

Choosing suitable instruments is often left to the discretion of the child and, depending on the purpose of the activity, this is a good method to follow, particularly in discovering a child's interest. In terms of child development, certain actions will generally be easier or more appealing to different age groups, and just as all the previous framework sections can be viewed as guidance in terms of ages and developmental opportunities, this section is also geared to general situations.

Instrument suitability for observers: 0–3 years

Infants are born with survival-dependent skills, one of which includes the grasping/holding reflex. With the potential strength to support their body weight if necessary, this grasping reflex is clearly expressed in the way that children aged 0–1 year hold onto egg shakers. Often to no easily observable rhythm, and sometimes actually matching the rhythm of their own heartbeat, the effect of shaking an instrument and experiencing the noise made can be used with great effect for these little ones, so it is useful to have a variety of instruments that are easy to hold and make a good shaking sound. It is surprisingly difficult to maintain a clear rhythm or keep a beat with an instrument that can be shaken, so useful songs to use with these instruments would be *directional* (up, down, around, in, out) or *naming* (tapping on body parts). Children quickly extend their grasping reflex towards tapping, so children from 1–2 years old do well with instruments that require beaters/sticks. It is useful to make a clear distinction between instruments that may or may not be tapped on the ground as a number of instruments that need a beater look interestingly like a hammer, producing a good tapping sound – and will break if repeatedly smashed on the floor (or struck by a particularly enthusiastic beater!). Introducing these instruments through careful demonstration and passing around individually is an effective non-verbal way to encourage respect of instruments. Children aged 2–3 years have developed more control and are now more confident in beating instruments like drums. Again, it is worth emphasising the value of the sound they are creating and the contribution that they make to the group so that you can clearly hear the beat without the instrument being damaged or drowning out the singing or other instruments.

Instrument suitability for participants: 3–7 years

Beating an object is a natural and integral part of early childhood development, and as gross motor skills become more stable and can be controlled to a better extent, the size of instrument that children are able to manipulate is also able to scale down. Most 3–4-year-old children will find that they have the control and patience needed in playing the triangle, whether dangling the triangle from a ribbon or hanging one corner on their finger (better control, same sound). Children aged 4–5 years will find that they are able to strike a cymbal confidently with a beater in time, and can judge the force and distance needed to compensate for the swinging weight. With the introduction of more activities with fine motor skills, children aged 5–6 years will be ready to strike the keys of a glockenspiel accurately with a beater, picking out simple tunes with few notes. As this is the first tuned (can play different notes) percussion (instrument to beat) that the children are introduced to as a group, beginning to identify and differentiate the ideas of "low" and "high" from either end is a good starting point. Level One songs in this book begin with two notes, the *nee-naw* ambulance sound using sol-mi (Kodály terminology), or the equivalent of G–E on a glockenspiel keyboard. Identified as common tones found in most Westernised countries, these notes are arguably the easiest notes to sing and recognise. There are different songs that can be played using these two simple notes, progressing a note at a time, and then in different note combinations, so that children are successfully able to sing the songs, play the games and then play the songs on instruments. Children aged 6–7 years start to have the finger strength and determination to play ukuleles. These are small guitar-shaped instruments that have four strings, originating in Portugal, and travelling with Portuguese sailors to Hawaii, where they were made famous. Although ukuleles can be tuned in two main ways, the most common is the GCEA tuning, which can be remembered using the mnemonic, God Can't Eat Ants. The G is the top string, the E is the second from the bottom, so these simple two note songs can be played on the ukulele without even having to press the string down onto the fretboard. (The songs can also be played using the ukulele as accompaniment by playing the chord of C, which is achieved by pressing the bottom string against the ukulele on the third fret.)

Language work

Like most things that children learn, language is acquired through modelling the people closest to the child. However, researchers, including the early childhood community, recognise that children communicate from birth. From focussed gazing and wordless cooing to directional pointing and changes in posture, children are adept at reading and communicating through body language, and much of what becomes their adult fallback behaviour is learnt during this quickly forgotten period. In a sense, adults have become reliant on language as an equaliser in communication, and so it has become a cause for concern and intervention when children have not begun to use language meaningfully within the first two years. Music, like body language, seems to be an instinctive form of communication, and children are quick to notice whether the music being heard meets adult approval, and therefore whether their response to the music heard will meet adult approval. Music appears to help the transition to language, with studies currently being carried out on the potential relationship between rhythm and dyslexia. With the variety of styles of language used in different pieces of music, it is worth using music with language.

Language work for observers: 0–3 years

Children aged 0–1 year use language in music by pointing. One effective exercise in developing a sense of rhythm with little ones is to use simple percussion, egg shakers for instance, to tap body parts to a beat while naming the body part. One option is to start either at the head or toes, for example:

Toes, toes, toes, toes, toes, toes, toes – toes, toes, toes, toes, toes and stop.

Then move on to knees, tummy, elbows, shoulders, neck, cheeks, nose – whichever you wish to choose (by choosing a direction to move up or down, you are unlikely to repeat a body part). Children aged 1–2 years may begin to repeat the body part names, and will enjoy the familiarity of the exercise, especially if an extension is used, such as using different instruments, starting at the cheeks, or asking different children to lead the exercise. Children aged 2–3 years will enjoy developing their use of language by dressing up (using scarves which could be used as props in a variety of ways) as characters in the song, or imitating the actions of the song. At this stage, all children enjoy the opportunity to act out all the characters, developing the language of the whole song. By watching each other, the children gather ideas on how to develop their first thoughts.

Language work for participants: 3–7 years

By 3–4 years old, children will be more likely to use language confidently, while still enjoying acting out characters and dressing up, with all the children still having the opportunity to act as the same character. Children aged 4–5 years and sometimes younger begin to develop a great sense of humour too and, recognising that laughter signals happiness, will try to start telling jokes. Songs with funny descriptions or unlikely events will go down really well, giving the children confidence in performing as well as in developing language. Children aged 5–6 years enjoy having different characters assigned within the same group, effectively taking turns when their performance is needed, but possibly still requiring the support of the group singing when they take their turn at performing. Children aged 6–7 years old will enjoy performing songs in character, perfecting their language for their part in the song or game, and taking on roles independently within a game context. Occasionally this may be in a performance context, but this will usually depend on the musical home background of the child.

Line work

The ability to follow is an essential part of social behaviour. From standing in queues and turn-taking to driving, cycling, education, and multiple types of jobs, the ability to follow can be the difference between financial success and failure. Even in reading, the ability to follow a line of writing means the difference between understanding a complete thought or struggling to understand a number of incomplete, random thoughts. Music is similar, from being able to follow a line of printed music, through following or repeating musical patterns, to being able to follow which parts to play and when to wait in silence. These are all concepts that we initially develop through early experiences and these can easily be reinforced through simple activities.

Line work for observers: 0–3 years

Children aged 0–1 year can begin to learn about moving in straight lines through physically rolling over, a skill that eventually leads to pushing up, sitting up and ultimately standing up. Children aged 1–2 years often start walking and can usually manage to walk in a line holding hands with another child or adult. From 2–3 years old, children are able to follow each other in a line, one behind the other, although this may require a considerable level of adult assistance, at least in the beginning. Opportunities to experience linear movement is also foundational to the writing experience, where a number of letters require the ability to write straight lines. This is another case where the gross motor experience preceding the fine motor experience acts as a physical example of what is expected.

Line work for participants: 3–7 years

From 3–4 years of age, children are individually able to follow each other in a winding line, even a line that develops into a spiral. (Using a dance technique, it is possible to uncurl from a spiral without having to let go and walk in reverse!) Physically experiencing shapes increases the potential for later success in fine motor skills and other abstract ways. From 4–5 years of age, children are able to walk successfully in a line and stop to create a bridge, under which the other children are able to walk. Children aged 5–6 years can use the dance technique to follow each other into a spiral and uncurl from the spiral (once the group is curled into a tight spiral, ensuring that hands are held tightly, the first two of the spiral create a "bridge" that travels over the line of dancers, effectively allowing for the rest of the group to walk under and escape the spiral to return to a circle). Children aged 6–7 years can join in games and dances that involve partners standing across from them in parallel lines. These are all shapes which they will come across in various aspects of life, from education (maths) to social situations. Having this practical experience creates the necessary situation for the brain to recognise and respond accordingly.

Musical rhythms

Some instrumental music teachers wait until children have started reading before they introduce music notation because of the Westernised concepts like reading from left to right and up to down. This is when the symbol is recognised for its importance, separate to the time and sound that it represents. Using music education experiences from Dalcroze, Kodály and Orff, children can begin to recognise not only the regular beat of the pulse, but also the difference between fast and slow, and the various levels within those two extremes. This is extremely useful preparation for mathematical skills like fractions, language skills for descriptions, as well as gross motor skills involving balance and fine motor skills requiring co-ordination.

Musical rhythms for observers: 0–3 years

In all musical sessions, the initial foundational teaching is on pulse, which is the regular on-going beat, like the heartbeat. In many songs, this coincides with the crotchet or quarter note beat, which can be thought of as a walking pace beat. Using different instruments and experiences, the children tap instruments and body parts to the crotchet/quarter note beat, and even as children begin to walk in their first or second year, they are encouraged to recognise the fluid, repetitive motion of walking by the teacher playing instruments to match their walking pace. In the second year, 1–2 years, teachers can emphasise the crotchet beat by passing around toys and patting them, or sitting opposite each other and tapping knees or clapping hands, further developing skills in co-ordination. During the 1–2 year stage, teachers can also introduce music that has clear changes in tempo or speed, and children can approximate their movements. It is useful to have a standard or walking pace, a faster pace and a slower pace, and because of natural muscular development, children will find it easier to approximate or match walking than they will clapping or tapping (research has shown that it would be unusual if 25–50 per cent of children were able to match rhythms perfectly at this stage). Children aged 2–3 years begin to experience the deliberate difference between crotchet/ quarter note and quaver/eighth note rhythms. These are literally double the speed of the normal walking rhythm. To help children with self-control, we term this a "jogging" rhythm (running implies a lack of timing), and the year is spent making them confident in recognising the difference and being able to adjust their personal movement, whether in feet or on instruments, to match the beat that they hear. It is possible to introduce these rhythms as symbols, using musical notation, and ask children to tap each beat as they hear it. The songs chosen in this book, particularly the ones with crotchet/quarter note and quaver/eighth note rhythms usually have clear lyrics that use one syllable per beat, making it easier for both the teacher and child to hear accurately. Note that the crotchet often has four beats per line or bar of music:

Twin-	*kle,*	*twin-*	*kle*

In contrast, quavers/eighth notes fill in the space between the crotchets/quarter notes:

Pol-	*ly*	*put*	*the*	*ket-*	*tle*	*on,*	*we'll*

Some early childhood music courses recommend using these rhythms printed on separate card or paper for children to tap, however, this is up to teacher discretion.

Musical rhythms for participants: 3–7 years

After becoming more confident in these rhythms using gross motor skills, primarily walking, children aged 3–4 years can begin to apply these different rhythms in fine motor skills, including clapping, tapping and shaking or scraping instruments. These demonstrations help to show the teacher instantly which children are listening or not paying attention, as well as which children understand and which children may need more support. The *self-rewarding* nature of music ensures that those children who can play accurately will continue to play, while the *peer effect* of music works to support those who may need a little more time or experience to gain the required skills. Children aged 4–5 years are able to learn the dotted rhythm in between walking and jogging: skipping. Notoriously tricky for adult music students who count every rhythm, skipping is the second-most natural movement for preschool children after walking, mirrored in the number of children's songs using this rhythm (e.g. *"Girls and boys go out to play"*). Being able to hear and then experience the difference between a walk, a jog and a skip makes reading the notation much easier. Mathematically explained, two quavers/eighth notes take the same length of time as a crotchet/quarter note. In the same way, a dotted-quaver-semiquaver or dotted-eighth-note-sixteenth-note takes the same overall length of time as a crotchet/quarter note. This is because a dotted note is longer by half of the note value before it, so a dotted quaver/eighth note takes three-quarters of the time of a single crotchet/quarter note, completed by a quick semiquaver or sixteenth note. How much easier to tap a pulse/on-going beat and, instead of tapping double-time to make quavers, tap one beat in for a slightly longer time than the second, so that you have a long-short, long-short, long-short rhythm! Like a skip! Children aged 5–6 years continue to refine their experience, putting the rhythm onto instruments and gaining the ability to play songs with any of the rhythms they have learnt. Children aged 6–7 will be in a position to use their increasing strength and self-control to slow down their walk to a minim or half note beat. Taking twice as long as the walking crotchets/quarter

151

notes, many analogies can be made to describe the concept of slow: snails, dragons, dinosaurs, moonwalks, elephants, trucks and other large objects that would have to move slowly because of their size or ability. Often these mental images are useful initial reminders of the rhythm: walk like you're going to the shops; jog like you're a spider creeping; skip like you're a fairy in a meadow; stride like you're a dragon in a castle. Children's TV characters are also helpful references for comparisons and can create a meaningful experience, even at the youngest age.

Musical intervals

Musical intervals are the differences in sound from one note to another. They are important because knowing them helps us to predict the tune or melody of the song. Predicting the tune of the song helps with planning where to place fingers on instruments, making music playing more accurate. Just as maths first considers the addition of whole numbers in a number sequence starting with the familiar idea of "one", understanding the relationship between musical notes starts with a familiar tune that is found in many Westernised countries: the ambulance *nee-naw* sound. In the do-re-mi sequence, the scale is: do-re-**mi**-fa-**so**-la-ti-do, and the *nee-naw* sound is *so* and *mi*. Singing songs that emphasise this progression gives children a lifelong foundation for singing clearly and accurately.

Musical intervals for observers: 0–3 years

Many songs for 0–3-year-olds are introduced as games so that as children develop their strength and vocabulary, they learn to play games while automatically learning to sing the correct pitch. Children naturally begin singing by using an approximation of the tune: notes that are near the tune. This is what can make their singing slightly unclear. By using only two notes, the children are more likely to sing successfully from the start. One of the most effective ways of teaching songs is by first singing the song to the children, then playing the game, and finally teaching the children to sing the song while they play the game. Children often like to learn about the background of the song, which is a great link into the humanities (e.g. history and geography), such as *Cobbler cobbler*, the old name for a shoe-maker. Using songs with two notes helps children to learn to sing one high note and one low note, and if you wish to measure their success, this is the fairest method to use – how many two note (minor third) songs can children aged 0–2 years sing accurately? For children aged 2–3 years, they could be introduced to songs with a small number of notes within the range of the perfect fifth, so songs including a limited number of notes within the *do-re-mi-fa-so* range. Some methods suggest that introducing *fa* may be problematic because the intonation is so near to *so*, but within the Western culture, it is a staple note for most contemporary music. It is still essential to introduce children to a wide variety of music of different genres, rhythms, instruments and melodies. New experiences encourage the brain to develop new pathways of information, and more familiar experiences help children to feel more confident. However, it would be unfair to expect young children to sing more complicated songs accurately without substantial musical experience or training, which is a contentious issue in itself. Finally, it is useful to remember that as children's vocal folds are undeveloped and immature until puberty at least, most are physically unable to sing as low as most adults find comfortable. Expecting them to do so is like expecting small children to reach high shelves – completely unreasonable. One way to find the most suitable pitch is to ask a relatively confident child to start off the song and join in at the same pitch as you, as the teacher, sing each individual note clearly as a model for the group.

Musical intervals for participants: 3–7 years

Children aged 3–7 years can start expanding their song list or repertoire by building on intervals with which they are already confident and familiar. Children aged 3–4 years can build on their *so-mi* experience by introducing *la*, a little higher than *so*. In fact, the chant, *"nah-nahnah-nah-nah, you can't catch me"* is often to the tune of: *so-mi-la-so-mi, so-mi-la-so-mi* (in music notes, it may be G–E–A–G–E, G–E–A–G–E), showing that *la* is quite a common part of children's original or made-up songs. Children aged 4–5 years can develop their singing from the minor third (*so-mi*; e.g. G–E) to the major third (*mi-do*; e.g. E–C). Children aged 5–6 years should be successful at learning songs with the major second interval (*re-do*; e.g. D–C), while children aged 6–7 years will be able to expand this to the full octave, recognising the relationship between *do*, (e.g. C') and *do'* (e.g. C''). Significant work was done over the last century in terms of identifying songs that children sang with tunes using these notes, and these are often identified as Kodály songs. While some were deliberately invented, others were already used as folk songs, often passed down through word of mouth. This is one of the key elements to Kodály music: its ability to transcend time and endure through different fashions and cultures. Kodály found that the songs that appeared to endure had small repetitive motifs or parts with a very specific range of notes, and also a good storyline, making them memorable and relatable to the culture where they were created. As he felt children should be exposed to the best, this included the best performances and songs so that the children would be capable of not only recognising but also replicating the best music.

Interval movements

From quite early on, children understand that a lot of what they need to learn involves sequences. From ordering numbers from smallest to largest to the sequence of the

153

alphabet, some schools use the practical experience of labelling staircases with the sequence to help children to memorise it. Music has been compared to language many times and, in some cases, even taught like language. One of the ways in which it is similar is the order of the notes in scales. In the most common scale today, the major scale (sometimes called the Ionian scale), has a:

- root note (do,)
- major second (re)
- minor third (mi)
- perfect fourth (fa)
- perfect fifth (so)
- major sixth (la)
- major seventh, and (ti)
- octave (same as the first) (do').

(The difference between *do,* and *do'*: the low *do* has a comma to show it is low, while the high *do* has an apostrophe, showing that it is high.)

Through this you can see that notes are numbered in sequence, and this concept was made quite famous in the film, *The Sound of Music* (1965) with *Doe a Deer*, which increased the knowledge and popularity of the Kodály scale. Using the concept of Orff's body percussion, associating these tones to body parts helps to visualise or experience the way the music goes up and down, for example:

Do   toes (stamp)
Re   knees (tap/patsch)
Mi   hip (tap)
Fa   hands (clap)
So   shoulders (tap)
La   head (tap)
Ti   clap overhead
Do   point overhead

Having pointed out in the previous section that some notes are easier to sing because they are more familiar, you will be aware that the notes *so* and *mi* are not in sequence. This can, however, be associated with movements that can gradually be increased as more tones are introduced. The best reason to use this concept is because of the inherent understanding that it brings to children in how music works – how notes work together, and how to put them onto just about any instrument. Teaching children patterns like sequences prepares them for many situations in life, from practical skills like forming queues in social situations to high-tech computer programming and data encryption. The ability to sequence and find patterns in apparent chaos adds a level of creativity, independence and leadership seen in the minds of the most successful entrepreneurs and inventors today.

Interval movements for observers: 0–3 years

Children aged 0–3 are still mainly developing their gross motor skills, so expecting stamping and tapping may be considered unreasonable. As children aged 0–1 year are singing songs using the minor third, these are two notes, up and down, so bouncing up and down to songs would help to associate high notes with up and low notes as down. Children aged 1–2 years are also primarily focussing on the same notes, but as they are becoming more confident in their gross motor abilities, jumping up and down shows the same concept of high and low. Children aged 2–3 years singing *Twinkle, Twinkle* can identify the perfect fifth showing the distance by either tapping shoulders or hips. It is important to remember that these music education ideas are *guidelines*: they are mere starting points or suggestions to help teachers use something concrete to describe an idea that only exists in the mind, that can be heard by the ear, and that is interpreted in many different ways by different people.

Interval movements for participants: 3–7 years

In every case, it is helpful to sing first, then play the game. After this, children are ready to get the melody and rhythm right. They will always learn by demonstration, and it is helpful to become familiar with sequences first before trying to teach them so that you know how fast you will need to sing for them to have enough time to change their actions. Children aged 3–4 years can demonstrate the *so-la* major sixth tone through tapping shoulders and head, for example, and many of the songs for that stage involve a combination of *mi-so-la*, allowing many opportunities to practise hip-shoulders-head actions. Children aged 4–5 years singing songs with the major third *mi-do* can copy the teacher in tapping hips and stamping/tapping toes when they hear those notes. Children aged 5–6 years can recognise the major second by tapping knees and toes, appreciating that the difference between these two notes is so close. Finally, children aged 6–7 years can identify the octave by demonstrating tapping/stamping toes and pointing overhead. As children become more familiar with the sounds and associated actions, it becomes easier to teach new songs by actions. Certainly by the end of each year, a good aim would be to introduce a completely new song through actions first, giving children the opportunity to associate the appropriate sound with the action. This form of action, much like the actions we use in familiar songs to remind children of the next words (like flickering hands and diamond shapes for *Twinkle, Twinkle*), introduces the idea of substitution to them. This concept is essential in developing language, where words

155

describe objects and ideas, and in mathematics, where figures and shapes represent quantity and operations.

Pulse

Pulse is the beginning of rhythm and is the underlying reason for musical counting. Being able to match another beat is an indication of external awareness of other minds, and shows the ability to choose to match the other beat. Often this is an underlying beat that we clap to when we join in with a song, or that we walk to when we hear a song playing in a shop or large area. It can be matched in a variety of ways once we have sufficient control over those body parts, and there is some argument that it begins with the ability to hear the heartbeat from the womb, then recognition of one's own heartbeat compared to others and, finally, the ability to recognise and play an external beat regardless of the heartbeat. In fact, in choirs, it has been found that when the entire choir are synchronised to sing together, even their individual heartbeats align and beat together in unity.

Pulse for observers: 0–3 years

Developing pulse in everyone is literally as easy as synchronising movement to the beat that you hear. Dancing, moving, rocking and swaying are all ways to keep the pulse, and these are such instinctive actions with children that Kodály is famously quoted as saying that the best time to teach a child music is nine months before the mother is born. Children aged 0–1 year can keep the pulse by clapping, although beating is more common at this age. Be aware that while not all children this age will clap or beat accurately, greater gross motor experience will improve this. In fact, there is no evidence to prove otherwise. Children aged 1–2 years will find clapping to a regular beat difficult and will be more successful at walking or stamping the beat with their feet because of the difference in the length of the limbs. Children aged 3–4 years still find clapping slowly difficult and are more accurate at walking to the beat, but they will find it easier to click or flick their fingers to the beat (e.g. *Twinkle, Twinkle* actions). This said, it is useful not to restrict actions to a specific age group but to explore the action that each child or group is most successful at using, and use success as a starting point to encourage greater success.

Pulse for participants: 0–3 years

Walking to the pulse is the most fundamental association of sound to movement working towards maintaining the on-going beat, and this is one of the most effective ways to begin a music session. In one fairly simple activity, as soon as children are able to walk independently, allowing children to walk around the room to the regular beat of a drum, the tap of a tambourine, or even the strum of the ukulele, immediately focuses the group in a common purpose and identifies children who made need support to catch up or be stretched. For children aged 3–4 years, this experience can be extended to developing their ability to hop. Whether holding on initially or relying on their own balance, it is useful for children to develop the skill of hopping on one foot and then the other for a number of counts because it is the precursor to skipping, another useful skill for children aged 4–5 years. Older children will also be more likely to maintain an accurate beat while clapping, and revisiting the previous skills of hopping and flicking/clicking to the beat are great activities for building co-ordination. Children aged 5–6 years will be able to move their clapping on to patching, or tapping their knees, while children aged 6–7 years will be more confident in using all methods, and even extending them.

Singing range

Children's singing range appears to have changed over time. At the beginning of the last century, music education specialists recommended using tones from the D above middle C, however, more recent research has suggested that children towards the end of the last century tended to naturally sing from the A below middle C to the A above middle C. One approach to identifying comfortable singing ranges is to ask one child to start the group off, giving children leadership opportunities as well as having the opportunity to determine whether they are singing the notes accurately. These opportunities are helpful in determining the next musical skills to teach, from dynamics like loud and quiet to rhythm and pitch. Despite the guidelines given, it is useful to remember that all children are different and some have much lower singing voices than others.

Singing range for observers: 0–3 years

Children who still behave as observers generally respond to higher singing, and this shows in them turning their head to pay closer attention; however, adults may find it easier to sing A' A". As a result, guidance would be to use the range between A'–A" for children aged 0–2 years, and with children aged 2–3 years, as they begin to sing back and match pitch, use songs in the range of D'–B'.

Singing range for participants: 3–7 years

Children aged 3–4 years begin to control their singing voices more, using a greater range between C'–C" (where C' is the lower C and C" is the higher C). As their confidence develops, children aged 4–7 years are best at singing between D' and D", with most songs in the key/chord of D.

Song range

In the same way that children are expected to learn a number of skills, such as alphabet for reading and writing, skills like left to right and up to down, numbers for mathematics, and skills like adding and subtracting, they are also able to sing and memorise a number of songs. This is an area in which teachers can identify whether more or less developmental work is needed.

Song range for observers: 0–3 years

Children aged 0–1 year should be able to recognise and join in at some level to three out of five songs based on the two minor third notes. Children aged 1–2 years should comfortably remember six out of ten songs, including the ones they learnt the year before. Children aged 2–3 years should be able to show recognition and complete the line for 11 out of 20 songs, including songs they have learnt previously.

Song range for participants: 3–7 years

As children are expected to sing a number of songs, it is useful to keep a record of the songs learnt in each year. This book contains several songs already analysed by tones and rhythms, but these are not the only songs that may be used, they are just songs that are able to help musical development in a progressive way. Most children aged 3–4 years should be able to sing 12 out of 28 songs, while most children aged 4–5 years should be able to sing 16 out of 35 songs. With the additional notes and rhythms of new songs, most children aged 5–6 years should be able to sing 22 out of 42 songs, while most children aged 6–7 years should be able to sing 28 out of 50 songs. Depending on the frequency with which children sing these songs, they should be able to sing closer to the total number of songs for their age. Repetition and new ways to sing, or changes to verses, keep songs fresh and interesting.

Session length

Many external music providers hold sessions for 30–45 minutes for convenience of timing and pricing, but everyday childcare workers may have difficulty arranging sessions this way in setting. While daily singing could be used as transition sessions between various activities, multiple sessions including a few songs would be useful.

Session length for observers: 0–3 years

Children aged 0–2 years would enjoy sessions of 10 minutes each, including a few different types of musical activities and songs. Children aged 2–3 years could comfortably manage regular sessions of 15 minutes.

Session length for participants: 3–7 years

Children aged 3–4 years could focus for sessions of 20 minutes, while children aged 4–5 years would benefit from at least two weekly sessions of 30 minutes each. By 5–7 years old, children would benefit from sessions held for 45 minutes.

Lesson or session delivery

A comprehensive framework of activities would include principles or elements based on research. I developed the following sequence and it has been trialled over 10 years and found to be sufficient for a 30–45-minute music session for any preschool age group, with small changes made to suit each developmental level:

- Hello song (routine)
- Fine motor action (vocal warm-up)
- Stretches (physical warm-up)
- Instrument play (establish pulse)
- Pattern dance (lines, circles, opposite lines, concentric circles)
- Story (act, game, imagination)
- Body percussion (stamp, clap, flick, patch, tap)
- Instrumental music (pulse/rhythm/tempo/dynamics)
- Free dance (movement improvisation)
- Instrument improvisation (explore instruments, sounds, rhythms)
- Relax (wind-down)
- Goodbye song (routine)

This session list was based on research findings of beneficial activities, which I trialled in different sequences with groups. I found that both children and adults engaged most with this particular sequence. The importance of establishing routine was identified as a type of time marker that aided children in preparing themselves emotionally for the next activity (Addessi, 2009). Songs that involved adults were found to enhance child play and involvement (Berger and Cooper, 2003), and creating opportunities to play were found to be necessary in developing a child's sense of agency and independence (Barrett, 2011). A number of activities were found to improve vocal awareness, including: following a musical story; tapping the beat to pictures; moving to musical ideas; performing simple actions and playing games; playing together as a group activity; exploring sound dynamics; and being introduced to a wide variety of songs (Cooper and Cardany, 2011). Encouraging the exploration of natural movement responses to music (Melville-Clark, 2006) was beneficial, with various researchers identifying stages of the development of movement (Moog, 1976b), rhythm (Frega, 1979) and tonality (Michel, 1973b). The extension of creating opportunities for children to compose or improvise original music was explored (Barrett, 2006), as well as the ways in which this could be done (Young, 1992).

Song material choice

The songs included in this book have been taken from numerous training sessions based on traditional Kodály materials, as well as from internet sources and books, including Sinor and Katalin (1988). They have been arranged to follow the systematic teaching of the approach, beginning with the minor third, gradually introducing the anhemitonic pentatonic scale and then the diatonic scale, incorporating common (Western) time signatures (2/2, 4/4, 3/4, 6/8) as well as the major and minor tonalities. Some music education circles are critical of this approach as some of these folk songs appear simplistic and repetitive compared to the variety of music that children are exposed to and able to sing today. Others criticise the songs for being unfamiliar and therefore difficult for adults to learn. In contrast, the arguments for using this approach are that this allows educators to introduce musical concepts clearly and sequentially, and that it makes it easier for both the educator and student to identify and confidently perform these musical skills in more complex songs. As professionals, early childhood educators can determine the most suitable approach to take with their own groups of children.

Curriculum design

Whether you follow a topical curriculum or an in-the-moment approach, these songs can be used to develop the ideas most important in your setting. Song choices can be topical or skill based, with word changes if necessary to establish the main idea of the session. It is possible to use these songs and designs to create a two-year rolling curriculum, the approximate length of time that children spend in each nursery room in England (0–2 years, 2–4 years), ensuring that children always have a new topic. Topical books have already been published based on child-appropriate interests, including food, transport, fairy royalty, animals, sea life and sports (Music Olympics!), with activity and equipment suggestions (Turnbull, 2013a, 2013b, 2013c, 2016a, 2016b).

The table of skills progression (Figure 3.9) summarises each of the ideas covered in this section in one straightforward table for quick and easy access. Each age is referred to as a colour-coded level, for example, 0–1 year is Red level, 1–2 years is Orange level. Songs from the various identified levels within the book will involve the responses seen in the table, teaching the concepts listed, and identifying the preceding and following skills for each age, which is useful for individual musical development.

Age	0–1 years	1–2 years	2–3 years	3–4 years	4–5 years	5–6 years	6–7 years
Awards	Red	Orange	Yellow	Green	Blue	Purple	Violet
Circle work	Sit and sway	Sit and tap knees	Hold hands and walk	Play circle games	Step forward and step back	Inner and outer circles	Dance with inner and outer circles
Line work	Roll over	Walk in pairs	Follow in a line	Follow in a spiral	Walk in line, create bridge	Walk in/out of spiral	Walk in line with partners
Memory work	Show surprise	Continue song through movement	Continue song vocally	Sing the last phrase	Sing the last 2 phrases	Sing the missing motif	Clap beat of missing motif
Listening work	Eyes follow movement	Eyes follow movement	Copy actions	Copy actions	Play partner games	Play partner games	Conduct songs in 2/4
Language work	Point at things	Point at body parts	Act song characters	Act song characters	Understand clever lyrics	Acting as different characters	Perform song in character
Instrument suitability	Shaking instruments	Tapping instruments	Drum and beater	Triangle and beater	Cymbal and beater	Glockenspiel (2 notes)	Ukulele (2 strings)
Pulse	Clapping	Stamping	Flicking/clicking	Hopping	Skipping	Patsching (knee tap)	Variety of methods
Musical rhythms	Crotchet	Crotchet	Crotchet, quaver	Crotchet, quaver	Crotchet, quaver, dotted rhythm	Crotchet, quaver, dotted rhythm	Crotchet, quaver, dotted rhythm, minim
Musical intervals	Minor 3rd (A–F# or sol-mi)	Minor 3rd (A–F# or sol-mi)	Major 6th (A–B or sol-la)	Perfect 5th (A–D, or sol-doh)	Major 3rd (F#–D or mi-doh)	Major 2nd (E–D, or re-doh)	Octave (D'–D, or doh'–doh,)
Interval movements	Bouncing up (A) and down (F#)	Jumping up (A) and down (F#)	Clap (A) and Shoulders (B)	Clap (A) to toes (D,)	Hips (F#) to toes (D,)	Knees (E) to toes (D,)	Overhead (D') to toes (D,)
Singing range	a,–a'	a,–a'	d,–b,	c,–c'	d,–d'	d,–d'	d,–d'
Song range	3 out of 5 songs	6 out of 10 songs	11 out of 20 songs	12 out of 27 songs	16 out of 35 songs	22 out of 42 songs	28 out of 50 songs
Session length	10 min	10 min	15 min	20 min	30 min × 2	45 min	45 min

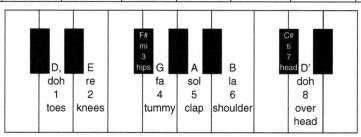

Figure 3.9 Early childhood music skills progression

Source: author

Figure 3.10 Song using la-so-fa-mi-re-do notes

Table 3.7 This old man rhythm table

⊓	│	⊓	│
This old	man,	he played	one
⊓	⊓	⊓	⊓
He played	knick-knack	on my	drum, with a
⊓	⊓⊓	⊓⊓⊓	│
Knick-knack,	paddy-whack,	give a dog a	bone
⊓	⊓	⊓	│
This old	man came	rolling	home

Song Level Six: This old man

Level Six songs use more combined rhythms than before, extending the notes to *do-re-mi-fa-so-la*.

> *This old man, he played one*
> *He played knick-knack on my drum, with a*
> *Knick-knack, paddy-whack, give a dog a bone*
> *This old man came rolling home!*
>
> *This old man, he played two, he played knick-knack on my shoe . . .*
> *This old man, he played three, he played knick-knack on my knee . . .*

This old man, he played four, he played knick-knack on my door . . .
This old man, he played five, he played knick-knack on my hive . . .
This old man, he played six, he played knick-knack on my sticks . . .
This old man, he played seven, he played knick-knack up to heaven . . .
This old man, he played eight, he played knick-knack on my gate . . .
This old man, he played nine, he played knick-knack on my spine . . .
This old man, he played ten, he played knick-knack on my hen . . .

We mainly used this song for the number development, printing out the figures of the numbers and pictures of the items, and stopping to count them too. If the children were very energetic, they had the opportunity to "roll home", either forward rolls or on their sides.

Summary

By looking at the current state of music education at the start of the 21st century, we can piece together the important areas in order to identify potential gaps in knowledge and to understand where music education may be headed. Music education has a growing number of groups with a vested interest in its development, but all with quite different agendas. From external investment groups who pay for music education services, including councils as well as the general public, through to the service delivery teachers, the delivery varies according to the purpose of the investment group, despite being broadly identified as early childhood music sessions. Regardless of the purpose of the group, the delivery of the music education sessions often includes the application of historical techniques, however, these are frequently adhered to in a "silo" mentality, towards promoting purity of the technique. Nevertheless, with little groundbreaking new research from any of the individual techniques, it may be useful to compare and contrast the techniques to use the best fit for each individual student group. Applying principles from both music education and child development leads to a potential new music education framework where these individual techniques may be combined, developing creative skills effectively from the earliest years. Included activities are justified by leading researchers and theorists, and summarised in a quick reference table (Figure 3.9). This way forward has the potential to be delivered by child development specialists in multiple settings. By understanding the theoretical reasoning for each activity, it becomes easier to identify children's spontaneous musical activities and see the progression and links where scaffolding may extend the child's natural interest and ability.

Song Level Seven: **My Bonnie**

Level Seven songs use more combined rhythms than the Levels One–Six songs and the full range of notes, *do-re-mi-fa-so-la-ti*.

Figure 3.11 Song using ti-la-so-fa-mi-re-do notes

Table 3.8 My Bonnie rhythm table

♪ ⊓ ♪	⊓ ♪	⊓ -	- - ♪
(My) Bonnie lies	over the	ocean,	my
⊓ ♪	⊓ ♪	I -	- - ♪
Bonnie lies	over the	sea,	my
⊓ ♪	⊓ ♪	⊓ -	- - ♪
Bonnie lies	over the	ocean,	oh
⊓ ♪	⊓ ♪	I -	- - -
Bring back my	Bonnie to	me	
I -	I ♪	I -	I ♪
Bring	back, oh,	bring	back, oh
⊓ ♪	⊓ ♪	I ♪	I -
Bring back my	Bonnie to	me, to	me
I -	I ♪	I -	I ♪
Bring	back, oh,	bring	back, oh
⊓ ♪	⊓ ♪	I -	- -
Bring back my	Bonnie to	me	

My Bonnie lies over the ocean
My Bonnie lies over the sea
My Bonnie lies over the ocean
Oh, bring back my Bonnie to me!

Bring back, oh, bring back, oh
Bring back my Bonnie to me, to me
Bring back, oh, bring back, oh
Bring back my Bonnie to me

Oh blow you waves over the ocean
Oh blow you waves over the sea
Oh blow you waves over the ocean
And bring back my Bonnie to me

As we were developing the rocking feel of this lovely 6/8 rhythm with non-walkers, we used a blanket to rock them (two adults hold each end of the blanket securely). With older children, we used musical instruments to develop the waltz-rhythm, preparing them by practising tapping HARD-soft-soft, HARD-soft-soft.

References

Addessi, A. R. (2009). The musical dimension of daily routines with under-four children during diaper change, bedtime and free-play. *Early Child Development and Care, 179*(6), 747–768. https://doi.org/10.1080/03004430902944122 (Accessed 7 April 2017).

Amini, E., Rafiei, P., Zarei, K., Gohari, M. and Hamidi, M. (2013). Effect of lullaby and classical music on physiologic stability of hospitalized preterm infants: A randomized trial. *Journal of Neonatal-Perinatal Medicine, 6*(4), 295–301.

Arterberry, M. E., Midgett, C., Putnick, D. L. and Bornstein, M. H. (2007). Early attention and literacy experiences predict adaptive communication. *First Language, 27*(2), 175–189.

Bachmann, M.-L. (1991). *Dalcroze Today: An Education Through and into Music.* Oxford: Clarendon Press.

Barrett, M. S. (1997). Invented notations: A view of young children's musical thinking. *Research Studies in Music Education, 8*(1), 2–14. https://doi.org/10.1177/1321103X9700800102 (Accessed 7 April 2017).

Barrett, M. S. (2006). Inventing songs, inventing worlds: The 'genesis' of creative thought and activity in young children's lives. *International Journal of Early Years Education, 14*(3), 201–220.

Barrett, M. S. (2011). Musical narratives: A study of a young child's identity work in and through music-making. *Psychology of Music, 39*(4), 403–423. https://doi.org/10.1177/0305735610373054 (Accessed 7 April 2017).

Barrett, M. S. (2012). Preparing the mind for musical creativity: Early music learning and engagement. In O. Odena (Ed.), *Musical Creativity: Insights from Music Education Research.* Farnham, UK: Routledge.

Barton, G. and Hartwig, K. (2012). Where is music?: A philosophical approach inspired by Steve Dillon. *Australian Journal of Music Education*, 2, 3–9.

Benedict, C. (2009). Processes of alienation: Marx, Orff and Kodaly. *British Journal of Music Education*, 26(2), 213. https://doi.org/10.1017/S0265051709008444 (Accessed 7 April 2017).

Berger, A. A. and Cooper, S. (2003). Musical play: A case study of preschool children and parents. *Journal of Research in Music Education*, 51(2), 151–165. https://doi.org/10.2307/3345848 (Accessed 7 April 2017).

Bialystok, E. and DePape, A.-M. (2009). Musical expertise, bilingualism, and executive functioning. *Journal of Experimental Psychology: Human Perception and Performance*, 35(2), 565–74.

Bierman, K. L., Nix, R. L., Greenberg, M. T., Blair, C. and Domitrovich, C. E. (2008). Executive functions and school readiness intervention: Impact, moderation, and mediation in the Head Start REDI program. *Development and Psychopathology*, 20(3), 821–843. https://doi.org/10.1017/S0954579408000394 (Accessed 7 April 2017).

Brown, E. D., Benedett, B. and Armistead, M. E. (2010). Arts enrichment and school readiness for children at risk. *Early Childhood Research Quarterly*, 25(1), 112–124. https://doi.org/10.1016/j.ecresq.2009.07.008 (Accessed 7 April 2017).

Bruner, J. S. (1966). *Toward a Theory of Instruction*. Cambridge, MA: Harvard University Press.

Bull, R. and Scerif, G. (2001). Executive functioning as a predictor of children's mathematics ability: Inhibition, switching, and working memory. *Developmental Neuropsychology*, 19(3), 273–293. https://doi.org/10.1207/S15326942DN1903_3 (Accessed 7 April 2017).

Casarow, P. (2012). *Uniting Orff and Kodály: Best of Both Worlds*. Clearwater, FL: Clearwater Christian College.

Choksy, L. (1999). *The Kodály Method I: Comprehensive Music Education*. Upper Saddle River, NJ: Prentice Hall.

Cooper, S. and Cardany, A. B. (2011). The importance of parents in early childhood music program evaluation. In S. L. Burton and C. C. Taggart (Eds.), *Learning from Young Children: Research in Early Childhood Music*. Lanham, MD: R&L Education.

Coppola, C. (2009). Two perspectives on method in undergraduate music education. *Teaching Music*, 17(1), 60.

Custodero, L. A. (2005). Observable indicators of flow experience: A developmental perspective on musical engagement in young children from infancy to school age. *Music Education Research*, 7(2), 185–209.

Degé, F., Kubicek, C. and Schwarzer, G. (2011). Music lessons and intelligence: A relation mediated by executive functions. *Music Perception*, 29(2), 195–201.

Elliott, D. J. (1995). *Music Matters: A New Philosophy of Music Education* (9th edition). New York: Oxford University Press.

Elliott, D. J. (2005). Musical understanding, musical works, and emotional expression: Implications for education. *Educational Philosophy and Theory*, 37(1), 93–103.

Findlay, E. (1971). *Rhythm and Movement: Applications of Dalcroze Eurhythmics*. Evanston, IL: Summy-Birchard Co.

Frega, A. L. (1979). Rhythmic tasks with 3-, 4-, and 5-year-old children: A study made in Argentine Republic. *Bulletin of the Council for Research in Music Education*, 59, 32–34.

Gault, B. (2005). Music learning through all the channels: Combining aural, visual, and kinesthetic strategies to develop musical understanding. *General Music Today*, 19(1), 7–9.

Gell, H., D. (2005). *Dalcroze Eurhythmics: Music through Movement: A Hundred Lessons and Thousands of Ideas for Early Childhood Education* (Joan Pope, Ed.). Perth: Heather Gell Dalcroze Foundation. http://trove.nla.gov.au/work/20194273?q&versionId=23815335 (Accessed 7 April 2017).

Gerry, D. W., Faux, A. L. and Trainor, L. J. (2010). Effects of Kindermusik training on infants' rhythmic enculturation. *Developmental Science, 13*(3), 545–551.

Gilbert, J. (1980). An assessment of motor music skill development in young children. *Journal of Research in Music Education, 28*(3), 167–175. https://doi.org/10.2307/3345234 (Accessed 7 April 2017).

Gordon, R. L., Shivers, C. M., Wieland, E. A., Kotz, S. A., Yoder, P. J. and Devin McAuley, J. (2014). Musical rhythm discrimination explains individual differences in grammar skills in children. *Developmental Science, 17*(6), 809–1049.

Gudmundsdottir, H. R. and Gudmundsdottir, D. G. (2010). Parent–infant music courses in Iceland: Perceived benefits and mental well-being of mothers. *Music Education Research, 12*(3), 299–309.

Hallam, S. (2010). The power of music: Its impact on the intellectual, social and personal development of children and young people. *International Journal of Music Education, 28*(3), 269–289. https://doi.org/10.1177/0255761410370658 (Accessed 7 April 2017).

Hargreaves, D. J. (2008). *Developmental Psychology of Music*. Cambridge and New York: Cambridge University Press.

Hargreaves, D. J. and Lamont, A. M. (2017). *The Psychology of Musical Development*. Cambridge: Cambridge University Press.

Ilari, B. (2015). Rhythmic engagement with music in early childhood: A replication and extension. *Journal of Research in Music Education, 62*(4), 332–343.

Jaques-Dalcroze, E. (1912). *The Eurhythmics of Jaques-Dalcroze*. London: Dodo Press.

Johnston, D. (2001). Scottish local government reform and instrumental music instruction. *Scottish Educational Review, 33*(2), 133–141.

Kaviani, H., Mirbaha, H., Pournaseh, M. and Sagan, O. (2014). Can music lessons increase the performance of preschool children in IQ tests? *Cognitive Processing, 15*(1), 77–84. https://doi.org/10.1007/s10339-013-0574-0 (Accessed 7 April 2017).

Keetman, O. (1954). *Orff-Schulwerk Music for Children*. Mainz: Schott & Co.

Kenny, A. (2011). Mapping the context: Insights and issues from local government development of music communities. *British Journal of Music Education, 28*(2), 213–226. https://doi.org/10.1017/S0265051711000088 (Accessed 7 April 2017).

King, M. E. (2016). *Comparing the Effects of Elementary Music and Visual Arts Lessons on Standardized Mathematics Test Scores*. Lynchburg, VA: Liberty University. http://digitalcommons.liberty.edu/doctoral/1210/ (Accessed 7 April 2017).

Kocabaş, A. (2009). Using songs in mathematics instruction: Results from pilot application. *Procedia – Social and Behavioral Sciences, 1*(1), 538–543. https://doi.org/10.1016/j.sbspro.2009.01.097 (Accessed 7 April 2017).

Kolb, D. A. (1983). *Experiential Learning: Experience as the Source of Learning and Development* (1st edition). Upper Saddle River, NJ: Financial Times/Prentice Hall.

Lesiuk, T. (2014). Music perception ability of children with executive function deficits. *Psychology of Music, 44*(4), 530–544. https://doi.org/10.1177/0305735614522681 (Accessed 7 April 2017).

Liao, M.-Y. (2002). *The Effects of Gesture and Movement Training on the Intonation and Tone Quality of Children's Choral Singing*. Sheffield: University of Sheffield.

Liao, M.-Y. (2008). The effects of gesture on young children's pitch accuracy for singing tonal patterns. *International Journal of Music Education, 26*(3), 197–211.

Liao, M.-Y. and Davidson, J. W. (2007). The use of gesture techniques in children's singing. *International Journal of Music Education, 25*(1), 82–94. https://doi.org/10.1177/0255761407074894 (Accessed 7 April 2017).

Loewy, J., Stewart, K., Dassler, A.-M., Telsey, A. and Homel, P. (2013). The effects of music therapy on vital signs, feeding, and sleep in premature infants. *Pediatrics, 131*(5), 902–918.

Maclean, L. M., Brown, L. J. E. and Astell, A. J. (2014). The effect of rhythmic musical training on healthy older adults' gait and cognitive function. *The Gerontologist, 54*(4), 624–633. https://doi.org/10.1093/geront/gnt050

Martin, A., Razza, R. A. and Brooks-Gunn, J. (2012). Specifying the links between household chaos and preschool children's development. *Early Child Development and Care, 182*(10), 1247–1263. https://doi.org/10.1080/03004430.2011.605522 (Accessed 7 April 2017).

Melville-Clark, P. (2006). *Music, Moving and Learning in Early Childhood: A Manual of Songs, Lesson Plans and Basic Theory for Teachers, Students and Parents of Young Children Aged 3-5 Years*. Darling Heights, QLD: Music & Movement Education Australia.

Michel, P. (1973a). The optimum development of musical abilities in the first years of life. *Psychology of Music, 1*(2), 14–20. https://doi.org/10.1177/030573567312002 (Accessed 7 April 2017).

Michel, P. (1973b). The Optimum Development of Musical Abilities in the First Years of Life. *Psychology of Music, 1*(2), 14–20. https://doi.org/10.1177/030573567312002 (Accessed 7 April 2017).

Miendlarzewska, E. A. and Trost, W. J. (2014). How musical training affects cognitive development: Rhythm, reward and other modulating variables. *Auditory Cognitive Neuroscience, 7*(279). https://doi.org/10.3389/fnins.2013.00279 (Accessed 7 April 2017).

Montessori, M. (1912). *The Montessori Method*. Radford, VA: Wilder Publications.

Montessori, M. (1914). *Dr. Montessori's Own Handbook*. New York: Knopf Doubleday Publishing Group.

Moog, H. (1976a). The development of musical experience in children of pre-school age. *Psychology of Music, 4*(2), 38–45. https://doi.org/10.1177/030573567642005 (Accessed 7 April 2017).

Moog, H. (1976b). *The Musical Experience of the Pre-school Child*. London: Schott Music.

Moreno, S., Bialystok, E., Barac, R., Schellenberg, E. G., Cepeda, N. J. and Chau, T. (2011). Short-term music training enhances verbal intelligence and executive function. *Psychological Science, 22*(11), 1425–1433. https://doi.org/10.1177/0956797611416999 (Accessed 7 April 2017).

Moreno, S., Friesen, D. and Bialystok, E. (2011). Effect of music training on promoting preliteracy skills: Preliminary causal evidence. *Music Perception, 29*(2), 165–172.

Ockelford, A. and Welch, G. F. (2012). Mapping musical development in learners with the most complex needs: The sounds of intent project. In G. E. McPherson and G. F. Welch (Eds.), *The Oxford Handbook of Music Education, Volume 2*. Oxford: Oxford University Press. www.oxfordhandbooks.com/view/10.1093/oxfordhb/9780199928019.001.0001/oxfordhb-9780199928019-e-2?mediaType=Article (Accessed 7 April 2017).

Phillips-Silver, J. and Trainor, L. J. (2005). Feeling the beat: Movement influences infant rhythm perception. *Science, 308*(5727), 1430–1430.

Phillips-Silver, J. and Trainor, L. J. (2007). Hearing what the body feels: Auditory encoding of rhythmic movement. *Cognition, 105*(3), 533–546.

Phillips-Silver, J. and Trainor, L. J. (2008). Vestibular influence on auditory metrical interpretation. *Brain and Cognition, 67*(1), 94–102.

Piaget, J., Inhelder, B. and Weaver, H. (1969). *The Psychology of the Child*. New York: Basic Books.

Rabinowitch, T.-C., Cross, I. and Burnard, P. (2013). Long-term musical group interaction has a positive influence on empathy in children. *Psychology of Music, 41*(4), 484–498. https://doi.org/10.1177/0305735612440609 (Accessed 7 April 2017).

Rainbow, E. (1981). A final report on a three-year investigation of the rhythmic abilities of pre-school aged children. *Bulletin of the Council for Research in Music Education, 66/67*, 69–73.

Rainbow, E. and Owen, D. (1979). A progress report on a three year investigation of the rhythmic ability of pre-school aged children. *Bulletin of the Council for Research in Music Education, 59*, 84–86.

Reimer, B. (2005). Philosophy in the school music program. *Philosophy of Music Education Review, 13*(2), 132–135.

Reimer, B. (2007). Roots of inequity and injustice: The challenges for music education. *Music Education Research, 9*(2), 191–204. https://doi.org/10.1080/14613800701384052 (Accessed 7 April 2017).

Rodrigues, A. C., Loureiro, M. A. and Caramelli, P. (2013). Long-term musical training may improve different forms of visual attention ability. *Brain and Cognition, 82*(3), 229–235. https://doi.org/10.1016/j.bandc.2013.04.009 (Accessed 6 July 2014).

Rutkowski, J. (1990). The measurement and evaluation of children's singing voice development. *The Quarterly, 1*(2), 81–95.

Sawyer, B. E., Justice, L. M., Guo, Y., Logan, J. A. R., Petrill, S. A., Glenn-Applegate, K., Kaderavek, J. N. and Pentimonti, J. M. (2014). Relations among home literacy environment, child characteristics and print knowledge for preschool children with language impairment. *Journal of Research in Reading, 37*(1), 65–83. https://doi.org/10.1111/jrir.12008 (Accessed 7 April 2017).

Schellenberg, E. G. and Trehub, S. E. (1996). Children's discrimination of melodic intervals. *Developmental Psychology, 32*(6), 1039.

Schlaug, G., Norton, A., Overy, K. and Winner, E. (2005). Effects of music training on the child's brain and cognitive development. *Annals of the New York Academy of Sciences, 1060*, 219–230. https://doi.org/10.1196/annals.1360.015 (Accessed 7 April 2017).

Schleuter, S. L. and Schleuter, L. J. (1985). The relationship of grade level and sex differences to certain rhythmic responses of primary grade children. *Journal of Research in Music Education, 33*(1), 23–29.

School Curriculum and Assessment Authority (SCAA). (1996). *Nursery Education: Desirable Outcomes for Children's Learning on Entering Compulsory Education.* London: SCAA. http://eric.ed.gov/?id=ED433091 (Accessed 7 April 2017).

Scott-Kassner, C. (1993). Musical characteristics. In M. Palmer and W. L. Sims (Eds.), *Music in Prekindergarten: Planning and Teaching* (pp. 7–14). Lanham, MD: R&L Education.

Seitz, J. A. (2005). Dalcroze, the body, movement and musicality. *Psychology of Music, 33*(4), 419–435.

Serafine, M. L. (1983). Cognition in music. *Cognition, 14*(2), 119–183. https://doi.org/10.1016/0010-0277(83)90028-8 (Accessed 7 April 2017).

Serafine, M. L. (2013). *Music as Cognition: The Development of Thought in Sound.* New York: Columbia University Press.

Sims, W. L. (1988). Movement responses of pre-school children, primary grade children, and pre-service classroom teachers to characteristics of musical phrases. *Psychology of Music, 16*, 110–127.

Sinor, J. and Katalin, F. (1988). *Music in preschool.* Budapest: Corvina.

Slevc, L. R., Davey, N. S., Buschkuehl, M. and Jaeggi, S. M. (2016). Tuning the mind: Exploring the connections between musical ability and executive functions. *Cognition, 152*, 199–211.

Standley, J. M. (1996). A meta-analysis on the effects of music as reinforcement for education/therapy objectives. *Journal of Research in Music Education, 44*(2), 105–133.

Standley, J. M. (1998). The effect of music and multimodal stimulation on responses of premature infants in neonatal intensive care. *Pediatric Nursing, 24*(6), 532–538.

Standley, J. M. (2000). The effect of contingent music to increase non-nutritive sucking of premature infants. *Pediatric Nursing, 26*(5), 493–499.

Strait, D. L., Parbery-Clark, A., O'Connell, S. and Kraus, N. (2013). Biological impact of preschool music classes on processing speech in noise. *Developmental Cognitive Neuroscience, 6*, 51–60.

Swanwick, K. (2010). Musical development theories revisited. *Music Education Research, 3*(2), 227–242.

Swanwick, K. and Tillman, J. (1986). The sequence of musical development: A study of children's composition. *British Journal of Music Education*, *3*(3), 305–339. https://doi.org/10.1017/S0265 051700000814 (Accessed 7 April 2017).

Tafuri, J. and Welch, G. (2008). *Infant Musicality: New Research for Educators and Parents*. Farnham, England, and Burlington, VT: Ashgate.

Tezer, M., Cumhur, M. and Hürsen, E. (2016). Reasoning states of children who play a musical instrument, regarding the mathematics lesson: Teachers' views. *Eurasia Journal of Mathematics, Science & Technology Education*, *12*(6).

Thresher, J. M. (1964). The contributions of Carl Orff to elementary music education. *Music Educators Journal*, *50*(3), 43. https://doi.org/10.2307/3390084 (Accessed 7 April 2017).

Tierney, A. and Kraus, N. (2013). Music training for the development of reading skills. In M. M. Merzenich, M. Nahum and T. M. Van Vleet (Eds.), *Progress in Brain Research* (Vol. 207, pp. 209–241). Burlington, VT: Academic Press.

Trainor, L. J. and Trehub, S. E. (1994). Key membership and implied harmony in Western tonal music: Developmental perspectives. *Perception & Psychophysics*, *56*(2), 125–132.

Tsang, C. D. and Conrad, N. J. (2010). Does the message matter? The effect of song type on infants' pitch preferences for lullabies and playsongs. *Infant Behavior and Development*, *33*(1), 96–100.

Turnbull, F. (2013a). *Magical Musical Kingdom: Musicaliti Nursery Series: Volume 1* (1st edition). Bolton: Musicaliti Publishers.

Turnbull, F. (2013b). *Musicaliti Nursery: Sharks, Fish, Shells: Musicaliti Nursery Series: Volume 2* (2nd edition). Bolton: Musicaliti Publishers.

Turnbull, F. (2013c). *Musicaliti Nursery: Yum, Yum, Yum: Musicaliti Nursery Series: Volume 3* (1st edition). Bolton: Musicaliti Publishers.

Turnbull, F. (2016a). *Magical Musical Kingdom Song Book*. Bolton: Musicaliti Publishers.

Turnbull, F. (2016b). *Music Gone Wild Song Book*. Bolton: Musicaliti Publishing.

UNESCO. (2012). *Expenditure on Education as % of Total Government Expenditure (%)*. http:// data.worldbank.org/indicator/SE.XPD.TOTL.GB.ZS (Accessed 24 October 2016)

Vongpaisal, T., Trehub, S. E., Schellenberg, E. G., van Lieshout, P. and Papsin, B. C. (2010). Children with cochlear implants recognize their mother's voice. *Ear and Hearing*, *31*(4), 555–566.

Welch, G. F. (2005). We are musical. *International Journal of Music Education*, *23*(2), 117–120. https://doi.org/10.1177/0255761405052404 (Accessed 7 April 2017).

Welch, G. F., Ockelford, A., Carter, F.-C., Zimmermann, S.-A. and Himonides, E. (2009). "Sounds of Intent": Mapping musical behaviour and development in children and young people with complex needs. *Psychology of Music*, *37*(3), 348–370.

Wilson, M. and Cook, P. F. (2016). Rhythmic entrainment: Why humans want to, fireflies can't help it, pet birds try, and sea lions have to be bribed. *Psychonomic Bulletin & Review*, *23*(1647) 1–13. https://doi.org/10.3758/s13423-016-1013-x (Accessed 7 April 2017).

Young, S. (1992). Physical movement: Its place in music education. *British Journal of Music Education*, *9*(3), 187–194. https://doi.org/10.1017/S0265051700009062 (Accessed 7 April 2017).

Zendel, B. R. and Alain, C. (2012). Musicians experience less age-related decline in central auditory processing. *Psychology and Aging*, *27*(2), 410–417.

Zhao, T. C. and Kuhl, P. K. (2016). Musical intervention enhances infants' neural processing of temporal structure in music and speech. *Proceedings of the National Academy of Sciences*, *113*(19), 5212–5217.

Zimmerman, M. P. (1971). *Musical Characteristics of Children*. Washington, DC: Music Educators National Conference. Retrieved from www-usr.rider.edu/~vrme/v17n1/visions/article8.pdf (Accessed 7 April 2017).

4 Resources for the practitioner

Introduction

There is a considerable amount of material available for the practitioner who wants to include music in the curriculum, but it is not always easy to access or clear to follow. Material is often advertised with specific results in mind; for example, *specialist music approaches* promote a better transition to instrumental music training, *academic music approaches* promote a better transition to school and acquisition of academic skill, while *rehabilitative music approaches* promote improved health-socio-emotional behaviour. Practitioners gauge the level of success of the programme by the goals they have set for their group and the subsequent changes they see; for example, passing instruments one by one develops patience, turn-taking and co-operative, teambuilding skills. Most approaches to music education include an element of moving, singing and tapping. By knowing how specific behaviours can be identified as *musical*, the informed practitioner can use and/or adapt almost any musical programme to essential early skills. This book has been written not as a specific programme to follow, but with the intention of identifying principles of musical development to enhance the teaching of general practitioners. In addition, this book recognises that children do not develop in a vacuum, and that their experience of living in the present makes every new experience a learning experience. By following best principles from child development as well as concepts from music education, essential musical skills like *singing in tune* and *keeping an accurate beat* can be taught successfully to all ages. Moreover, by recognising children's developmental levels, appropriate activities can be chosen which give children the opportunity to love music, and teachers the opportunity to enjoy delivering music sessions.

Song Level One: 'Round and 'round

Level One songs start with two notes, the ambulance ni-naw sound, *so-mi.*

Figure 4.1 Song using so-mi notes

Table 4.1 'Round and 'round rhythm table

I	I	I	I
'Round	and	'round	the
I	I	I	-
Wheel	goes	round	
I	I	I	I
As	It	goes	the
I	I	I	-
corn	is	ground	

> 'Round and 'round the wheel goes round
> As it goes the corn it ground

We played this game with younger children by walking around in a circle, taking care to step as we said each word. With the older children, we formed an inner and outer circle, and walked in opposite directions.

Applying theory to practice: SPACE

This section considers the theory behind the different areas of development based on the acronym SPACE (social, physical, academic, creative, emotional), chosen because of the importance of children moving when learning.

Social development theory

Developing personal and social skills pays huge dividends in helping children learn how to learn, as well as making behaviour management easier. Understanding the reasons for behaviour not only allows practitioners to be more patient, it also helps practitioners to devise strategies to support families in a journey that is as life-changing for parents as it is for children. Bronfenbrenner (1994) created a comprehensive social ecological model that factors in the multiple influences on a child, and this model was used in the development of the American Head Start programme, which was introduced to the UK as Sure Start in 1998. The model involves concentric circles, with the centre circle focussed on the specific circumstances of the individual child, such as gender, age and health. Surrounding the child is the microsystem of direct influences on the child, including family, health care, religious groups, local neighbourhood, peers and education. A mesosystem of influences are the ways in which these social groupings interact

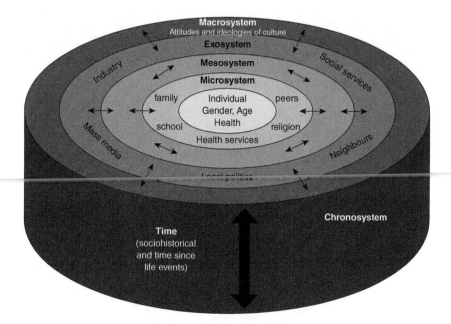

Figure 4.2 Socioecological model

Source: Bronfenbrenner, 1994

with each other. The next sphere of influence includes the extended groups, friends of the family, mass media, local government, legal offices and neighbours. This exosystem is directly affected by the macrosystem, which are the attitudes and ideologies of the culture, like political parties and cultural heritage (Figure 4.2). Although these are a considerable distance from the child, they still have an impact on the individual situation of the child and can work to support or worsen the opportunities of the child. Added on to this system is the chronosystem of time, which is the sociohistorical development of events that occurs within the child's lifetime, whether largely international like the Berlin wall coming down, or personal, like family changes.

A comparative model for early childhood music could arguably involve similar levels of impact (Figure 4.3). Surrounding early childhood music, for example, would be the microsystem of direct foundational factors of music and child development, essential components to a successful early childhood music programme, and in fact the two main topics discussed in this book. The mesosystem would involve the disciplines in which the foundations find themselves, music being part of the arts, and child development forming part of the study of human development. The exosystem would describe the

Figure 4.3 Socioecological model of early childhood music influence

Source: author

contexts in which they are found, for example, the arts fall within the context of creativity, while human development falls within the context of community. The macrosystem could describe the conceptual qualities of early childhood music, where creativity is included in the concept of flow, and community falls within the concept of culture. Within the time-related chronosystem, the ideologies of flow could fall within heritage, while culture could fall within (social) policy. Finally, a biological consideration could be made, where heritage would fall within the order of the human condition, while (social) policy would fall within the order of human advancement. The implications are that music, like other early experiences, has far-reaching, interactive consequences on situations far larger than the individual.

Physical/gross motor movement theory

Some practitioners may not expect or even see the relevance of the next aspect of music education that this book introduces, but *movement* is one of the most effective ways to experience music and learn to create it. The word *movement* is deliberately used rather than *dance* because although dance is included within the term *movement*, movement to rhythms or melodies may not necessarily look like dance (it may look more automated or less aesthetically pleasing than dance). Practitioners can be reluctant to introduce physical movement partly due to the additional clear space that is needed, and partly because a group of young children moving independently can feel unruly, whereas children sitting in fixed positions seem easier to manage. A few factors support the idea of using movement, including: the fact that most people learn more effectively by doing rather than only hearing or watching; children develop gross motor skills before fine motor co-ordination; children naturally tend to move when hearing music. It takes some practice to use gross motor movement to teach, but music can be used effectively to manage the behaviour of a group. Most music sessions or groups begin by sitting in a group or circle, but small ideas can be used to gradually introduce movement in music, for example, introducing one movement song per session. This could involve singing while rolling a ball and then bouncing the ball to each child while they are sitting in a circle, and then they roll and bounce the ball back. This can be extended to children rolling the ball to each other in pairs, gradually increasing the space that children can confidently use, all while singing the song and developing the control to roll on the first word of the line.

Haywood and Getchell (2009) wrote extensively on the way that motor development develops over a lifetime. They identified principles of motion and stability, and noted that these are limited by three aspects of Newell's constraints model: individual structural and functional constraints (e.g. growth and aging); environmental constraints (including weather and terrain); task constraints (i.e. the goal of the motion). Awareness of constraints gives the practitioner insight into the control that a child could potentially exert over specific parts of the body, identifying possible areas of development that the practitioner could address. In practice, with young children, individual constraints would mean assessing the task performance in terms of the child's size and growth, with implications from any birth complications (e.g. premature birth) as well as opportunities that they may experience through their own family (e.g. climbing, rough and tumble play, etc.). Environmental constraints would include taking into consideration the changes in weather and seasons as well as the physical area that children can access, and the obstacles they may encounter. Task constraints would include the over-riding challenge which musically often involves matching an external event, for example, walking to the beat, singing quietly, tapping quickly. These skills develop through first experiencing the event together (walking, singing, tapping), then individually (at different paces and timings), and finally asking the child to match the external sound.

Assessment of musical ability can be very subjective, however, Haywood and Getchell's principles of assessing motor development can be used to assess musical skill performance. The principles involve: observing complete skills; analysing each phase and its elements; using knowledge of mechanics (parabolic principle, Newton's laws of motion, rotational motion, locomotor movement, inertia, kinetic chain, balance, centre of gravity, stability); identifying errors and solutions. A wide range of physical activities can be used to develop musical principles (see Tables 4.2 and 4.3). Through physical activities, children can learn about theoretical concepts by first allowing them to experience sensations of musical principles, like high-low, fast-slow, solo-ensemble.

As such, the typical development of gross motor movement is shown in Tables 4.2 and 4.3.

Table 4.2 Table of movement of children aged 3 months–2 years

3–6 months	6–9 months	9–12 months	12–18 months	18 months–2 years
Randomly move arms/legs	Start rolling back to front	Crawl over and around objects	Walk independently	Stand on tiptoe with support
Put hands near eyes, touch mouth	Sit independently	Cruise around furniture	Run with stiff posture	Run fairly well
Lift head while on stomach	Turn and creep on stomach	Move from sitting to lying down	Squat to pick up things	Jump with feet together
Move head from side to side on back	Stand while holding on to furniture (stiff legs)	Pull on furniture to stand	Step on ball of foot to kick	Jump down and forwards
Hold head steady when sitting		Walk with both hands held	Crawl upstairs, creep down	Walk up/down stairs holding hands

Sit with little waist support	Sit on small chair	Squat to play
Turn from back to side and try to roll over	Pull a toy from behind	Use ride-on toys
Reach for toys, straight in mouth	Throw underhand while sitting	Throw ball in box
From stomach, lift head, weight on arms and move head side to side		Kick ball forwards
Stand when held, knees bent		
From back, touch knees and feet with hands		

Table 4.3 Table of movement of children aged 2–7 years

2–2.5 years	2.5–3 years	3–4 years	4–5 years	5–7 years
Stand on tiptoe	Walk on tiptoe	Run around obstacles	Somersaults	Team games
Stand on balance beam	Kick ball forwards	Walk on line	Walk on balance beam	Ball skills
Catch ball (arms straight)	Catch ball (arms bent)	Balance (on one foot) 5–10 seconds	Balance (on one foot) 8–10 seconds	Hop scotch/ rope
Tricycle using feet	Tricycle using pedals	Tricycle	Throw ball to target	Two-wheel bike
Jump from bottom step	Walk up/down stairs two feet on each step	Alternate feet up/ down stairs	Skipping rope	Run up/ down stairs
	Stand on one foot	Hop	Hop five times	
		Skip (gallop)	Skip alternating feet	
		Jump from 12", feet together	Jump back	
		Slide independently	Swing independently	
		Climb (not ladders)	Climb playground ladder	

Academic experiential learning theory

Devised originally as a way of teaching adults business concepts and promoting lifelong learning, Kolb's experiential learning theory (1983) has much application within the early childhood curriculum. Developing the ideas of prominent educators including Piaget and Dewey, Kolb has created an on-going cycle of learning that involves concepts from philosophy, psychology and physiology.

Through my own exploratory work with preschoolers, it was clear that concepts and activities that maintained the children's attention most effectively were ones in which they were all actively involved, from creating shapes together like circles or parallel lines, to individual activities where each child explored movements and expressed individual emotions, such as flying like a fairy or stomping like dragon. This worked well when followed up by an activity that gave the children an opportunity to observe reflectively, so allowing half the group to participate while the rest watched, and then swapping over. Introducing the concept through another activity, whether loud/quiet or short/long, contrasts in a different way, and the children were able to see the link relatively easily, often proudly aware of the new skill or knowledge that they gained.

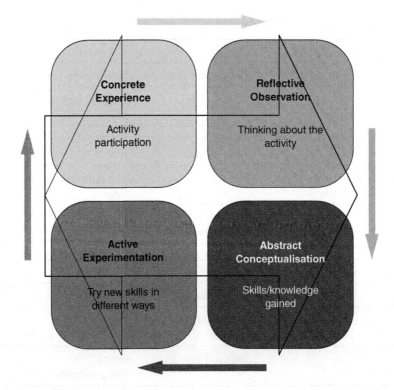

Figure 4.4 Experiential learning theory

Source: Kolb, 1983

The process could only be considered complete once the children were given alternative materials again, whether a mixed box of instruments or even scarves, and given the freedom to experiment actively with their new skill in different ways.

Creative flow theory

Csikszentmihalyi's (2008) concept of flow was identified through his studies on creativity, where he recognised the zone of being completely immersed in a specific interest. According to this theory, this is the state in which people are happiest, where they lose track of time, food needs, and even ego. In order to get to this state, there must be a balance between the level of skill that the individual has developed, and the level of challenge that the task demands. High states of skill and challenge lead to flow, whereas low states of challenge and flow lead to apathy. Csikszentmilhalyi pinpointed eight different mental states from combinations of low, medium and high levels of challenge and skill that are possible; for example, high challenge but low skill level often leads to anxiety, whereas high skill level with low challenge results in relaxation. Figure 4.5 is useful

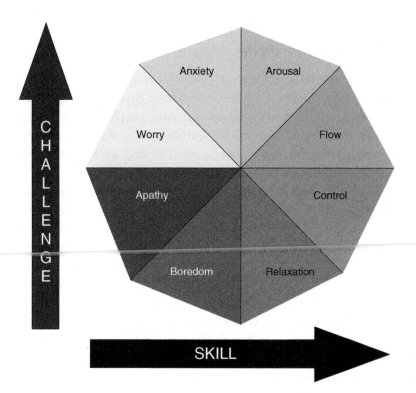

Figure 4.5 Theory of flow

Source: Csikszentmilhalyi, 1990

in identifying the reason for student apathy, anxiety, boredom and control, allowing the educator to adjust the level of challenge or skill suitably.

In order to achieve flow, nine states were identified as essential, including:

- Balancing the challenge and skill involved
- Combining awareness with action
- Being clear about the goals of the challenge
- Immediate feedback
- Concentration on present task
- Paradox of control
- Loss of awareness of time
- Loss of ego
- Autotelic experience (engaging in an activity for its own sake)

If these states were all involved in an activity, this theory states that the student will be immersed in it and avoid distraction.

Emotional intelligence theory

Salovey and Mayer (1990) described four essential components included in the skill of emotional intelligence. These are organised from basic psychological processes to more complex processes, to recognise the ability that some people develop in order to work more effectively with people (Figure 4.6). Seen as a skill, emotional intelligence is an ability that can be encouraged and developed in all and, as with all early childhood experience, modelling is the most effective way to develop this.

The first branch component, perception, appraisal and expression of emotion, describes the ability to identify one's own and others' emotions, as well as being able to express and discriminate between honest and dishonest expressions of emotion. As young children necessarily communicate most effectively through body language, they are often able to recognise honest and dishonest expressions more accurately than adults.

The second branch component describes the emotional facilitation of thinking. This describes the ability to prioritise emotions over thinking when balancing the importance of information and to recall memories related to emotions experienced. This also includes the ability to recognise different emotional perspectives and the way that emotions can affect problem-solving decisions. Acting out characters from stories is an effective way to develop this aspect.

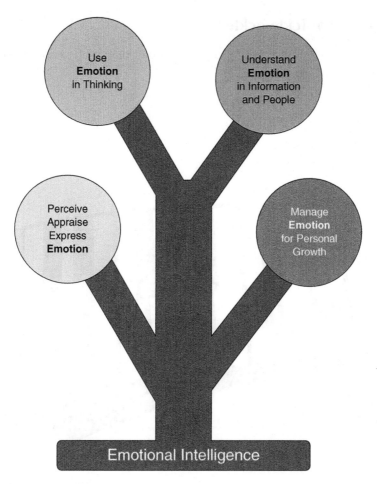

Use
Emotion
in Thinking

Understand
Emotion
in Information
and People

Perceive
Appraise
Express
Emotion

Manage
Emotion
for Personal
Growth

Emotional Intelligence

Figure 4.6 Emotional intelligence

Source: Mayer and Salovey, 1995

The third branch component, understanding and analysing emotions and employing emotional knowledge, describes the ability to name and see relationships between emotions, both opposites and similar. It includes interpreting meanings, feeling multiple emotions at once and, finally, recognising the journey of emotions and the way they may change.

Finally, the last branch component of emotional intelligence is reflective regulation of emotion to promote emotional and intellectual growth. This involves being open to feeling positive and negative emotions, choosing to accept or reject emotions based on the results they will achieve, monitoring emotions within interactions, and managing emotions by enhancing the positive and moderating unpleasant emotions. This interactive facilitation of teamwork is an on-going lesson throughout all social interactions, with clear co-operative benefits.

Song Level Two: Ickle ockle

Level Two songs use simple rhythms and three notes that are far enough apart to hear the difference clearly, *so-mi-do*.

> *Ickle ockle blue bottle*
> *Fishes in the sea*
> *If you want a partner*
> *Just choose me*

Figure 4.7 Song using so-mi-do notes

Table 4.4 Ickle ockle rhythm table

⊓	⊓	I	⊓
Ickle	ockle	blue	bottle
⊓	⊓	I	-
Fishes	in the	sea	
⊓	⊓	I	I
If you	want a	part-	ner
I	I	I	-
Just	choose	me	

With the younger children, we used shakers in the shape of fish to tap the beat. With older children who were walking, we played this song as a variation of duck-duck-goose. This can be extended for more capable children by creating one circle of children inside another circle of children, and walking in a circle until the end of the song, when the inside and outside circles turn to face the other.

NB: "Duck-duck-goose" is a traditional circle game where one child walks around a circle of seated children, tapping them lightly on the head, naming each child, "duck . . . duck . . . duck . . .", until choosing one child to be the "GOOSE". The first child tries to run around the circle to take the place of the "GOOSE", while the "GOOSE" jumps up and chases the first child to try to catch them. If the first child is caught, they either sit in the middle, or must take another turn at being the picker (depending on the age of the children and which is the worse consequence!). Most often, with younger children, they all take turns regardless of who is caught.

Original research

I undertook a small-scale exploratory study (to be published), in Bolton in England in 2015, investigating the effect of physical movement training through music on pre-school (3–4 years) learning. Using video recording (on iPad and iPhone, with parental consent), a group of preschool children were split into two groups, matched for gender, ability and government-funded places, and invited to music sessions (at no cost to the nursery). Children were assessed for their participation in eight individual activities held over eight weekly, 30-minute sessions:

- Greeting
- Shape game
- Gross motor rhythmic preparation
- Gross motor performance
- Fine motor instrument preparation
- Fine motor performance
- Gross motor independent movement
- Close

The activities included generic games found in most preschool music groups, with a specific sequence that acted as an introduction to the overarching concept of developing and maintaining an accurate rhythm. The greeting activity involved the group singing hello to each child, and asking them to respond by telling the group the name of the child next to them. The shape game had children forming shapes as a group;

for example, holding hands in a circle, standing in lines facing each other and crossing over, walking in lines and creating bridges, and forming two circles, one within the other (these were repeated over two weeks). Gross motor rhythmic preparation involved listening to an instrumental rhythm/beat and matching it, either slowly or quickly. Gross motor performance had children responding to recorded or sung music, working towards matching the tempo/speed. Fine motor instrument preparation involved either all playing the same instrument by imitation or passing round an instrument and taking turns, whereas fine motor performance involved children choosing different instruments and playing together. Gross motor independent movement had children moving to music with a prop, usually a scarf, with suggestions given but no specific instructions. Finally, the close involved singing goodbye to each child with the opportunity for each child to wave or sing goodbye, receiving a sticker at the end. Each session was held by the same instructor, and a familiar member of staff accompanied each session. No session involved more than 10 children, although attendance averaged at nine children per session.

The intention of this pilot study was to use Kolb's theory of experiential learning to determine which activities children responded to best within preschool music sessions. Overall, individual participation was high, however, out of all the activities, the highest level of participation was found in gross motor performance, followed by fine motor instrument play and fine motor instrument performance. This finding matched Kolb's theory, as children began by physically becoming or creating musical rhythm. Providing opportunities to prepare for both gross and fine motor activities allowed time for reflective observation (shown by the slightly lower participation level, potentially indicating time taken to think) and active experimentation (again, shown by the slightly lower participation level, potentially indicating time taken to think).

The next step to this enquiry will be to determine whether children maintain a rhythm more accurately after the intervention. Rhythmic accuracy could be measured both through movement using the children's gross motor muscles, and on instruments using their fine motor muscles after experiencing those rhythms through their gross motor muscles. This step will involve a different group of children, creating an opportunity to either corroborate or contradict the initial findings as the sample was so small.

The overarching intention of this study seeks to investigate whether the gross motor movement experience impacted the children's fine motor co-ordination. This would not only provide an alternative solution to the usual practice of improving fine motor skills through repetition (by developing gross motor skills to support fine motor development), but it would also potentially provide evidence that executive function could be impacted through gross motor training, allowing for further study to determine whether musical training had any benefit over non-musical training, such as martial arts. With executive function linked to concepts of school readiness, these findings could hold interesting prospects for those developing the early education curriculum.

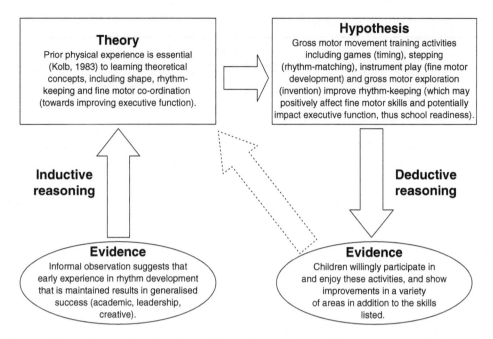

Figure 4.8 Investigation into the effect of physical movement training on preschool learning

Source: author

Song Level Three: Who's that?

Level Three songs use simple rhythms and four notes that are closer together than the Level One and Two songs, *so-mi-re-do*.

Figure 4.9 Song using so-mi-re-do notes

Table 4.5 Who's that? rhythm table

I	I	♫	♪
Who's	that	knocking on my	window
I	I	♫	I
Who's	that	knocking on my	door
I	I	♫	♪
I	am	knocking on your	window
I	I	♫	I
I	am	knocking on your	door

> *Who's that knocking on my window*
> *Who's that knocking on my door*
> *I am knocking on your window*
> *I am knocking on your door*

We played this as a listening game, with children sitting in a circle with one child in the middle, either eyes closed or blind-folded. The child in the middle sang the first two lines, while another child sang the last two lines. The child in the middle tried to guess whose voice they heard. This game could be extended to one child sitting in front of the group, not able to tell the direction of the voice.

Instruments

Percussion instruments are the most popular choice in the early years because of children's instincts to tap or beat things. Often only one of each instrument is offered in, but this can be extremely limiting and can cause competition and upset depending on personalities. It is strongly recommended that each nursery has a class set of identical instruments per child, usually sticks/claves or egg shakers. The benefits of having a class set of instruments are that all children can play together at the same time, children can find different ways to play instruments, and songs can even be extended into turn-taking. More expensive instruments can also be grouped by type, developing additional skills. Suggested instruments are listed below in their instrument groups.

Resources for the practitioner

Group sets

- Egg shakers
- Rhythm sticks/claves
- Sandblocks
- Jingle bells
- Small drums

Woods

- Guiro
- Shaker/scraper
- Maracas
- Castanets
- Two-tone guiro
- Clatterpillar

Skins

- Drums
- Tambour
- Monkey drum
- Djembe

Metals

- Triangles
- Cymbals
- Tambourine
- Cow bell
- Vibraslap
- Cabasa

Tuned percussion

- Glockenspiel
- Xylophone
- Boom whackers
- Tuned bells
- Ocarinas
- Steel pans
- Thumb piano

Strings

- Guitar
- Ukulele
- Violin

Song Level Four: Pumpkin, pumpkin

Level Four songs use simple rhythms and the whole anhemitonic pentatonic scale, *la-so-mi-re-do*. This means that all the notes are at least a tone away from each other, so they are easier to sing and repeat successfully.

> *Pumpkin, pumpkin round and fat*
> *Turns into a jack-o-lantern just like that – BOO!*

With younger children, we played instruments to the beat and the children pulled scary faces. We played this game with older children by all walking or tapping to the beat of the words and then, on the last line, turning around and pulling a scary face (like a pumpkin carved for Halloween).

Figure 4.10 Song using la-so-mi-re-do notes

Table 4.6 Pumpkin pumpkin rhythm table

I	I	I	I
Pump-	kin,	pump-	kin
I	I	I	-
Round	and	fat	
⊓	⊓	⊓	⊓
Turns in-	to a	Jack-o-	lantern
I	I	I	I
Just	like	that!	ARR!

Materials

Additional materials can be used to demonstrate musical phenomena quite easily, and the more standardised they are, the more versatile they are.

Examples of these include the following.

- Scarves or ribbons can be used to demonstrate high/low, fast/slow, can be made to be wide or narrow, can join children together without holding hands, and can be used as dressing up, fireworks, etc.

- Small soft balls are great for rolling back and forth until children are able to understand the idea of rolling balls in time.

- Tennis balls with a small bounce are great props to help children show that they can identify specific words or beats by bouncing them, or throwing them in a box/bucket at a particular part of the song.

- Long feathers can be used to move creatively or to play mirror games.

- Disposable cups can make the sound of horse hooves by tapping them on the floor or together.

- Tin foil can be used to explore mirror effects and shiny surfaces.

- Water can be used to explore flow and contrasts like hot and cold and wet and dry.

- Bean bags can be passed around or dropped behind people (like duck-duck-goose).

- Play dough with herbs/spices/grains can demonstrate items, especially those found in older songs, and this adds tactile and scented experience to the songs.

- Parachute, for circle dances, bouncing toys and rolling balls.

- Plastic or metal spoons as an alternative to sticks/claves.

- Hula hoops to identify space (move to a space, throw a bean bag in the middle).

Song Level Five: Oats and beans

Level Five songs include simple time and introduce the 6/8 timing, like rocking songs, with the notes limited to *so-fa-mi-re-do*.

Oats and beans and barley grow
Oats and beans and barley grow
Not you nor I nor anyone knows how
Oats and beans and barley grow

First the farmer sows the seed
Stands up tall and takes his ease
Stamps his foot and claps his hand
And turns around to view the land

Looking for a partner
Looking for a partner
Not you nor I nor anyone knows we're
Looking for a partner

Figure 4.11 Song using so-fa-mi-re-do notes

Table 4.7 Oats and beans rhythm table

♫	♫	♫	l
Oats and	beans and	barley	grow
♫	♫	♫	♫
Oats and	beans and	barley	grow, not
♫	♫	♫	♫
You nor	I nor	anyone	knows how
♫	♫	♫	l
Oats and	beans and	barley	grow

> *Dancing with a partner*
> *Dancing with a partner*
> *Both you and I and everyone knows we're*
> *Dancing with a partner*

With younger children, we used this song during extended instrument play, utilising the change in verses to swap instruments. With older children, we used this song as a circle dance, walking around in a circle for the first verse. The second verse involved stopping and acting out the actions. During the third verse, children walked around each other until they chose a partner on the last line of the verse. For the final verse, children danced (usually jumping up and down) together.

Games (formations)

Different formations are used in the songs in this book, introducing children to the experience of shapes and spatial relationships that is essential for optimal mental development. These involve both sitting and standing positions in various arrangements but, as it is a game, a level of timing is involved that requires the co-operation of all the children involved. Often a large group provides a better experience because the expectation to participate and make a personal contribution is what makes the game so enjoyable. Children that are bored either find the game too difficult or too easy – most often too difficult – so it is useful to go back a step to re-engage their interest. It is also worth bearing in mind that different groups play different games better or worse, and it is worth exploring ways in which your group may like to personalise their experience – perhaps by using a familiar word, personalised names, or changing various aspects of the game. While the game/song combinations suggested below are perhaps the traditional version, it is worth considering that the same song can be used to focus on different skills – children may sing the same song but play different games depending on their age group. Examples of formations are as follows.

ACTING OUT

Using versatile props (e.g. scarves), children take turns to act out parts of the story, and end up dancing with a partner.

BALL ROLLING

Rolling balls is a game that children can play sitting opposite each other. Rolling the ball on the first word of the line helps children to identify the beginning of the line, which is also usually the first beat of the bar, in important skill in music education. This game can be extended by asking children to roll the ball for four counts, two counts and one count, learning how to use more energy or change the distance to get the ball where it needs to be in time. This game can also develop timing through accurate bouncing and catching skills.

Rolling balls from the teacher to each child is a fun way to demonstrate the timing needed to roll or bounce a ball accurately in time. This can be used to develop musical skills like recognising the beginning of a new song line (usually the first beat of the bar) as well as beats in a bar (roll the ball for four counts, two counts and one count), and using more force or moving closer together or further apart to roll or catch the ball accurately.

Figure 4.12 Ball rolling

BODY PART TAP

This can be as easy as two note songs clapping and tapping knees, to three note songs (shoulders, clapping, knees), to four note songs (shoulders, clapping, knees, stamping) to five note songs (tap head, shoulders, clapping, knees, stamping). This helps children to gradually identify the level of the notes, whether high or low, as well as the musical interval – how many steps away the notes are from each other.

BRIDGES

After forming a line and all holding hands, the first two children create a bridge, holding hands in an upward arch for the line of children to walk underneath. Once all the children have walked through, the next two children can create a new bridge until all children have had a turn at being a bridge and walking underneath a bridge. Alternatively, children can be captured by the bridge at the end of the song!

CIRCLE DANCES

Circle dances begin with holding hands and practising walking in a circle, keeping the empty space clear. This develops co-ordination, spatial awareness, balance and body awareness (proprioception), which are essential skills not only for sports but for higher level thinking.

Figure 4.13 Bridges

Figure 4.14 Standing circle

Figure 4.15 Concentric circles

CONCENTRIC CIRCLES

Walking in a circle can be encouraged through creating an inner circle that can move around the same direction or in the opposite direction. This is a great alternative for duck-duck-goose songs where children need to find a partner on the last line of the song.

FIND THE THIMBLE

This musical take on an old game involves hiding the object of the song, ideally a small version of it, and asking the children to sing a given song louder when the seeker is near or quieter when the seeker is further away.

FOLLOWS

Many musical pieces involve repetition of some kind, and one type of repetition is where one instrument plays same tune as another a little bit later or a little bit slower or faster. This can be physically demonstrated, developing spatial awareness and body awareness by playing follow games. Using a hula hoop, one child stands inside the hoop while another child holds onto it from the outside, and both must move at a pace where they keep up. Alternatively, scarves or purpose-made wide elastic hoops can be used, one child in front and one behind, learning how to move and work together by copying body language cues.

Figure 4.16 Hula follow

GO FOR A RIDE

This fun activity involves a washing basket, box, bucket or blanket – something sturdy enough for a child to sit in or on while another drags them around. Children swap over as they sing the song again.

HAND CLAPS

Older children will enjoy holding their hands up and taking turns clapping against a partner. This is a great activity to develop turn-taking as well as establishing the skill of keeping a beat and working together.

Figure 4.17 Basket follow

Figure 4.18 Standing hand clap

INSTRUMENT PLAY

All songs can and should involve instrument play at some stage. Instruments used can be metals only, woods only, skins only (drums), or a mixture, depending on the experience you wish to develop. Instrument play can involve identical instruments or different ones, instruments played one by one or altogether, or instruments passed around or self-chosen.

JUMPING TO THE BEAT

Songs involving counting or suspense (peek-a-boo songs) are great for jumping songs. They give children the opportunity to physically match the beat relatively slowly as they lift their whole bodies up and down. They can also be used to develop concentration through quick responses by building up the anticipation and then releasing it in physical activity.

LISTENING AND WALKING

Older children create a circle with a large gap ("door"). The teacher brings in the child who is "on" and, with their eyes closed, they have to walk inside the circle trying to find the "door" of the "house" in order to walk out of the circle.

LOVE LETTER

Any topical object of interest can be used, but the point of the game is to sing one line of the song, and only take four steps to the beat towards a nearby person before passing on the topical object. This works well when all the children are sitting in different places around the room (and should not move around), with the challenge that every child has to have a turn. This teaches essential musical skills including timing, turn-taking and an understanding of the effort needed to cross large and small areas.

MELODY PLATES

Using the same number of plates as notes in the song, place them in order, and have children choose the plate that is the "high note" and the "low note" (if a two note song). Children choose which plate to stand on to start and, while the group sing, jump to the appropriate plate. Plates named "do-re-mi" names or different colours have proven to be most effective.

NOTATION/RHYTHM STICKS

Using songs with crotchets/quarter notes, quavers/eighth notes and rests, children stand in a circle holding up drum sticks, rhythm sticks, beaters, chopsticks etc., half of the children hold up either no sticks for rests, one stick for one syllable words, or two sticks for two syllable words, showing the rhythm of the song. The rest of the children tap the rhythm that they see.

ONE TO MANY

This game develops independence and confidence in solo performance by having one child call the important line. It can be used for "catching" songs, where the one child has to catch others.

This is also a game strategy that can be used for listening songs, where one child faces in the opposite direction to the others and has to identify another child singing one line.

PARALLEL DO-SI-DO

With children standing opposite each other in two lines, each side sings a line of the song until the last two lines. Then the second side walks over to their opposite partner, walks around them and walks back to their original spot, after which the sides swap turns.

PARALLEL LINES

These games suit "call and response" songs where all children can be involved regularly. One group sings the first line, the group opposite sings the next line, and so on, until the final line, which may end in a chase or merely swapping sides.

Figure 4.19 Standing one to many

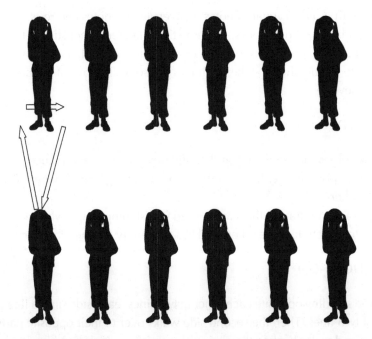

Figure 4.20 Parallel do-si-do

PARALLEL PROMENADE

With children standing opposite each other in two lines, the head couple dances down the centre aisle and joins the end of the lines.

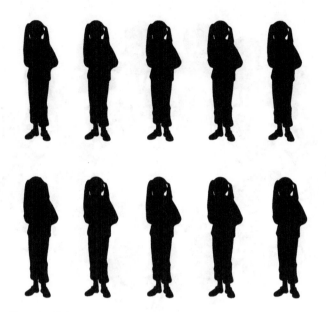

Figure 4.21 Standing parallel

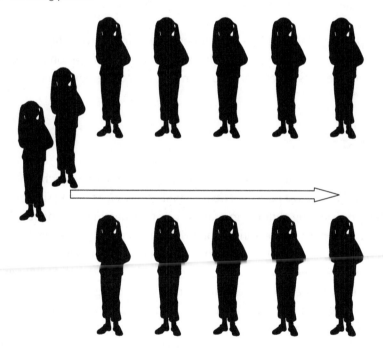

Figure 4.22 Parallel promenade

PARTNER CIRCLE DANCES

For older children, one group forms a circle facing inwards. The other group creates a concentric circle inside, facing a child on the outside. Using a simple hand clap (clap

Figure 4.23 Partner circles

hands, clap partner, clap hands, clap partner), the pairs alternate between hand claps and linking elbows and turning in a circle until the last line of the song, when the inside circle waves to the outside circle, who all move left to the next person, and sing the song again.

PASS THE INSTRUMENT

Like pass the parcel, children sit in a circle and pass instruments to each other. However, in this game, children must pass on a beat. Whether it is sticks or egg shakers, bean bags or balls, it is worth getting children to practise carefully passing from right to left, picking up the object in front of the person on their right, and carefully placing it in front of the person on their left. Note that they are not handing the instrument to the next person. When children have this concept, another item can be introduced to the circle, meaning that children will need to concentrate on not only singing the song but on two items that may be nearby that they will need to pick up and pass on. More advanced groups will enjoy each having an object to pick up and pass along all through the song. This teaches the children to automate some actions while focussing on another, an essential skill for time management and prioritisation. Alternative games involve passing toys/objects around, and the teacher can decide whether this should be to the beat (one beat per bar) or to the rhythm. With younger children, simply tapping the toy or bouncing it on your knee is useful, either for the whole song or a line of the song, developing skills in turn-taking and self-control.

Figure 4.24 Pass the instrument

PEEKABOO

Peekaboo games with scarves are fun for babies and younger children because the children learn that objects out of sight have not disappeared forever and will return. Older children enjoy the sensation of the scarf over their heads but be aware that not all children will enjoy the sensory experience. They may prefer to hold the scarf in front of them like a curtain and should be given the option. These games are valuable to develop a sense of timing through anticipation, as children wait for their turn or the line of the song before they remove the scarf.

ROCKING/RESTING

Rocking toys or dolls in blankets or even rocking the children in a blanket (one adult on each side) helps children to experience the three/four "waltz" timing that encourages relaxation. Other resting ideas include gently singing while children lie on the floor, taking turns to pass around a torch in a darkened room, or cuddling children close enough for them to feel your humming or singing along.

SITTING IN A CIRCLE

Games may involve tapping on your neighbours' shoe or knee, which helps children to individually develop their rhythm-keeping. While they experience the tapping from the child next to them, they create the tapping experience for the child on the other side of them.

Figure 4.25 Circle sitting

SITTING OPPOSITE EACH OTHER

Tapping your neighbour's knees is the first step to sharing a beat, and this can easily progress to clapping your neighbour's hands, which requires an extraordinary amount of co-ordination and skill.

Figure 4.26 Sitting opposite

SPIRAL DANCES

Creating a spiral is a lot of fun with a large group, especially as the spiral gets tighter. Often it needs to be abandoned, *but* there is a beautiful way to get out of it without abandoning it. Mainly for older groups, this relies on children keeping hold of hands, and the leader creating an arch with the second person, under which the rest of the group walk, still holding hands. Really exciting!

STOP-START REACTIONS

As toddlers develop their ability to move confidently, stop-start games can be a lot of fun because children enjoy the anticipation of sudden changes. Whether they hear a particular sound or word (e.g. triangle or drum), see a particular colour (e.g. traffic

Figure 4.27 Standing spiral

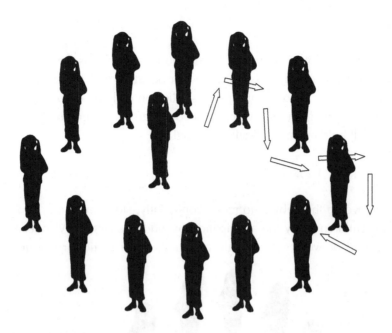

Figure 4.28 Weaving circle

lights), or have to stand somewhere special (in a corner, or on a colour), games can be adapted to suit the learning situation you are developing. This activity also helps to develop self-control and prepares children for musical turn-taking.

WEAVING

The children stand in a circle and one child weaves in between the others, being careful to go in and out of the circle until reaching the point in the song where they dance or swap places with another child. This develops many senses: children are singing, the child is moving in and out, and the rest of the children must be aware that they could be chosen to be next at any point.

Song Level Six: Twinkle, twinkle

Level Six songs use more combined rhythms than before, extending the notes to *la-so-fa-mi-re-do*.

> *Twinkle, twinkle, little star*
> *How I wonder what you are*
> *Up above the world so high*
> *Like a diamond in the sky*
> *Twinkle, twinkle, little star*
> *How I wonder what you are*

Figure 4.29 Song using la-so-fa-mi-re-do notes

Table 4.8 Twinkle, twinkle rhythm table

⊓	⊓	⊓	⏐
Twinkle,	twinkle,	little	star
⊓	⊓	⊓	⏐
How I	wonder	what you	are
⊓	⊓	⊓	⏐
Up a-	bove the	world so	high
⊓	⊓	⊓	⏐
Like a	diamond	in the	sky
⊓	⊓	⊓	⏐
Twinkle,	twinkle,	little	star
⊓	⊓	⊓	⏐
How I	wonder	what you	are

We used this song for relaxation for all children. With younger children, we used it as a song to sing along with baby massage. With older children, we lay on the floor with scarves and all took turns passing around a torch, creating patterns on the ceiling.

Summary

This book provides theory-based ideas on how to plan an early childhood musical curriculum, in both the long and short term. Additional repertoire ideas are included in the next section, broken down by ease of levels. Ease refers to the number of notes used, and the types of beats used. Game suggestions have been given, but these are all starting points. All songs can be used:

- to develop the on-going pulse, or the rhythm or syllables of the words
- to develop different instrument techniques
- to develop musical dynamics like loud and quiet, fast and slow
- to accompany the exploration of wood, metal or skin instruments.

Finally, all songs can be found online on www.musicaliti.co.uk.

Song Level Seven: Muffin man

Level Seven songs use more combined rhythms than the Levels One–Six songs and the full range of notes, *ti-la-so-fa-mi-re-do.*

Figure 4.30 Song using ti-la-so-fa-mi-re-do notes

Table 4.9 Muffin man rhythm table

⊓	⌐⊓	⊓	⌐⊓
Do you	know the	muffin	man, The
⊓	⌐⊓	⊓	I
Muffin	man, the	muffin	man?
⊓	⌐⊓	⊓	⌐⊓
Do you	know the	muffin	man, Who
⊓	⊓	I	-
Lives on	Drury	Lane?	

Do you know the muffin man
The muffin man, the muffin man?
Do you know the muffin man
Who lives on Drury Lane?

Yes, I know the muffin man
The muffin man, the muffin man
Yes, I know the muffin man
Who lives on Drury Lane

We used this song for both younger and older children as an instrumental song, with opportunities to exchange instruments between verses.

Additional repertoire

Song Level One

Figure 4.31 Songs using la-so-mi notes

Table 4.10 Star light rhythm table

Star	light,	star	bright
	⊓	⊓	
First	star I	see to-	night
⊓		⊓	
Wish I	may,	wish I	might
⊓	⊓	⊓	
Have the	wish I	wish to-	night

Star light

Star light, star bright
First star I see tonight
Wish I may, wish I might
Have the wish I wish tonight

We used this song to give older and younger children the opportunity to solo sing, useful in identifying children who need additional support or additional challenges, as well as for learning to pass an individual object on the beat. Passing around a star (tin foil/toy) on the beat, the child left holding the star on the last line gets to make a wish, which they must sing out loud ("or it won't come true!").

Level One songs start with two notes, the ambulance ni-naw sound, *so-mi*. Then they develop to the note above "so", and include *la-so-mi*. By teaching using a limited number of notes, children begin to hear and sing more accurately, the same way that we teach number and letter recognition gradually. When children are introduced to music notation later, they have a better understanding of how notes work together to create music.

Roll here

Roll here, roll there
Roll the ball to Leicester Square
Bounce high, bounce low
Bounce the ball to Shiloh

We played this game the same way with both younger and older children. We began this game with the teacher/leader rolling the ball to and from each child, and then bouncing the ball to and from each child, demonstrating that the rolling and bouncing started on those words (roll; bounce). Then children were asked to sit opposite each other (like *Row, row, row your boat*), and each pair had a ball to roll and bounce to each other.

Table 4.11 Roll here rhythm table

Roll	here,	roll	there,
П	П	П		
Roll the	ball to	Leicester	Square
Bounce	high,	bounce	low
П	П			
Bounce the	ball to	Shi-	loh

Table 4.12 *We are dancing* rhythm table

Π	Π	Π	Π
We are	dancing	in the	forest
Π	Π	Π		
While the	wolf is	far a-	way
Π	Π	Π	Π
Who knows	what may	happen	to us
Π	Π	Π		
If he	finds us	at our	play?
		Π			-↰
Wolf,	are you	there?	I'm
Π					-
combing	my	hair!	

We are dancing

> We are dancing in the forest
> While the wolf is far away
> Who know what may happen to us
> If he finds us at our play ?
> Wolf, are you there?
> "I'm combing my hair!"

With younger children, we used this song as a bouncing game, changing the last line from "I'm combing my hair" to "I'm coming to get you!", and tickling them. With older children, they learnt the song and sang it to the "wolf" (teacher), asking if the "wolf" was there. The wolf delays catching them for a bit, combing hair, brushing teeth, washing the dishes, picking up toys, etc., until answering, "I'm coming to get you!" The first child caught then becomes the new "wolf".

Snail, snail

Table 4.13 *Snail snail* rhythm table

Snail,	snail,	snail,	snail,
Π	Π	Π		
Creep a-	round and	round and	round

Table 4.14 Lucy Locket rhythm table

∏	∏	∏	∏
Lucy	Locket	lost her	pocket
∏	∏	I	I
Kitty	Fisher	found	it
∏	∏	∏	∏
Not a	penny	was there	in it
∏	∏	I	I
Only	ribbon	'round	it

> *Snail, snail, snail, snail*
> *Creep around and round and round*

With younger children, we used this in baby massage, tracing a spiral on tummies and hands and feet. With older children, we walked in a long line holding hands as we turned into a tight spiral.

Lucy Locket

> *Lucy Locket lost her pocket*
> *Kitty Fisher found it*
> *Not a penny was there in it*
> *Only ribbon 'round it*

With younger children, we let each child hold a "pocket" (purse with a ribbon) for the length of the line or song (depending on how many were in the group). With older children, we used the "pocket" in a variation of duck-duck-goose.

Bobby Shaftoe

> *Bobby Shaftoe went to sea*
> *Silver buckles on his knee*
> *He'll come back and marry me*
> *Bonny Bobby Shaftoe*

> *Bobby Shaftoe's fit and fair*
> *Combing back his yellow hair*
> *He's my love forever more*
> *Bonny Bobby Shaftoe*

Table 4.15 Bobby Shaftoe rhythm table

П	П	П		
Bobby	Shaftoe	went to	sea
П	П	П		
Silver	buckles	on his	knee
П	П	П		
He'll come	back and	marry	me
П	П				
Bonny	Bobby	Shaf-	toe

With younger children, we used this as a rhythm tapping song on identical instruments, with variations of loud and quiet. With older children, we turned this into a sailor dance, so children stood with hands on hips for the first two lines, then danced with another child for the last two lines.

I had a dog

I had a dog, his
Name was Rover
Every time I called his name, he
Rolled over and over

Roll over, Rover, roll over, Rover
Roll over, Rover, pass him on

Table 4.16 I had a dog rhythm table

		П				
		had a	dog,	his
Name	was	Ro-	ver
П	П	П	П
Every	time I	called his	name, he
		П				
Rolled	over and	o-	ver

Table 4.17 Bell horses rhythm table

&#124;	&#928;	&#124;	&#928;
Bell	horses,	bell	horses
&#124;	&#928;	&#124;	-
What	time of	day?	
&#928;	&#124;	&#928;	&#124;
One o'	clock,	Two o'	clock
&#928;	&#928;	&#124;	-
Time to	run a-	way	

With both younger and older children, we played this game by passing a toy dog and each child bouncing the dog on their knee. To develop the idea of the dog rolling over, and to have the opportunity to develop the co-ordination of rolling the dog over and over, we added the chant at the end.

Bell horses

Bell horses, bell horses
What time of day?
One o'clock, two o'clock
Time to run away

With younger children, we used bells to keep a steady beat as we sang this song. With older children, we used scarves, elastic or hula hoops as "reins". With children in pairs, one child in front/in the hoop would lead as the child holding the "reins" followed. Children walked to the beat for the song and then tried running on the last line, and then swapped, giving both children the opportunity to lead and follow.

Doggy doggy

Table 4.18 Doggy doggy rhythm table

&#928;	&#928;	&#928;	&#124;
Doggie,	doggie	where's your	bone?
&#928;	&#928;	&#928;	&#124;
Someone	took it	from your	home
&#124;	&#928;	&#124;	&#124;
Who	took your	bo-	ne?
&#124;	&#928;	&#124;	&#124;
"I	took your	bo-	ne!"

Doggy, doggy, where's you bone?
Someone took it from my home!
Who took your bone?
"I took your bone!"

With younger children, we sang every line, passing around a toy bone and then a little later a toy dog, ensuring each child had a turn with each toy. With older children, we chose one child to sit in the middle blind-folded. The group sang the first line, the child in the middle sang the second line, the group sang the third line, and a secret person sang the last line on their own. This gives the teacher the opportunity to assess children's singing on their own, as well as giving children confidence in a non-threatening environment.

Red rover

Rover, red rover
We call Jenny over

With younger children, we divided the box of instruments and called them over, "We call the triangle over". With older children, we played this old playground game very carefully, with them standing in two parallel lines opposite each other. The line singing the words all held hands and "Jenny" had to run through their hands to break their grasp. If she broke through, she returned to her team; if not, she had to join the opposite side. Children should be approximately the same size for this to be played successfully.

Here we come

Here we come!
Where from?
Bolton!
What's your trade?
Cotton mills and lemonade
Give us some if you're not afraid!

Table 4.19 Red rover rhythm table

I	Π	I	I
Ro-	ver, red	Ro-	ver
Π	Π	I	I
We call	Jenny	o-	ver

213

Table 4.20 Here we come rhythm table

⊓	I	I	I
Here we	come!	Where	from?
I	I	⊓	I
Bol-	ton!	What's your	trade?
⊓	⊓	⊓	I
Cotton	mills and	lemon-	ade
⊓	⊓⊓	⊓	I
Give us	some if you're	not a-	fraid!

We played this game in two parallel lines, with each group taking a turn to sing a line. With younger children, adults sang and carried them, while older children held hands until the last line. After the last line of the song, the groups swapped places, and played it again.

A-tisket a-tasket

A-tisket, a-tasket, a
Blue and yellow basket, I
Wrote a letter to my love and
On the way, I dropped it, I
Dropped it, I dropped it

Table 4.21 A-tisket a-tasket rhythm table

♪ I	⊓	I	⊓
(A) Tis-	ket, a	tas-	ket, a
⊓	⊓	I	⊓
Blue and	yellow	bas-	ket, I
⊓	⊓	⊓	⊓
Wrote a	letter	to my	love and
⊓	⊓	I	⊓
On the	way I	dropped	it, I
I	⊓	I	I
dropped	it, I	dropped	it

Table 4.22 See saw Margery Daw rhythm table

| -	| -	⊓♪	| -
See	saw,	Margery	Daw
⊓♪	⊓♪	| -	| -
Johnny shall	have a new	mas-	ter
| ♪	⊓♪	⊓♪	| ♪
He shall	earn but a	penny a	day, be-
⊓♪	⊓♪	| -	| -
Cause he can't	work any	fas-	ter

   With younger children, we used this song to keep the beat with different instruments. With older children, we used this song like duck-duck-goose, dropping a "letter" behind one of the children to pick up and try to catch the one who dropped it before they sat down in the new space.

See saw Margery Daw

   See saw, Margery Daw
   Johnny shall have a new master
   He shall earn but a penny a day
   Because he can't work any faster

With younger children, we rocked them in a blanket individually, with two adults holding each end of the blanket. With older children, we used scarves and asked them to rock stuffed toys, helping them to feel the rocking rhythm.

Song Level Two

Level Two songs use simple rhythms and three notes that are far enough apart to hear the difference clearly, *so-mi-do*. This develops to include the fourth note, *la-so-mi-do*.

Ring a rosies

   Ring a ring a rosies
   A pocket full of posies
   A tishoo, a tishoo
   We all fall down

Figure 4.32 Songs using so-mi-do and la-so-mi-do notes

Table 4.23 Ring a rosies rhythm table

I ♪	I ♪	I -	I ♪
Ring a	ring a	ro-	sies, a
I ♪	I ♪	I -	I ♪
Pocket	full of	po-	sies, a
I -	I ♪	I -	I ♪
Ti-	shoo, a	tish-	Oo, we
I -	I -	I -	- - -
All	fall	down!	

> *Fishes in the water*
> *Fishes in the sea*
> *We all jump up with a*
> *One-two-three!*

We played this song the traditional way with both groups holding hands and walking around in a circle. At the end of the first verse, the children crouched down and wiggled their fingers as they began the chant of the second verse.

Hot cross buns

> *Hot cross buns*
> *Hot cross buns*

Table 4.24 Hot cross buns rhythm table

I	I	I	-
Hot	cross	buns	
I	I	I	-
Hot	cross	buns	
⊓	⊓	⊓	⊓
One a	penny,	two a	penny
I	I	I	-
Hot	cross	buns	

One a penny, two a penny
Hot cross buns

If you have no daughters
Give them to your sons
One a penny, two a penny
Hot cross buns

We used tapping instruments (sticks) with both younger and older children, exploring different ways to play them, as we kept the beat.

I have lost

I have lost my closet key
In some lady's garden

Table 4.25 I have lost rhythm table

⊓	⊓	⊓	I
I have	lost my	closet	key
⊓	⊓	I	I
In some	lady's	gar-	den
⊓	⊓	⊓	I
Help me	find my	closet	key
⊓	⊓	I	I
In some	lady's	gar-	den

> *Help me find my closet key*
> *In some lady's garden*

With younger children, we used this as a song to play with different instruments. With older children, once they sang the words they had to search for a small object. The teacher kept singing the song, singing louder when they were close to finding it, and quieter when they went further away.

Hop old squirrel

> *Hop old squirrel, eideldum, eideldum*
> *Hop old squirrel, eideldum, dee*
> *Hop old squirrel, eideldum, eideldum*
> *Hop old squirrel, eideldum, dee*

With pre-walkers, we used scarves and bounced them up and down. With older children, they tucked the scarf in the back of their skirts or trousers like squirrel tails, and hopped around the room.

Table 4.26 Hop old squirrel rhythm table

ǀ	ǀ	Π	-
Hop	old	squirrel	
Π	ǀ	Π	ǀ
Eidel-	dum,	eidel-	dum
ǀ	ǀ	Π	-
Hop	old	squirrel	
Π	ǀ	ǀ	-
Eidel-	dum,	dee	
ǀ	ǀ	Π	-
Hop	old	squirrel	
Π	ǀ	Π	ǀ
Eidel-	dum,	eidel-	dum
ǀ	ǀ	Π	-
Hop	old	squirrel	
Π	ǀ	ǀ	-
Eidel-	dum	dee	

Table 4.27 Riding in a buggy rhythm table

♫♫	♫	⊓	⊓
Riding in a	buggy, Miss	Mary	Jane, Miss
⊓	⊓	⊓		
Mary	Jane, Miss	Mary	Jane
♫♫	♫	⊓	♫
Riding in a	buggy, Miss	Mary	Jane, we're a
⊓	-↾			-
Long way	from	home	

Riding in a buggy

Riding in a buggy, Miss Mary Jane
Miss Mary Jane, Miss Mary Jane
Riding in a buggy, Miss Mary Jane
We're a long way from home

With both older and younger children, we used washing baskets (sturdy boxes or buckets could be used too). Placing blankets inside them, each child had a turn "riding in the buggy".

On a log

On a log, Mister Frog
Sang his song the whole day long
Croak, croak, croak
Croak, croak, croak

Table 4.28 On a log rhythm table

⊓			⊓		
On a	log,	Mister	Frog
⊓	⊓	⊓		
Sang his	song the	whole day	long
						-
Croak,	croak,	croak,	
						-
Croak,	croak,	croak	

Table 4.29 Apple tree rhythm table

⊓	I	⊓	I
Apple	tree,	apple	tree
⊓	⊓	⊓	I
Will your	apple	fall on	me
⊓	⊓	⊓	I
I won't	cry and	I won't	shout
⊓	⊓	⊓	I
If your	apple	knocks me	out

With younger children, we used the frog-shaped guiro to pass and play, particularly on the "croak, croak, croak" parts. With older children, we asked them to hop on the spot if they were not playing the guiro.

Apple tree

Apple tree, apple tree
Will your apple fall on me?
I won't cry and I won't shout
If your apple knocks me out

We played this game with both younger and older children by passing an "apple" (egg shaker, etc.) to the beat, and the person to hold the "apple" on the last word ("out") sits to the side shaking their own instrument to the beat.

Song Level Three

Level Three songs use simple rhythms and four notes that are closer together than the Level One and Two songs, *so-mi-re-do*.

How many miles to Babylon?

How many miles to Babylon?
Three score and ten
Will I get back before you do?
Yes, and back again

Figure 4.33 Songs using so-mi-re-do notes

Table 4.30 How many miles to Babylon? rhythm table

⊓	⊓	⊓	I
How many	miles to	Baby-	lon?
I	⊓	I	-
Three	score and	ten	
⊓	⊓	⊓	I
Will I get	back be-	fore you	do?
⊓	⊓	I	-
Yes, and	back a-	gain	
⊓	⊓	⊓	I
Open the	gates and	let us	through!
⊓	⊓	⊓	I
Not with-	out a	beck and	bow
⊓	I	⊓	I
Here's the	beck	here's the	bow
⊓	⊓	⊓	I
Open the	gates and	let us	through!

> *Open the gates and let us through*
> *Not without a beck and bow*
> *Here's the beck, here's the bow*
> *Open the gates and let us through!*

With younger children, we sat in parallel lines, taking turns to play the instruments per line. With older children, we stood up in parallel lines facing each other and took turns in singing each line – the final two lines are sung by one group. Children then crossed over to the other side, with the opposite group starting the game.

Mary had a little lamb

> *Mary had a little lamb*
> *Little lamb, little lamb*
> *Mary had a little lamb*
> *Its fleece was white as snow*
>
> *And everywhere that Mary went*
> *Mary went, Mary went*
> *Everywhere that Mary went*
> *The lamb was sure to go*

Table 4.31 Mary had a little lamb rhythm table

Π	Π	Π	I
Mary	had a	little	lamb
Π	I	Π	I
Little	lamb,	little	lamb
Π	Π	Π	Π
Mary	had a	little	lamb, Its
Π	Π	I	- ↑
fleece was	white as	snow,	And
Π	Π	Π	I
every-	where that	Mary	went
Π	I	Π	I
Mary	went,	Mary	went
Π	Π	Π	Π
Every-	where that	Mary	went The
Π	Π	I	-
lamb was	sure to	go	

It followed her to school one day
School one day, school one day
It followed her to school one day
Which was against the rules

It made the children laugh and play
Laugh and play, laugh and play
It made the children laugh and play
To see a lamb at school

With younger children, we passed around a toy lamb while playing instruments that developed skills in keeping the beat. With older children, we stood in a circle with one child holding a lamb, weaving in and out between the other children. At the end of the verse, the lamb was passed to a nearby child until all children had had a turn.

Bought me a cat

Table 4.32 *Bought me a cat* rhythm table

|	∏	|	-↑
Bought	me a	cat,	the
|	|	|	-↑
cat	pleased	me	I
|	|	|	∏
Fed	that	cat	under
|	|	|	-↑
yon-	der	tree	The
|	|	∏	|
cat	went	fiddle-	i,-
∏	|	∏	|
fiddle-	i,	fiddle-	i
|	|	∏	|
Cat	went	fiddle-	i-
∏	|	|	-
fiddle	i-	fee!	

Bought me a cat, the cat pleased me
I fed that cat under yonder tree
The cat went fiddle-i, fiddle-i, fiddle-i
Cat went fiddle-i-fiddle-i-fee!

Bought me a hen, the hen pleased me
I fed my hen under yonder tree
The hen went chipsy-chopsy
Cat went fiddle-i-fiddle-i-fee!

Bought me a duck, the duck pleased me
I fed that duck under yonder tree
The duck went slishy-sloshy, hen went chipsy-chopsy
Cat went fiddle-i-fiddle-i-fee!

Bought me a goose, the goose pleased me
I fed that goose under yonder tree
The goose went quaaa, duck went slishy-sloshy
Hen went chipsy-chopsy, cat went fiddle-i-fiddle-i-fee!

With both younger and older children, we passed around instruments and changed at each verse. Younger children could pick and choose, while older children passed their instruments to the left.

John Kinacker

Table 4.33 *John Kinacker* rhythm table

♪ |	-♪	|	♪
I heard	I	heard	the
|	|	|	-
Old	man	say	
|	-♪	⊓	⊓
John	Ki-	nacker	nacker
|	|	|	♪
Do-	rye	aye	To-
|	-♪	|	-♪
Day,	To	day's	a
|	|	|	-

Ho-	li-	day	
I	-♪	⊓	⊓
John	Ki-	nacker	nacker
I	I	I	-
Do	rye	aye	
I	I	I	-
Do	rye	aye	
I	I	I	-
Do	rye	aye	
I	-♪	⊓	⊓
John	Ki-	nacker	nacker
I	I	I	-
Do	rye	aye	

I heard, I heard the old man say
John Kinacker-nacker, do-rye-aye
Today, today's a holiday
John Kinacker-nacker, do-rye-aye
Do-rye-aye, do-rye-aye
John Kinacker-nacker, do-rye-aye

With younger children, we used this as a suspense song, only playing instruments on "John Kinacker-nacker, do-rye-aye". With older children, they did a simple partner dance, facing each other and clapping their partner's hands. On the fifth line, "Do-rye-aye, do-rye-aye," children waved goodbye and found a new partner.

Hickory dickory buttercup

Hickory dickory buttercup
How many fingers do I hold up? [4]
Four you see and four you say
Please count four with me today
One, two, three, four

With younger children, we kept the number of fingers down to three, and played instruments along to the song. With older children, we played instruments or we moved to the number of fingers that the teacher/leader held up – great for maths reinforcement.

Table 4.34 Hickory dickory rhythm table

∏♪	∏♪	│♪	│ -
Hickory	dickory	butter-	cup
∏♪	∏♪	│♪	│ -
How many	fingers do	I hold	up
│♪	│♪	│♪	│ -
Four you	see and	four you	say
│♪	│♪	│♪	│ -
Please count	four with	me to-	day

Hush little baby

Table 4.35 Hush little baby rhythm table

∏	∏	∏	│
Hush little	baby,	don't say a	word
∏∏	∏	∏	│
Mamma's gonna	buy you a	mocking	bird
∏	∏	∏	│
If that	mocking	bird don't	sing,
∏∏	∏	∏	│
Mamma's gonna	buy you a	diamond	ring
∏	∏	∏	│
If that	diamond	ring turns	brass
∏∏	∏	∏	│
Mamma's gonna	buy you a	looking	glass
∏	∏	∏	│
If that	looking	glass gets	broke
∏∏	∏	∏	│
Mamma's gonna	buy you a	Billy	goat
∏	∏	∏	│
If that	Billy	goat don't	pull
∏∏	∏	∏	│

Mamma's gonna	buy you a	cart and	bull
♫	♫	♫	♫
If that	cart and	bull turn	over
♬	♫	♫	♫
Mamma's gonna	buy you a	dog named	Rover
♫	♫	♫	|
If that	dog named	Rover don't	bark
♬	♫	♫	|
Mamma's gonna	buy you a	horse and	cart
♫	♫	♫	♫
And if that	horse and	cart fall	down, you'll
♫	♬	♫	|
Still be the	sweetest little	baby in	town

Hush little baby, don't say a word
Mamma's gonna buy you a mocking bird
And if that mocking bird don't sing
Mamma's gonna buy you a diamond ring

If that diamond ring turns brass
Mamma's gonna buy you a looking glass
If that looking glass gets broke
Mamma's gonna buy you a Billy goat

If that Billy goat don't pull
Mamma's gonna buy you a cart and bull
If that cart and bull turn over
Mamma's gonna buy you a dog named Rover

If that dog named Rover don't bark
Mamma's gonna buy you a horse and cart
If that horse and cart fall down
You'll still be the sweetest little baby in town

With both older and younger children, we used this as a rocking song. Younger children were rocked in blankets (held by two adults), or had the opportunity to rock toys in blankets or scarves, like the older children.

Table 4.36 The little bells rhythm table

♪ ⊓	⊓	⊓	⊓
(The) little	bells of	Westmin-	ster go
|	|	⊓	|
Ding,	dong,	ding-dong	dong

The little bells

> The little bells of
> Westminster go
> Ding, dong
> Ding, dong-dong

With both younger and older groups, we used bells to play the beat to the song.

Poor little kitty cat

> Poor little kitty cat
> Poor little feller
> Poor little kitty cat
> Lost in the cellar

With both older and younger children, we sang this song while playing instruments, keeping the steady beat.

Table 4.37 Poor little kitty cat rhythm table

|	⊓	⊓	|
Poor	little	kitty	cat
|	⊓	⊓	-
Poor	little	feller	
|	⊓	⊓	|
Poor	little	kitty	cat
|	⊓	⊓	-
Lost	in the	cellar	

Table 4.38 *Old mister rabbit* rhythm table

I	Π	I	Π
Old	Mister	Rab-	bit, you've
Π	Π	I	Π
Got a	mighty	ha-	bit of
Π	Π	I	Π
Jumping	in my	gar-	den and
Π	Π	I	I
Eating	all my	cab-	bage!

Old mister rabbit

Old mister rabbit
You've got a mighty habit
Of jumping in my garden and
Eating all my cabbage

With younger children, we passed around a toy rabbit and a toy cabbage to the beat, passing on each line. With older children, like *Oranges and lemons*, we had two children form a bridge while the rest passed through in a straight line. On the last line, the children forming a bridge bring their arms down to catch the "rabbit" (the child under the bridge), who then becomes part of the bridge, until all children have had a turn.

Come butter come

Table 4.39 *Come butter come* rhythm table

I	Π	I	-
Come	butter,	come	
I	Π	I	-
Come	butter,	come	
Π	I	Π	I
Mary	stands	at the	gate
Π	Π	Π	I
Waiting	for a	butter	cake

Come butter, come
Come butter, come
Mary stands at the gate
Waiting for a butter cake

With both younger and older children, we gave each child a turn to tap the beat on a drum ("cake"), and then pass it around the circle until everyone has had a turn.

Rosie darling

Rosie darling, Rosie
Ha-ha, Rosie
Rosie darling, Rosie
Ha-ha, Rosie
Way down yonder by Baltimore
Ha-ha, Rosie
Need no carpet on the floor
Ha-ha, Rosie

With both older and younger children, we used this as a suspense song, only playing our instruments on "Ha-ha, Rosie".

Table 4.40 Rosie darling rhythm table

⊓	⊓	I	I
Rosie	darling,	Ro-	sie
⊓	-	I	I
Ha-ha,		Ro-	sie
⊓	⊓	I	I
Rosie	darling,	Ro-	sie
⊓	-	I	I
Ha-ha,		Ro-	sie
⊓	⊓⊓	⊓	I
Way down	yonder by	Balti-	more
⊓	-	I	I
Ha-ha,		Ro-	sie
⊓	⊓	⊓	I
Need no	carpet	on the	floor
⊓	-	I	I
Ha-ha,		Ro-	sie

Song Level Four

Level Four songs use simple rhythms and the whole anhemitonic pentatonic scale, *la-so-mi-re-do*. This means that all the notes are at least a tone away from each other, so they are easier to sing and repeat successfully.

Tideo

Through one window, tideo
Through two windows, tideo
Through three windows, tideo
Jingle at the windows, tideo

Figure 4.34 Songs using la-so-mi-re-do notes

Table 4.41 *Tideo* rhythm table

⊓	⊓	⊓	I
Through one	window,	tie-dee-	oh
⊓	⊓	⊓	I
Through two	windows,	tie-dee-	oh
⊓	⊓	⊓	I
Through three	windows,	tie-dee-	oh
⊓⊓	⊓	⊓	I
Jingle at the	windows,	tie-dee-	oh

With younger children, we used bells to keep the beat as we sang this song. We played the song as a circle game with older children, with the children all standing in a circle holding hands with arms raised. Another child weaves in and out between the children in the circle according to the words of the song. At the last line, the weaving child swaps places with the nearest child in the circle, who then starts the weaving and singing all over again until every child has had a turn.

Built my baby

> Built my baby a fine brick house
> Built it in a garden
> I put him in but he jumped out
> So fare thee well, my darling

We played a circle game with this song with both younger and older children. With younger children, adults with babies stood and bounced them while one baby/adult couple walked around the group. On the third line, the group lets the couple in and, on the fourth line, the couple chooses another couple to take their place for the next time. With the older children, they made two equal circles, one inside the other. They walked in opposite directions until the third line, when they stopped and swapped places with the person opposite them, then kept walking for the fourth line, starting the song again.

Down the road

> Down the road and across the creek
> Can't get a letter but once a week

Table 4.42 Built my baby rhythm table

∏	∏∏	∏	I
Built my	baby a	fine brick	house
∏	∏	∏	I
Built it	in a	garden,	I
∏	∏	∏	∏
Put him	in but	he jumped	out, so
∏	∏	∏	-
Fare thee	well, my	darling	

232

Table 4.43 *Down the road* rhythm table

⊓	⊓⊓	⊓	|
Down the	road and a-	cross the	creek
⊓⊓	⊓⊓	⊓	|
Can't get a	letter but	once a	week
⊓	|	⊓	|
Ida	Red,	Ida	Blue,
⊓	⊓	⊓	|
I got	stuck on	Ida	too

> *Ida Red, Ida Blue*
> *I got stuck on Ida too*

With younger children, we played this song using red and blue instruments. With older children, we played a circle game as a variation of duck-duck-goose. One child walked around the circle with a red and blue envelope. On the last line, they stopped and handed the envelopes to the two nearest children. In the envelopes were pictures of animals, and the two chosen children had to go around the circle like those animals – the winner (who guessed the animal correctly) was the next person to take a turn at walking around the circle with the envelopes.

Do pity my case

> *Do, do pity my case*
> *In some lady's garden*
> *My clothes to wash when I get home*
> *In some lady's garden*

Table 4.44 *Do pity my case* rhythm table

|	|	⊓⊓	|
Do,	do	pity my	case
⊓	⊓	|	⊓
In some	lady's	gar-	den, my
⊓	⊓	⊓	|
Clothes to	wash when	I get	home
⊓	⊓	|	|
In some	lady's	gar-	den

233

We played this song with younger children using instruments and on the third line, the grown-ups took turns singing a chore. With older children, we did the same, but each child made up a chore. (We found it useful to have a standard chore to sing about if the child could not think of an alternative.)

This way Valerie

This way Valerie
That way Valerie
This way Valerie
All day long

Here comes another one
Just like the other one
Here comes another one
All day long

We played this game the same way with both younger and older children by standing in two lines facing each other. At one end, the lead couple walked/danced/twirled between the lines and joined the ends of the lines during the first verse. The next couple copied the first pair going down between the lines, joining the end of the line, until everyone had a go. With younger children, we allocated one adult per one/two babies, and followed the dance pattern described.

Sally go 'round the sun

Sally go 'round the sun
Sally go 'round the moon

Table 4.45 *This way Valerie* rhythm table

⊓	⊓⊓	⊓	⊓⊓
This way	Valerie,	that way	Valerie,
⊓	⊓⊓	I	⊓.
This way	Valerie,	all	day long
⊓⊓	⊓⊓	⊓⊓	⊓⊓
Here comes a-	nother one,	just like the	other one
⊓⊓	⊓⊓	I	⊓.
Here comes a-	nother one,	all	day long

Table 4.46 Sally go 'round the sun rhythm table

⊓♪	∣♪	∣ -	- - -
Sally go	'round the	sun	
⊓♪	∣♪	∣ -	- - -
Sally go	'round the	moon	
⊓♪	∣♪	∣♪	⊓♪
Sally go	'round the	chimney	top on a
∣♪	∣♪	∣ -	-
Sunday	after-	noon	BOOM!

> *Sally go 'round the chimney top on a*
> *Sunday afternoon, BOOM!*

This circle song/game was played the same way for both younger and older children. Walking around in a circle holding hands, we sang the song and, on the word BOOM, we jumped to face the opposite direction and kept singing.

Phoebe

> *Phoebe in her petticoat*
> *Phoebe in her gown*
> *Phoebe in her petticoat*
> *Going down to town*

With younger children, we used scarves to play at dressing up, using them as capes, dresses, hats, etc. With older children, we stood facing each other in two parallel lines, dressing up with scarves. The couple at one end walked/promenaded between the lines then outside the lines and back to their place. The next couple walked/promenaded down between the lines, around the top couple and back, and so on until each couple had a turn.

Table 4.47 Phoebe rhythm table

♫♫	♫	♫♫	∣
Phoebe in her	petticoat	Phoebe in her	gown
♫♫	♫	♫♫	∣
Phoebe in her	petticoat	going down to	town

Table 4.48 Jim-a-long rhythm table

♫	Ι	♫♫	♫
Hey Jim-a-	long	Jim-a-long	Josie
♫	Ι	♫♫	Ι
Hey Jim-a-	long	Jim-a-long	Joe

Jim-a-long

Hey Jim-a-long
Jim-a-long Josie
Hey Jim-a-long
Jim-a-long Joe

We used this short song as a quick instrument pass around for younger children, giving each child a turn to play and then pass the instrument to the next child, while everyone else claps or taps their knees. For older children, we used this as a skipping game in parallel lines, with one pair skipping to the end of the line, with the children at the side clapping their hands to the beat until every pair has had a turn.

Down came a lady

Down came a lady
Down came two
Down came "George's" friend
And he was dressed in blue

Table 4.49 Down came a lady rhythm table

Ι	♫	Ι	Ι
Down	came a	la-	dy
Ι	Ι	Ι	-
Down	came	two	-
Ι	Ι	♫	♫
Down	came	"George's"	friend and
♫	♫	Ι	-
He was	dressed in	blue	-

We used this song with both younger and older children standing in parallel lines opposite each other (babies carried by adults). One pair walked or danced down the centre of the lines to the end of the lines, then the next pair would start to walk or dance down the centre of the lines.

Jolly miller

There was a jolly miller and he
Lived by himself, when the
Wheel went round he made his wealth, with
One hand in his pocket and the
Other in his bag, when the
Wheel went round he
Made his grab!

With younger children, we sang this song while we found creative ways to make circles using scarves, balls and tin foil. With older children, we formed two circles, a smaller one inside the larger circle. Walking in opposite directions gave the children the feeling of being within a wheel, and we extended this by changing direction each time we sang the song.

Table 4.50 Jolly miller rhythm table

♪⊓	⊓	⊓	⊓
(There) was a	jolly	miller	and he
|	⊓	|	⊓
Lived	by him-	self	when the
|	|	|	|
Wheel	went	round	he
|	|	|	-♪
Made	his	wealth	with
⊓	⊓	⊓	⊓
One hand	in his	pocket	and the
⊓	⊓	|	⊓
Other	in his	bag	when the
|	|	|	|
Wheel	went	round	he
|	|	|	-
Made	his	grab!	

Circle right

> Circle right, do-oh, do-oh
> Circle right, do-oh, do-oh
> Circle right, do-oh, do-oh
> Shake 'em 'simmons down
>
> Circle left, do-oh, do-oh
> Circle left, do-oh, do-oh
> Circle left, do-oh, do-oh
> Shake 'em 'simmons down

With both older and younger children, we followed the actions of the song by walking in a circle. On the last line, adults holding babies lowered the babies down, while older children lowered their hands to the ground.

Mummy loves

> Mummy loves and
> Daddy loves and
> Everybody loves little
> Baby
>
> Brother loves and
> Sister loves and
> Everybody loves little
> Baby

With both younger and older children, we used this song as a rocking song. With smaller children, two adults rocked a baby placed in the centre of a blanket, while older children used scarves to rock soft toys.

Table 4.51 *Circle right* rhythm table

♫	♬	♫	♬
Circle right,	do-oh, do-oh	circle right	do-oh, do-oh
♫	♬	♬	ǀ
Circle right,	do-oh, do-oh	shake 'em 'simmons	down

Table 4.52 Mummy loves rhythm table

	-♪			
Mum-	my	loves	and
	-♪			
Dad-	dy	loves	and
Π	Π			Π
Every-	body	loves	little
			-	-
Ba-	by		
	-♪			
Bro-	ther	loves	and
	-♪			
Sis-	ter	loves	and
Π	Π			Π
Every-	body	loves	little
			-	-
Ba-	by		

Old brass wagon

Circle to the left, old brass wagon
Circle to the left, old brass wagon
Circle to the left, old brass wagon
You're the one, my darling

Circle to the right, old brass wagon
Circle to the right, old brass wagon
Circle to the right, old brass wagon
You're the one, my darling

Everybody down, old brass wagon
Everybody up, old brass wagon
Everybody down, old brass wagon
You're the one, my darling

Table 4.53 *Old brass wagon* rhythm table

᚛ᚌᚌᚌ	I	⊓	⊓
Circle to the	left,	old brass	wagon
ᚌᚌᚌ	I	⊓	⊓
Circle to the	left,	old brass	wagon
ᚌᚌᚌ	I	⊓	⊓
Circle to the	left,	old brass	wagon
ᚌ᚛	⊓	I	I
You're the	one, my	dar-	ling

> *Everybody in, old brass wagon*
> *Everybody out, old brass wagon*
> *Everybody in, old brass wagon*
> *You're the one, my darling*

We played this circle game the same way for both younger and older children, younger children being carried by adults. Walking in a circle, we followed the directions in the song, cuddling ourselves on the last line. The third verse involved everybody crouching down, standing up, and crouching down again, while the last verse involved everyone walking to the middle of the circle, walking out and walking back in and out again.

Old King Glory

Table 4.54 *Old King Glory* rhythm table

I	I	⊓	⊓
Old	King	Glory	on the
I	-	I	-♪
Moun-		tain,	the
⊓	⊓	I	-♪
Mountain	was so	high,	it
⊓	⊓	I	⊓
Almost	touched the	sky,	and it's
I	-	I	-
One,		two,	
I	⊓	I	-
Three,	follow	me	

Old King Glory on the
Mountain, the
Mountain was so high, it
Almost touched the sky, and it's
One, two,
Three, follow me

Both younger and older children played this game the same way, with younger children carried by an adult. Choosing one child to be king or queen, the group followed the leader until the last line. The king/queen then went to the end of the line, allowing a new king/queen to lead until all children had a turn.

Charlie over the ocean

Charlie over the ocean
Charlie over the sea
Charlie caught a big fish
Can't catch me

Younger children used fish-shaped shakers and took turns with a fish-shaped guiro when we sang this song, while older children sang this while sitting in a circle and playing a game similar to duck-duck-goose.

Lil' Liza Jane

I know a girl that you don't know
Lil' Liza Jane

Table 4.55 *Charlie over the ocean* rhythm table

♫	♫	|	|
Charlie	over the	o-	cean,
♫	♫	|	-
Charlie	over the	sea,	
♫	♫	|	|
Charlie	caught a	big	fish
|	|	|	-
Can't	catch	me	

Table 4.56 Lil' Liza Jane rhythm table

⊓̄	⊓	⊓	l
I know a	girl that	you don't	know
♪ l	- ♪	l	-
Lil' Li-	za	Jane	
⊓	⊓	⊓	l
Way down	south in	Balti-	more
♪ l	- ♪	l	-
Lil' Li-	za	Jane	
l	- ♪	l	l
Oh,	E-	li-	za
♪ l	- ♪	l	-
Lil' Li-	za	Jane	
l	- ♪	l	l
Oh,	E-	li-	za
♪ l	- ♪	l	-
Lil' Li-	za	Jane	

> Way down south in Baltimore
> Lil' Liza Jane
> Oh, Eliza
> Lil' Liza Jane
> Oh, Eliza
> Lil' Liza Jane

With younger children, we used this as an instrumental exploration song. With older children, we made up a clapping routine for the words "Lil' Liza Jane": Clap, Tap Knees, Stamp, Tap Knees. Singing the song, we had to remember to use the routine each time we sang the words.

My paddle

> My paddle's keen and bright
> Flashing like silver
> Follow the wild goose flight

Table 4.57 My paddle rhythm table

♪ |	- ♪	⊓	|
My pad-	dle's	keen and	bright
♪ |	- ♪	|	|
Flashing	like	sil-	ver
♪ |	- ♪	⊓	|
Follow	the	wild goose	flight
♪ |	- ♪	|	-
Dip-dip	and	swing	
♪ |	- ♪	|	-
Dip-dip	and	swing	
|	|	-	|
Dip	dip		and
|	-	-	-
Swing			

> *Dip-dip, and swing*
> *Dip-dip, and swing*
> *Dip-dip, and swing*

With little ones, we explored the long sound of chime bars and other metal instruments, tapping them at the beginning of each line. With older children, we all sat in a long line, one behind the other, as if sitting in a long canoe. Leaning forward and backward to the beat, we alternated this with rocking side to side depending on the person in front.

Song Level Five

Level Five songs include simple time and introduce the 6/8 timing, like rocking songs, with the notes limited to *so-fa-mi-re-do*.

Go 'round the mountain

> *Go 'round the mountain*
> *Toadie diddle-um, toadie diddle-um*
> *Go 'round the mountain*
> *Toadie diddle-um dee*

Figure 4.35 Songs using so-fa-mi-re-do notes

Table 4.58 Go 'round the mountain rhythm table

⎮	⊓	⊓	-
Go	'round the	mountain	
⊓	⊓⊓	⊓	⊓⊓
Toadie	diddle-um,	toadie	diddle-um
⎮	⊓	⊓	-
Go	'round the	mountain	
⊓	⊓⊓	⎮	-
Toadie	diddle-um	dee	

> *Tiptoe 'round the mountain*
> *Toadie diddle-um, toadie diddle-um*
> *Tiptoe 'round the mountain*
> *Toadie diddle-um dee*
>
> *Stomp 'round the mountain*
> *Toadie diddle-um, toadie diddle-um*
> *Stomp 'round the mountain*
> *Toadie diddle-um dee*

Tap 'round the mountain
Toadie diddle-um, toadie diddle-um
Tap 'round the mountain
Toadie diddle-um dee

Tickle 'round the mountain
Toadie diddle-um, toadie diddle-um
Tickle 'round the mountain
Toadie diddle-um dee

With the older children, we walked around in a circle, pretending there was a big mountain in the way. Children took turns inventing different ways to walk around the circle. With younger children, we found different ways to make sounds or perform actions around the circle.

Once a man

Once a man fell in a well
Splish, splash, splosh it sounded
If he had not fallen in
He would not have drownded

With both younger and older children, we played the same type of game with this song, with younger children being carried by adults. Standing up in pairs, we clapped our partner's hand four times for the first line, opposite hand four times for the second line,

Table 4.59 Once a man rhythm table

⊓	⊓	⊓	Ⅰ
Once a	man fell	in a	well
⊓	⊓	Ⅰ	Ⅰ
Splish, splash	splosh it	soun-	ded
⊓	⊓	⊓	Ⅰ
If he	had not	fallen	in
⊓	⊓	Ⅰ	Ⅰ
He would	not have	drown-	ded

Table 4.60 Row, row, row rhythm table

| -	| -	| ♪	| -
Row,	row,	row, your	boat
| ♪	| ♪	| -	- - -
Gently	down the	stream	
∏♪	∏♪	∏♪	∏♪
Merrily,	merrily,	merrily,	merrily,
| ♪	| ♪	| -	- - -
Life is	but a	dream	

both hands for the third line, and waved goodbye to find someone else in the last line. With younger children, adults helped babies to tap each other's hands four times for the first line, elbows four times for the second line, feet four times for the third line, and waved goodbye to find someone new for the last line.

Row, row, row your boat

> Row, row, row your boat
> Gently down the stream
> Merrily, merrily, merrily, merrily
> Life is but a dream

We used this song to do the traditional rocking together in pairs, but also to roll balls to each other, both for older and younger children.

Song Level Six

Level Six songs use more combined rhythms than before, extending the notes to *la-so-fa-mi-re-do*.

London Bridge

> London Bridge is falling down
> Falling down, falling down
> London Bridge is falling down
> My fair lady

Figure 4.36 Songs using la-so-fa-mi-re-do notes

Table 4.61 London Bridge rhythm table

⊓	⊓	⊓	I
London	Bridge is	falling	down
⊓	I	⊓	I
Falling	down,	falling	down
⊓	⊓	⊓	I
London	Bridge is	falling	down
I	I	⊓	-
My	fair	lady	

Wood and clay will wash away
Wash away, wash away
Wood and clay will wash away
My fair lady

Bricks and mortar will not stay
Will not stay, will not stay
Bricks and mortar will not stay
My fair lady

Iron and steel will bend and bow
Bend and bow, bend and bow

Iron and steel will bend and bow
My fair lady

Silver and gold will be stolen away
Stolen away, stolen away
Silver and gold will be stolen away
My fair lady

Send a man to watch all night
Watch all night, watch all night
Send a man to watch all night
My fair lady

With younger children, we had two teachers initially hold hands to make an arch while children walked through or were carried through. As children got older, we asked half the children to hold hands and make bridges for the others to walk through, like dot-to-dot, and then swapped over so that all children had the opportunity to walk under a bridge.

Farmer in the dell

The farmer in the dell
The farmer in the dell
E-I-endio
The farmer in the dell

Table 4.62 *Farmer in the dell* rhythm table

♪	♪	♪		♪		-	- - ♪
(The) farmer	in the	dell,	the
	♪		♪		-	- - -
Farmer	in the	dell	
	-		-		♪		♪
E		endi-	O, the
	♪		♪		- -		
Farmer	in the	dell	

The farmer wants a wife
The farmer wants a wife
E-I-endio
The farmer wants a wife

The wife wants a child
The wife wants a child
E-I-endio
The wife wants a child

The child wants a dog
The child wants a dog
E-I-endio
The child wants a dog

The dog wants a cat
The dog wants a cat
E-I-endio
The dog wants a cat

The cat wants a mouse
The cat wants a mouse
E-I-endio
The cat wants a mouse

The mouse wants some cheese
The mouse wants some cheese
E-I-endio
The mouse wants some cheese

We all pat the cheese
We all pat the cheese
E-I-endio
We all pat the cheese

With younger children, we sang the song playing different instruments. With older children, we played the song traditionally, standing in a circle, gradually building a smaller circle inside the larger one. The final verse involved everybody gently patting the cheese in the middle.

Table 4.63 *'Round the mountain* rhythm table

П П	П	П	П
(She'll be) coming	'round the	mountain	when she
I	-	-	П
Comes			she'll be
П	П	П	П
Coming	'round the	mountain	when she
I	-	-	П
Comes			she'll be
П	П	П	-
Coming	'round the	mountain,	
П	П	П	-
Coming	'round the	mountain,	
П	П	П	П
Coming	'round the	mountain	when she
I	-	-	
Comes			

'Round the mountain

> She'll be coming 'round the mountain when she comes
> She'll be coming 'round the mountain when she comes
> She'll be coming 'round the mountain, coming 'round the mountain
> Coming 'round the mountain when she comes
> Singing I-I-yippee-yippee-I
> Singing I-I-yippee-yippee-I
> Singing I-I-yippee, I-I-yippee
> I-I-yippee-yippee-I

> She'll be riding six white horses when she comes
> She'll be riding six white horses when she comes
> She'll be riding six white horses, riding six white horses
> Riding six white horses when she comes
> Singing I-I-yippee-yippee-I
> Singing I-I-yippee-yippee-I
> Singing I-I-yippee, I-I-yippee
> I-I-yippee-yippee-I

And we'll all go out to see her when she comes
And we'll all go out to see her when she comes
And we'll all go out to see her, all go out to see her
All go out to see her when she comes
Singing I-I-yippee-yippee-I
Singing I-I-yippee-yippee-I
Singing I-I-yippee, I-I-yippee
I-I-yippee-yippee-I

With younger children, we used this song to explore short wood or plastic instrument sounds, including sounds that can be made with everyday things like spoons and plastic cups. With older children, we walked in a circle for the first verse, galloped like horses for the second verse and waved and walked for the last verse. Each time we sang the chorus, we stamped our feet for the first line, tapped our knees for the second line, clapped our hands for the third line, and ended with tapping our knees for the last line.

Song Level Seven

Level Seven songs use more combined rhythms than the Levels One–Six songs and the full range of notes, *ti-la-so-fa-mi-re-do*.

What shall we do?

What shall we do when we all go out?
All go out? All go out?

Figure 4.37 Songs using ti-la-so-fa-mi-re-do notes

Table 4.64 *What shall we do? rhythm table*

♬	♬	♫	|
What shall we	do when we	all go	out?
♫	|	♫	|
All go	out?	All go	out?
♬	♬	♫	♬
What shall we	do when we	all go	out? When we
♫	♫	|	-
All go	out to	play?	

> What shall we do when we all go out?
> When we all go out to play ?
>
> Let's all play on the see saw
> The see saw, the see saw
> Let's all play on the see saw
> When we all go out to play
>
> Let's all play on the climbing frame
> The climbing frame, the climbing frame
> Let's all play on the climbing frame
> When we all go out to play

With younger children, we used this song to explore movement with scarves or dancing around the room with grown-ups. With older children, we acted out the movements with a partner, with children giving their own suggestions of how to play by using their imaginations.

Drunken sailor

> What shall we do with a drunken sailor?
> What shall we do with a drunken sailor?
> What shall we do with a drunken sailor?
> Earl-y in the morning
> Wey hey and up she rises
> Wey hey and up she rises
> Wey hey and up she rises
> Earl-y in the morning

Table 4.65 Drunken sailor rhythm table

♫♫	♫♫	♫	♫
What shall we	do with a	drunken	sailor?
♫♫	♫♫	♫	♫
What shall we	do with a	drunken	sailor?
♫♫	♫♫	♫	♫
What shall we	do with a	drunken	sailor?
♫	♫	♩	♩
Earl-y	in the	mor-	ning
♩	♫.	♫	♫
Way	hey and	up she	rises
♩	♫.	♫	♫
Way	hey and	up she	rises
♩	♫.	♫	♫
Way	hey and	up she	rises
♫	♫	♩	♩
Earl-y	in the	mor-	ning

Make him work and make him bail her
Make him work and make him bail her
Make him work and make him bail her
Earl-y in the morning
Wey hey and up she rises
Wey hey and up she rises
Wey hey and up she rises
Earl-y in the morning

With both groups, we used this as an instrumental exploration session, using different sounds to accompany the singing, playing in different ways, quietly and loudly, quickly and slowly.

Pretty little Susie

Where oh where is pretty, little Susie?
Where oh where is pretty, little Susie?
Where oh where is pretty, little Susie?
Way down yonder on the paw-paw patch

Table 4.66 Pretty little Susie rhythm table

♫	♫	♬	♫
Where oh	where is	pretty, little	Susie?
♫	♫	♬	♫
Where oh	where is	pretty, little	Susie?
♫	♫	♬	♫
Where oh	where is	pretty, little	Susie?
♫	♬	♫	♩
Way down	yonder on the	paw-paw	patch
♫	♩	♫	♫
Come on	friends,	let's go	find her
♫	♩	♫	♫
Come on	friends,	let's go	find her
♫	♩	♫	♫
Come on	friends,	let's go	find her
♫	♬	♫	♩
Way down	yonder on the	paw-paw	patch
♫♫	♫	♬	♫
Picking up	paw paws,	put 'em in your	pocket
♫♫	♫	♬	♫
Picking up	paw paws,	put 'em in your	pocket
♫♫	♫	♬	♫
Picking up	paw paws,	put 'em in your	pocket
♫	♬	♫	♩
Way down	yonder on the	paw-paw	patch

Come on friends, let's go find her
Come on friends, let's go find her
Come on friends, let's go find her
Way down yonder on the paw-paw patch

Picking up paw paws, put 'em in your pocket
Picking up paw paws, put 'em in your pocket
Picking up paw paws, put 'em in your pocket
Way down yonder on the paw-paw patch

We played this game the same way with both younger and older children, with two groups of children facing each other in parallel lines. We sang the first verse clapping our hands standing in place. In the second verse, the two at the end of each line walked around the outside of the lines and up the middle back to their spot, leading to the next couple walking around the outside and back up the middle. In the final verse, the first couple walked down the middle, bending down to pretend to pick up fruit on the ground, joining the end of the line.

Home on the range

Oh give me a home
Where the buffalo roam
Where the deer and the antelope play
Where seldom is heard
A discouraging word
And the skies are not cloudy all day

Table 4.67 *Home on the range* rhythm table

│ │ │ │	│ - Π	│ │ │	│ - Π
(Oh) give me a	home, where the	buffalo	roam, where the
│ - Π	│ │ │	│ - -	- - │
Deer and the	antelope	play,	where
│ │ │	│ - Π	│ │ │	│ - Π
Seldom is	heard a dis-	couraging	word, and the
│ - Π	│ │ │	│ - -	- - -
Skies are not	cloudy all	day	
│ - -	│ │ │	│ - -	- -Π
Home,	home on the	range,	where the
│ - Π	│ │ │	│ - -	- - │
Deer and the	antelope	play,	where
│ │ │	│ - Π	│ │ │	│ - Π
Seldom is	heard a dis-	couraging	word, and the
│ - Π	│ │ │	│ - -	- - -
Skies are not	cloudy all	day	

Home, home on the range
Where the deer and the antelope play
Where seldom is heard
A discouraging word
And the skies are not cloudy all day

We used instruments to explore sounds that felt like home and sounded like buffalo feet, deer and blue skies. We then took turns moving from instrument sets, playing in groups, in turn, according to the lyrics.

References

Bronfenbrenner, U. (1994). Ecological models of human development. In *International Encyclopedia of Education* (2nd edition, Vol. 3, pp. 1643–1647). Oxford: Elsevier.

Csikszentmihalyi, M. (1990). *Flow: The Psychology of Optimal Performance*. New York: Cambridge University Press.

Csikszentmihalyi, M. (2008). *Flow, the Secret to Happiness*. www.ted.com/talks/mihaly_csikszent-mihalyi_on_flow.html (Accessed 9 January 2014).

Haywood, K. and Getchell, N. (2009). *Life Span Motor Development*. Champaign, IL: Human Kinetics.

Kolb, D. A. (1983). *Experiential Learning: Experience as the Source of Learning and Development* (1st edition). Upper Saddle River, NJ: Financial Times/Prentice Hall.

Salovey, P. and Mayer, J. D. (1990). Emotional intelligence. *Imagination, Cognition and Personality*, 9(3), 185–211.

Appendix

Sample annual lesson plans

Annual music lesson plans should aim to include all of the principles of the age group involved. Table A.1 indicates that along with rhythm, pitch, SPACE (social, physical, academic, creative, emotional) and props, the number of songs should be considered in terms of how many songs to introduce per age group and how many children should be able to easily demonstrate that they recognise them (bouncing, vocalising, repeating). While these key songs should fall within the rhythm and pitch guidelines, additional songs should be used to enhance the musical experience – from classical to pop – and children should not be expected to be able to repeat/perform these accurately (this depends on home or additional experience).

Table A.1 Annual lesson plan: 0–5 years

Age	Rhythms	Pitches	SPACE	Props	Recognised songs
0–1 year	crotchet	a–f# (sol-mi)	S – bounce P – roll A – point at objects C – shake instruments E – sway	Shaking instruments	3 out of 5 (learn 5 new)
1–2 years	crotchet	a–f# (sol-mi)	S – walk in pairs P – stamp A – point at body parts C – tap/jump E – eyes follow movement	Tapping instruments	6 out of 10 (learn 5 new)

(continued)

Table A.1 (continued)

Age	Rhythms	Pitches	SPACE	Props	Recognised songs
2–3 years	crotchet, quaver	a–b (sol-la)	S – hold hands P – flick A – copy actions C – tap and sing E – act as character	Drum and beater	11 out of 20 (learn 6 new)
3–4 years	crotchet, quaver	a–d' (sol-do)	S – circle games P – hopping A – spiral C – sing last line E – act as characters	Triangle and beater	2 out of 28 (learn 7 new)
4–5 years	crotchet, quaver, dotted rhythm	f#–d' (mi-do)	S – bridges P – skip A – clever lyrics understood C – sing two lines E – partners	Cymbal and beater	16 out of 35 (learn 8 new)

Sample termly lesson plans

Termly lesson plans involve more detail, such as the specific songs to be used. These can be arranged according to personal preference: by reading material; group topic; musical focus; national holiday; or any other way appropriate to the setting. Rotating or alternating instrument sets like woods, skins and metals can be useful in maintaining interest, as well as helping to preserve instruments for longer and assisting children to focus on the types of sounds (timbre) that different materials produce.

Table A.2 Termly lesson plan: 0–5 years

Age	Topic	Props	Instruments	Games	Songs
0–1 year	Animals	Cups	Skins (drums)	Sit/circle	5 repertoire songs + others
1–2 years	Under the sea	Water play	Woods	Sit/stand own	5 repertoire songs + others

2–3 years	Space	Tin foil	Metals	Sit/pairs	6 repertoire songs + others
3–4 years	Spring time	Flowers/ fruit	Plastics	Stand/pairs	7 repertoire songs + others
4–5 years	Hungry caterpillar	Scarves	Tuned	Stand/circle	8 repertoire songs + others

Sample daily lesson plans

Daily lesson plans involve the sequence of the songs that have been chosen. Having a clear beginning and end helps children to anticipate what to expect and therefore focus more clearly and for a longer period. Alternating movement with sitting is another useful technique for promoting concentration and involvement. Moreover, being sensitive to group needs can often mean the difference between a successful or unsuccessful music session. Preparation helps the educator to be flexible to the group needs by aiming to maintain all the useful principles and elements, while being aware that there are many ways to achieve the same goal, for example, keeping a beat through walking or tapping instruments.

Table A.3 Daily sample lesson plan: babies 0–18 months

Activity	Song	Rhythms	Pitches	SPACE	Props
Greeting	Hello			Emotional	Scarves
Physical warm-up	Snail snail	Crotchet	So-mi		Massage
Vocal warm-up	Doggy doggy	Quavers	So-mi	Social	Toy dog
Bounce	Bell horses	Crotchet, quavers	So-mi-la	Physical	Lap bounce
Explore	Bell horses			Creative	Cups
Instruments	We are dancing	Crotchet, quavers	So-mi-la	Academic	Ball rolling
Free play	I had a dog	Crotchet, quavers	So-mi-la		Skins
Close	Goodbye			Emotional	

Table A.4 Daily sample lesson plan: toddlers 18 months–3 years

Activity	Song	Rhythms	Pitches	SPACE	Props
Greeting	*Hello*			Emotional	
Vocal warm-up	*Round and round*	Crotchet, quavers	So-mi-do		
Physical warm-up	*Ring a rosies*	Crotchet, quavers	So-mi-do	Physical	Circle dance
Instrument play	*All around the buttercup*				Woods
Explore	*Apple tree*	Crotchet, quavers	So-mi-do	Academic	Apples (sensory)
Instrument pass around	*A-tisket a-tasket*	Crotchet, quavers	So-mi	Social	Instruments in a basket
Creative movement	*On a log*	Crotchet, quavers	So-mi-do	Creative	Hopping
Close	*Goodbye*			Emotional	

Table A.5 Daily sample lesson plan: preschoolers 3–5 years

Activity	Song	Rhythms	Pitches	SPACE	Props
Greeting	*Hello*			Emotional	
Shape game	*Andy Pandy*	Crotchet, quavers	So-mi-do	Academic	Circle game
Gross motor rhythmic preparation	*Hot cross buns*	Crotchet, quavers	So-mi-do		Tapping sticks/ knees
Gross motor performance	*Jolly Miller*	Crotchet, quavers		Physical	Circle game
Fine motor instrument preparation	*Johnny works*	Crotchet, quavers	So-mi-re-do		Hands as hammers
Fine motor performance	*Pease porridge*	Crotchet, quavers	So-mi-re-do	Social	Plastic instruments
Gross motor independent movement	*Polly put the kettle on*	Crotchet, quavers		Creative	Scarves
Close	*Goodbye*			Social	

Index